Images of the Enemy

Communication and Society

General editor: James Curran

IMAGES OF THE ENEMY

Reporting the new cold war

Brian McNair

ROUTLEDGE
London and New York

For my parents, Pat and Norrie

First published in 1988 by Routledge
a division of Routledge, Chapman and Hall
11 New Fetter Lane, London EC4P 4EE

Published in the USA by Routledge
a division of Routledge, Chapman and Hall, Inc.
29 West 35th Street, New York, NY 10001

Printed in Great Britain by Biddles Ltd, Guildford

British Library Cataloguing in Publication Data

McNair, Brian, 1959–
Images of the enemy: reporting the new Cold War.
1. Soviet Union. Political events. Reporting by television in Great Britain
I. Title
070.4'499470854

ISBN 0–415–00645–7
ISBN 0–415–00646–5 Pbk

Library of Congress Cataloguing-in-Publication Data

McNair, Brian, 1959–
Images of the enemy.
Based on the author's thesis (Ph. D.)—University of Glasgow.
Bibliography: p.
Includes index.
1. Television broadcasting of news—Great Britain. 2. World politics—1975–1985. 3. World politics—1985–1995. 4. Soviet Union—Foreign relations—1975– . 5. Great Britain—Politics and government—1979– . 6. Soviet Union—Foreign public opinion, British. 7. Public opinion—Great Britain. I. Title. II. Title: Reporting the new cold war.

PN4784.T4M37 1988 947.085'4 88–2022

ISBN 0–415–00645–7
ISBN 0–415–00646–5 (pbk.)

Contents

Preface

For suggesting the title of this book, I am grateful to Margaret Thatcher. It was she who in the 1983 General Election campaign spoke of the Soviet Union as 'our sworn enemy'. In 1987 she was elected to a third term as British Prime Minister, committing us to a further five years of 'strong' defence premised on the assumption of a Soviet threat.

This book is about the way in which the idea of the Soviet threat, and the many issues relating to it, have been reported by British television news.

Chapter 7, which looks at recent developments associated with the rise of Mikhail Gorbachov in the Soviet Union and their effects on western media coverage of the USSR, also contains a short study of Soviet news media, focused on the Chernobyl crisis of April 1986.

I am grateful to the University of Glasgow for the postgraduate scholarship which made the research for this book possible, and to the British Council for supporting an extended period of research in Moscow.

I would especially like to thank Greg Philo, who supervised the Ph.D. on which this book is based, and the other members of staff in the Department of Sociology at Glasgow who provided help and guidance.

I should also mention the many journalists, British and Soviet, who co-operated with the research by providing interviews.

For inspiration, thanks to Kathy Granger and Jim O'Rourke.

I typed it myself.

'If we tell the truth, without fear or favour, the BBC can hold its head high as a vital engine of this great democracy.'

George Howard, Chairman of the BBC, in reply to Mrs Thatcher's criticisms of Falklands War coverage

'ITN's impartiality is a matter of public record.'

ITN's director of News and Current Affairs, August 1985, in reply to criticism of news coverage of the miners' strike

Part I

Introductions

1

Television news: 'a vital engine of this great democracy'

Returning from a trip to Moscow in 1984 I recall picking up a copy of the *London Evening Standard* at Heathrow airport, to be greeted with the headline – 'Red War Fleet Sails!'

War, fortunately, had not broken out on that warm July day. The headline and the photograph of warships accompanying it were simply the *Standard*'s way of informing its readers of a routine Soviet naval exercise in the Baltic. In doing so the newspaper had constructed a classic 'image of the enemy' – a grim vision of Soviet military might threatening and menacing our freedom.

Such images are important, because they relate in a very real way to an ongoing political debate which continues to dominate public life.

Since the beginning of the 1980s the issues of nuclear weapons, the arms race, and east–west relations have been the site of intense ideological and political conflict in Britain. The detente between NATO and the Warsaw Pact has broken down and been replaced by what some have called 'a new cold war'. The temperature of the new cold war may vary from time to time, but relations between east and west remain dangerously tense.

Partly as a result of the perceived dangers of this conflict among the population the British government from the early 1980s onwards experienced a major domestic challenge to the legitimacy of its national security policies. By the 1983 General Election, the subject of Chapter 9, only one party supported the Conservative government's proposed replacement of Britain's independent nuclear deterrent with the Trident system. The main opposition party fought that election on a defence platform which included the removal of all US nuclear bases from British territory and the adoption of a non-nuclear defence strategy for Britain. In the 1987 election campaign the three main parties again differed radically in their defence policies. The post-war consensus on defence had clearly and irrevocably broken down.

Despite the obvious importance of this debate to our lives we are largely ignorant of the complex issues which it raises. What people know about the Soviet Union – our future adversary, if NATO strategists are to be believed – is limited. Few have been there, and there are few opportunities to meet Soviet citizens here. Popular culture, a major source of images of the USSR, trades largely in caricatures and stereotypes. In fiction, cinema, and television entertainment the Soviet threat has become a staple theme. *Rambo*, *Red Dawn*, *Amerika*, and *The Fourth Protocol* exemplify a type of cultural production where the assumed evils of communism and the red menace are regularly and lucratively pitted against freedom 'n' democracy.

As a child growing up in the 1960s I remember playing at soldiers, with the Nazis as the bad guys. Now children's computer games simulate World War Three, where the objective is to nuke Moscow.

As for the issues, how are we to judge the value of a Zero Option, an Interim Zero Option, or a Double Zero Option? How are we to assess the true extent of the Soviet threat, the correctness of the political parties' very different defence policies, or the appeals of the peace movement for unilateral disarmament? How are we to respond to the western rejection of a Soviet arms control proposal, or to the Soviets angrily storming out of a conference room at Geneva?

Clearly, we cannot rely on Frederick Forsyth or Sylvester Stallone to give us answers to such questions. Nor can we rely on the *London Evening Standard* and the other elements of a largely right-wing press. We turn, increasingly, to one source – television news.

Studying news

Television is, without doubt, the most important news medium in Britain today. Television news, as Dahlgren puts it, 'has become the major source [of information] for a majority of the population, and the only news source for many; moreover it has become the medium most trusted by the public' (1981: 101).[1] According to an IBA study conducted in 1986 and reported in *Broadcast* magazine of 23 January 1987, 'TV is fair and unbiased in its coverage of news and current affairs, according to 74 per cent of the population.'

While the printed media, such as the *Standard*, make no secret of their partisanship, television news claims for itself the status of an objective and impartial information source. These claims (and the fact, as surveys repeatedly show, that they are accepted by the audience) are the basis of broadcasting's primacy as a news source.

They have, of course, been the subject of fierce and sometimes bitter debate for several years. The New Right in the Conservative party has accused the broadcasting institutions, and the BBC in particular, of left-wing bias, most notably in coverage of the US bombing of Libya in 1986.[2] The Liberal–Social Democratic Alliance has periodically accused the broadcasters of bias in favour of the two established parties, while the Labour party and the trade unions have complained since the 1970s about right-wing bias in television news. Academic studies such as those by the Glasgow University Media Group (1976), and Schlesinger, Murdock, and Elliot (1983), have sought to establish bias by empirical means while others, such as Hetherington (1985), Harrison (1985), and Anderson and Sharrock (1980) have attempted to refute their findings.[3]

This book follows in that tradition by asking if television news coverage of the east–west debate has been neutral, balanced, and impartial.

To assist in answering that question, the analyses of news content which form the bulk of the book are informed by the views of journalists who report east–west issues.

Images of the Soviet Union on British television are at the heart of this book. Consequently, interviews were conducted with television journalists from both BBC and ITN based in London who regularly report on Soviet and east European affairs. In addition, lengthy interviews were conducted in Moscow with the BBC's radio and television correspondents based there (at the time of the visit, ITN had no permanent presence in the Soviet capital).

In Moscow a number of British *press* correspondents were also interviewed. While the experiences of broadcasting journalists in Moscow were different in some ways from those reported by the press correspondents, interviews revealed that they shared many problems and constraints. While press coverage of the USSR is not the direct concern of this book, much of what the press correspondents had to say was clearly of relevance to an understanding of how news about the Soviet Union is constructed.

The purpose of the interviews was to establish the existence of constraints on news coverage of the Soviet Union which could not be ascribed to subjective factors on the part of the journalists themselves, but which might help to account for some of the observed features of coverage.

It was considered important, for example, to know if there were any physical limitations on the work of Moscow correspondents, such as travel restrictions, difficulty in gaining access to Soviet sources, or simply at the level of filming and interviewing Soviet citizens, which could explain the relative absence or presence of certain categories of news story about the USSR.

If what follows is often critical of public service broadcasting's 'impartiality, neutrality, and objectivity' in coverage of east–west issues, by speaking with some of the journalists who produce the news it was intended to isolate any external constraints on the coverage so that these could be taken into account in the overall analysis.[4]

Interviews were also conducted in Moscow with a number of Soviet journalists and media specialists. These helped to assess the extent and significance of the recent changes in Soviet news management practices introduced by the Gorbachov administration.

These changes have been encapsulated within the slogan of *glasnost*, the Russian word which approximates to the English 'openness' or 'publicity'. As Chapter 7 shows, they have significantly affected the way in which the Soviet Union is presented in the western media.

The interview materials and analyses of content which form the bulk of the book are preceded by a brief review of the east–west debate, setting out the main lines of contention, and based on background material from a wide range of academic, political, and military sources.[5]

The availability of these sources reflects the importance of the east–west debate during the 1980s. They include the publications of independent research institutes such as the International Institute of Strategic Studies and the Stockholm International Peace Research Institute (SIPRI), published articles by present and past leaders of the western politico-military command structure such as those by Robert McNamara in the US journal *Foreign Affairs* and by NATO Secretary-General Lord Carrington in *NATO Review*, as well as British, American, and Soviet defence documents.

In addition, television documentaries and current affairs programmes provided valuable sources of information on the events being reported on the news. Programmes by the *Horizon* and *Panorama* documentary teams discussed, at various times, the Soviet defence budget, the strategic significance of the Cruise and Pershing II missile deployments, and the arms control policies of the

Reagan administration. Television journalists produced material on such themes as *The Cold War Game* (Jonathan Dimbleby) and *The Truth Game* (John Pilger).

The categories of coverage

When the work for this book began in 1982 it was not possible to anticipate how the defence debate would develop and how it would be reflected, quantitatively and qualitatively, on the news. Thus an approach to sampling was adopted which would enable the research to incorporate the several 'axes' or levels of the debate, and the differing time frames of the newsworthy events to which it gave rise.

Interest focused initially on three themes in coverage. It was clear that the defence debate was, first and foremost, a debate about the nature of the USSR. Different approaches to this question seemed to underly all views on policy matters. Thus it was decided to study television news coverage of the USSR – *Soviet news*.

Soviet news appeared in two forms. In a given sample of television news, coverage of the Soviet Union would occupy a given proportion of news time – × number of items. This was categorized as *routine Soviet news*. The object of analysis of routine Soviet news was to establish the existence of patterns and tendencies in coverage of the USSR.

But the death of Leonid Brezhnev in November 1982 allowed for an extension to this project. It became possible to generate a category of *in-depth Soviet news*, by virtue of the large quantities of news devoted to this single event. Routine Soviet news items were generally brief and insubstantial. By contrast, coverage of Brezhnev's death was substantial and detailed, amounting to many hours of news time. The subsequent deaths of Yuri Andropov and Konstantin Chernenko were included in the sample.

A second theme of coverage was the peace movement, from which a content category labelled *peace movement news* was identified. As we note below, conflict between the anti-nuclear protest movement and NATO was one of the three 'axes' of the nuclear debate. Peace movement news became a significant quantitative category on television. Again, a sub-category of *routine* peace movement news was identified, from the routine, day-to-day coverage of the movement's activities, while specific events such as the Easter demonstrations of 1983 produced *in-depth* coverage of the peace movement.

A third theme of coverage concerned the superpower arms control dialogue – *disarmament news*. Disarmament news reported major events in the US–Soviet dialogue between 1981 and 1983. By a fortunate coincidence, the news samples from which Soviet and peace movement coverage was extracted also contained some of the most important events in the superpower dialogue, such as the Zero Option and START proposals, and the Soviet freeze and no-first-use proposals.

In September 1983, a 'special case' of superpower dialogue exploded around the Korean airliner disaster. This was propaganda warfare at its most bitter, and it was decided on the spot to record television coverage of the event. Two weeks of news coinciding with the incident's peak newsworthiness were recorded.

The Chernobyl disaster produced another bout of east–west propaganda warfare. However, when Chernobyl erupted in April 1986 the author had the bad luck (or good, depending on whose reassurances about radiation one chose to believe) to be in Moscow. Consequently, the analysis of British television news coverage of the event presented in Chapter 7 was limited by the lack of a proper sample. On the other hand, the author's presence in Moscow for the duration of the crisis means that Chapter 7 contains a detailed account of how the Soviet media reported Chernobyl, valuable in the context of *glasnost* and Gorbachov's reforms in the sphere of information.

Finally, as it became clear that the 1983 General Election, announced on 9 May, would be a 'nuclear' election largely fought around the issues of defence and disarmament, it was decided to record as much of its coverage on television as was practically possible. This generated a category of *election defence news*, which reported on the party political debate, with some limited reference to the peace movement's participation in the campaign. The 1987 General Election campaign came too late for a detailed analysis of its coverage to be included in this book. Others, I am sure, will fulfil that task.

The need for these content categories, and the variability of the sampling methods needed to generate workable quantities of them, reflect the scope and intensity of a debate which continues to occupy the centre stage of British and world politics.

2

The nuclear debate

In the 1970s east–west and nuclear issues were not matters of great public debate. This chapter examines how they became so in the 1980s, who was involved in the debate, and what their basic positions were.

The death of detente and the rise of the nuclear debate

Mary Kaldor observes that until 1981 'there was very little coverage of military issues and what coverage there was tended to be along orthodox lines' (1982a). She suggests that 'lack of coverage reflected lack of public debate'. During this period defence debates centred on 'orthodox' intra-service disputes. Major strategic issues were not up for discussion. So tightly was the veil of silence drawn around defence issues that the Labour government under Jim Callaghan was able to make decisions of great importance – such as the deployment of the Chevaline warhead on Polaris submarines – without informing its own Cabinet, let alone the country as a whole.

The low political profile of the defence issue reflected the relative stability and improved international atmosphere of the period we characterize as 'detente'. In the 1970s the conflict-ridden years of the first cold war had given way to an era of coexistence between the superpowers. Arms control, economic and cultural links, the acceptance by each superpower of the 'legitimate interests' of the other were all features of detente. Throughout these years the anti-nuclear protest movement, which had been a significant political force in the 1950s and 1960s, remained a fringe group. The breaking down of the 'consensus of silence' and the development of the current nuclear debate were responses to events which undermined and reversed these comforting trends, in particular the erosion of detente and the onset of a new arms race.

President Carter, as early as 1976, had begun to move United States foreign policy away from the detente of the Nixon–Ford administrations. It was he who in 1980 made the first large-scale increases in defence spending and initiated what Noam Chomsky calls 'one of the most remarkable propaganda campaigns in recent history ... the human rights crusade' directed against the USSR (1982: 32).[1] It was President Carter who sought permission from western European governments to deploy neutron weapons on their territories, and on 12 December 1979 NATO, under the leadership of Jimmy Carter, took the decision to modernize American long-range theatre nuclear weapons with Cruise and Pershing II missiles. These trends away from detente in US foreign policy were evident before the Soviet invasion of Afghanistan or the Iranian hostage crisis, although these events accelerated the process.

But the onset of what has been called 'the new cold war' and the present nuclear debate began in earnest with the coming to power in Britain and the United States of politicians who themselves broke most decisively with the consensus of the 1970s. Margaret Thatcher, Ronald Reagan, and the political forces which they represented initiated a qualitative leap in defence thinking.

Subsequently, a fiercely contested public debate developed in the NATO countries, and particularly in those which, like Britain, were to be recipients of the new Cruise and Pershing weapons. The debate produced three very broadly defined groups, whom we shall label the *conservatives*, the *pragmatists*, and the *disarmers*. These groups and the frameworks within which they argued were not new to the period under discussion, but the late 1970s and early 1980s saw a major realignment between them.

The era of detente can be seen as one in which the pragmatists held sway, while the conservatives and the disarmers remained on the political sidelines. The passing of detente saw the pragmatists ejected from office and replaced by radically conservative governments on both sides of the Atlantic: in Britain, decades of 'consensus' gave way to Thatcherism; in the United States Ronald Reagan became President, scornful of both his Democratic and Republican predecessors.

The conservatives

The conservatives have been variously referred to as the 'ideologues', the New Right, and the radical right. In Britain the term 'dries' is sometimes used to distinguish a conservative Conservative from the more pragmatic variety. These labels proclaim their bearers to be confident, assertive champions of the capitalist system, as compared with the much-reviled 'liberals' or 'wets'.

In the sphere of defence and foreign policy the conservatives argued that the years of detente and coexistence between NATO and the Warsaw Pact were a disaster for the west, for two reasons.

First, it was argued that while NATO had shown restraint in military spending, the Soviet Union had engaged in a huge military build-up. Arms control agreements such as SALTs I and II were castigated for permitting the USSR to catch up with and even overtake the west militarily. It was suggested that as Soviet confidence in its own military superiority grew, so would the risk of confrontation and war.

Second, the conservatives argued that while the west had shown restraint in the sphere of foreign intervention, the USSR had continued to intervene in foreign conflicts and had increased its influence in the Third World. The examples of Angola, Mozambique, and Ethiopia were invoked to illustrate the consequences of a detente which inhibited the US from pursuing its interests in the world while allowing the USSR to do what it liked.

The feeling that America (and by extension the west, freedom, democracy, etc.) had been 'taken for a ride' by detente characterized the conservative view and made it deeply suspicious of any form of co-operation or coexistence that resembled it.

Two main lines of policy were derived from this framework. On the one hand, the United States required a vast modernization and expansion of its military capability. The conservatives did not publicly dispute the theory of nuclear deterrence – although some were openly advocating the adoption of a nuclear war-fighting strategy[2] – but argued that 'effective' deterrence involved 'catching up' with the USSR.

On the other hand, because of the perceived global consequences of detente for US and western interests, the US and its allies had to engage in open military and ideological struggle with the Soviet Union and its 'proxies' in the Third World. 'It is a question of whether or not you compete politically with your opponent and do so in a way which deals with morality, with values, with natures of systems, and we are going to engage in that with a good deal of vigour, and we hope with a certain amount of spirit,' as US State Department official Mark Palmer put it on Jonathan Dimbleby's documentary *The Eagle and the Bear*.

The main objective of these policies was to reverse what was perceived to be a dangerous decline in the strength and prestige of American capitalism. Strong leadership – which Ronald Reagan promised to provide – and increased defence budgets were the means by which the decline could be halted and the damage made good. The experience of Vietnam was positively redefined.

The corollary of these developments was a revived anti-Sovietism. Nixon, Ford, and Carter had always been anti-communist. They tended, however, to forego rhetorical denunciations and to engage in 'normal' diplomatic relations. Each met Soviet leaders. Reagan, by contrast, denounced the Soviet Union as an 'evil empire' and expressed his hope to 'leave Marxism–Leninism on the ashheap of history'. Unlike all post-war Republican and Democratic Presidents, Reagan refused any contact with his Soviet counterpart during his first term of office. His first meeting with a member of the Soviet leadership took place with Foreign Secretary Gromyko a few days before the Presidential election of November 1984. He met Gorbachov for the first time in November 1985.

In most respects the British conservatives in government followed the Reagan administration in these policies, although disagreements were in evidence when Britain's own interests were transparently ignored. During the US invasion of Grenada and the US boycott of the Soviet gas pipeline project in 1983, both of which directly infringed British sovereignty, friction was evident between the two powers.

The pragmatists and the disarmers

Both the pragmatists and the disarmers opposed the conservatives' approach to defence and foreign policy. Many of their reasons for doing so were similar, while in other respects they differed significantly.

The pragmatists, in power and in opposition to the conservatives, believed in the natural superiority of the capitalist system and tended in general to perceive the Soviet Union as an enemy. But where Reagan, Thatcher, and the conservatives believed that Soviet gains could be reversed by military, political, economic, and ideological struggle the pragmatists argued that the new global balance of power – the 'rough equivalence' codified by the SALT agreements – precluded such a strategy. Confrontation and conflict, they argued, could not in the era of nuclear weapons be considered as a practical solution to the historic antagonism between east and west, since it would mean the destruction of both.

The pragmatists criticized several aspects of NATO policy as it was being conducted under conservative leadership. Although sharing with the conservatives a fundamental belief in the value of and need for NATO, the pragmatists disagreed on questions of strategy and tactics. On Channel 4's *Comment* programme of 4 October 1982, former Commander-in-Chief of the United States Pacific Forces and leading pragmatist Admiral Noel Gaylor disputed the wisdom of NATO's policy of first-use – the threat to use nuclear weapons first in the event of a Soviet conventional attack – as did former US Defence Secretary Robert McNamara in the American journal *Foreign Affairs*:

> Having spent seven years as Secretary of Defence dealing with the problems unleashed by the initial nuclear chain reaction forty years ago, I do not believe we can avoid serious and unacceptable risk of nuclear war until we recognize that *nuclear weapons serve no military purpose whatsoever. They are totally useless* [his emphasis].
>
> (1983)

The pragmatists argued that self-preservation be the guiding principle of superpower relations. Peace in their view was a *practical* necessity based on the realities of nuclear warfare. The disarmers, however, mounted a more fundamental critique of the conservatives' position.

The rise of the disarmament lobby was the most visible indicator of the breakdown of 'consensus' around defence. Its members were both numerous and diverse in their social and political backgrounds. They included groups with names such as Tories Against Cruise and Trident, the Christian Campaign for Nuclear Disarmament, and the Medical Campaign for the Prevention of Nuclear War.

The disarmers consequently had many different reasons for opposing nuclear defence, and differed also in their practical suggestions as to how 'disarmament' should proceed. The Labour party, for example, opposed Cruise and Trident missiles, was somewhat ambiguous about the future of Polaris, and supported Britain's membership of NATO. CND opposed nuclear weapons absolutely in the British context. They suggested unilateralism in Britain as the first step in a longer process of multilateral disarmament, and campaigned for Britain's withdrawal from NATO.

Many of the pragmatic arguments were welcomed and used by the disarmers. By the same token, it was partly the campaigning activities of the peace movement which led many who had previously accepted NATO strategies to 'break ranks' and dissent in public. The difference between the disarmers and the pragmatists lay not so much in the content of their positions as in their style. The disarmers campaigned in massive demonstrations throughout the NATO countries, translating pragmatic concerns for the future into a potent social protest movement. The women of Greenham Common exemplified this phenomenon, capturing the imagination of the world with their vigil at the US Cruise missile base.

The range of public debate during these years showed that the consensus of the 1970s on defence policy had been shattered. A radical shift in NATO's stance, accompanied by an upsurge in popular demands for arms control had made the issue the key one of the decade. The defence establishment was split between those currently in power who advocated the new assertiveness of the west and those – like Denis Healey, Robert McNamara, Admiral Gaylor – who called for an alternative approach. Millions of ordinary people gathered in political demonstrations against NATO policy.

Central to the debate were competing perceptions of the nature of the Soviet Union, and it is to that subject which, briefly, we now turn.

Perceptions of the Soviet threat

In 1983 the British government's Central Office of Information produced a video pack for use in British schools. It was called *The Peace Game*, and dealt with the subject of the Soviet Union and Britain's defence needs. It typifies conservative attitudes on the issue:

> As early as 1949 Russia was plainly showing her belief that Soviet ideology must dominate the world, and her readiness to use military force to achieve that. By 1971 Russia was already outstripping America as the world's biggest arms spender, and her arsenal today, nuclear and conventional, is many times greater than anything she could ever need for defence. So NATO too is forced to keep both a nuclear and a conventional deterrent. Firstly to show the Russians that they can gain nothing by attacking us, and secondly to encourage them to keep talking

towards world nuclear disarmament, because Russia has shown time and time again that she won't negotiate seriously with military weaklings.

Conservatives argued that the Soviet Union was approaching or had already attained a position of military superiority *vis-à-vis* the NATO alliance.

This superiority, it was claimed, derived from a Soviet defence budget which far outstripped that of any NATO country, including the United States. The following presentation by the US Defence Department was typical:

> In recent years, the military has absorbed 15 per cent of the Gross National Product as compared to less than 7 per cent for the United States – and if current trends continue, the Soviet military's share of the GNP will approach 20 per cent by the late 1980s. The cumulative dollar costs of Soviet investment for the decade were 80 per cent higher than US investment outlays. The estimated dollar costs for the Soviets were more than twice the US outlays in the mid-1970s.
>
> (1983: 74)

The UK Ministry of Defence echoed this figure in its 1983 *Defence Estimates*:

> The Soviet military build-up in recent years is well-illustrated by the steady increase in military expenditure. NATO's current estimate is that since 1970 this has risen by an average of 4 per cent a year in real terms, while NATO expenditure during the 1970s showed an overall slight decline. Soviet defence expenditure now accounts for some 14–16 per cent of GNP in current prices, over twice the level of any NATO country.
>
> (1983: 1)

Official Soviet statistics claimed that defence spending accounted for a mere 6.2 per cent of budget spending in 1979 – a sum of 17.2 billion dollars (see Hutchings 1983: 115). So which side was right on this crucial issue? Evidence suggests that the real extent of Soviet defence spending lies somewhere in between these two extremes.

Two methods of assessing Soviet defence spending are commonly used in the west. The first of these is to take the official Soviet figure (as quoted above) and add to it certain other categories in the Soviet budget which are known but not acknowledged by the Soviets to encompass military production. One such budget category is *machine building and metal working*. The difficulty here lies in the uncertainty surrounding the categories, and the fractions within them which should be counted as 'defence spending'.

A more commonly used method involves the quantification of Soviet military hardware and other items of expenditure, and their subsequent translation into 'dollar costs'. This was the method used by the CIA, whose figures the US Defence Department, the British government, and NATO as a whole subsequently adopted as authoritative.

A number of objections to this method were raised.

First, it made no allowance for the unreliability of estimating the extent of Soviet military hardware. US satellites, for example, calculate the number of tanks in the Soviet armoury by photographing the number of Soviet tank sheds. Andrew Cockburn (1983) points out that these estimates are always exaggerated since planners assume that each tank shed is full of tanks 'ready to go', when in reality many are not in working order.[3]

More importantly, the CIA's rouble-to-dollar ratio, on which estimated dollar costs are based, is not an absolute quantity. It simply measures how much a given item of Soviet military equipment would cost an American military planner at current *commercial* American prices. As the BBC *Horizon* documentary *Race to Ruin* explained:

> American analysts ask American companies how much it would cost them to produce a tank to the specifications of the Russian model, and they cost out each Russian serviceman as if he were paid an American salary, that's between 17 and $20,000 a man. So they end up with a high value for the things that are cheap and plentiful in the Soviet Union: men and tanks. They've concluded that the Soviets have been outspending by 50 per cent all these years, a figure that's grossly inflated.

Thus, if an American GI received a pay rise, the CIA increased its estimate of Soviet defence spending. The American serviceman earns a salary of about $700 dollars a month, while the Soviet soldier earns only $6. American government sources nevertheless count the cost of the Soviet soldier as equivalent.

In addition, by estimating the cost of a given quantity of military equipment in American dollars the CIA makes an assumption about the efficiency of Soviet industry and the productivity of

Soviet labour-power. Consequently, should it be decided that Soviet industry is less efficient than was previously thought, this appears as a massive increase in Soviet defence spending. This was precisely what happened in 1975 when, under pressure from the Committee on the Present Danger (a powerful conservative alliance whose members included Ronald Reagan), the CIA raised its estimate of Soviet defence spending 'from approximately 25 billion roubles to 50–60 billion, and from 6–8 per cent of GNP to 11–13 per cent' (Holloway 1983: 115). Though on paper this suggested a doubling of Soviet defence spending, the new figure represented no real increase in Soviet military capability.

The unreliability of these NATO figures was confirmed on 19 February 1984 when the *Observer* reported a 'major downward reassessment of Soviet defence spending by the CIA', and conceded that 'estimating Soviet defence spending is an imprecise science':

> Russia's defence spending has been increasing at less than half the rate previously thought, according to a confidential NATO study. It says that a change took place in 1976 [the very year when the figures were revised *upward*], since when growth in defence spending has been lower than the current annual increases in defence spending by the United States, Britain and a number of other NATO countries.

A further objection to the CIA figures argued that by expressing defence spending as a proportion of GNP the CIA failed to take into account the relative productive capacities of each country. By NATO's own admission, 12–14 per cent of Soviet GNP amounted in 1982 to $107.3 billion, while the 5 per cent of United States' GNP devoted to defence that year represented a sum of $111.2 billion. The Soviet economy produces only half as much as the American.

In addition, the figures failed to compare Warsaw Pact spending as a whole with that of NATO as a whole. Jacobsen (1983) cites the western commercial banks' mean estimates of Soviet defence spending in 1982 ($94.6 billion) which combines with spending in the rest of the Warsaw Pact ($20.66 billion) to give a total of $115.26 billion. The United States in 1982 spent $215.9 billion, which combined with the other NATO countries' spending of $106.144 billion to give a NATO total of $322.044 billion, approximately $207 billion dollars in excess of Warsaw Pact spending that year. The US Senate Committee on Armed Services also pointed out that:

> of the sixteen nations with the largest defence budgets as of 1978, seven are members of NATO, one (Japan) has a bilateral defence treaty with the United States, and three (China, Saudi Arabia, and Israel) are strongly anti-Soviet or pro-western in orientation. Only three of these countries (USSR, East Germany, and Poland) are members of the Warsaw Pact.
>
> (1981: 25)

The figures produced by the US and British governments showing NATO behind the Warsaw Pact in defence expenditure were debatable and, indeed, ultimately rejected by NATO itself. Independent studies suggest that even at the low point of United States and western defence expenditure – the mid- to late 1970s – NATO military spending exceeded that of the Warsaw Pact. As for the future, according to the SIPRI *Yearbook 1983*, 'the picture [for the Warsaw Pact] is of a steady, not particularly rapid, upward trend'. The United States for its part embarked with Ronald Reagan on a defence programme which, if followed through, would mean that 'by 1988 military spending in the United States would have almost doubled in volume within a decade' (1983a: 135).

A common justification for increases in western military power has been that the Soviet Union has a lead in particular – and crucial – technologies. In the 1940s speculation centred on particle accelerators; in the 1950s it was ballistic missiles; and most recently President Reagan personally championed the theory that the Soviet Union had gained a significant lead in laser technology, using this argument as one of the justifications for his 'Star Wars' project. Historically, such claims have preceded US efforts to 'catch up' with the USSR, although there has been no instance in which they were verified. Indeed, the US Defence Department boasts that 'the US continues to lead the Soviets in most basic technologies, such as the militarily critical area of electronics' (1983: 3). SIPRI cites a US study which corroborates this claim:

> While the Soviet Union has numerical superiority, it is inferior in advanced military technology. US weapons designers conducted a comparative analysis of US and Soviet design practices over the past forty years. In electronics – the key component of western technological superiority in weaponry – the study found that the initial Soviet utilization of different generations of electronic components lagged behind that of the United States by 10–15 years.
>
> (1983b: 150)

As of 1982 it was estimated by Holloway that 'as much as 30 per cent of American military technology was beyond the technological capacity of the Soviet Union to produce' (1983: 130).

Despite this, NATO continues to claim overwhelming Soviet military superiority. General Rogers, in an interview for Channel 4, defended his call for increased spending on conventional weapons with the argument that if attacked conventionally, 'we cannot sustain ourselves for very long with manpower, ammunition, and war reserve stock'. NATO's long-term objective in Europe, he continued, should be 'by the end of this decade to have developed a conventional capability that bolsters our deterrent by providing a reasonable prospect of defeating a conventional attack by the Warsaw Pact'.

Particular concern is often expressed about Soviet superiority in tanks and manpower, but as more than one author on this subject has noted, such comparisons generally ignore the fact that Warsaw Pact equipment is older than and technologically inferior to that of the USA and NATO.

On the specific issue of tanks the assertion of Soviet superiority is only possible if one downplays NATO's historic and deliberate emphasis for its defence of Europe on *anti-tank* weapons, in which it enjoys a huge superiority over the USSR. In general, it is possible to distort the actual balance of conventional forces by including *quantitative* measures which point to Soviet superiority, and excluding *qualitative* measures which tip the balance in favour of NATO.[4]

Mary Kaldor concludes that Soviet conventional superiority has been overstated. Even in Europe, she suggests, where Soviet military power is at its strongest, 'by no stretch of the imagination could the Soviet Union win a war against NATO forces' (1982b: 33).

Evidence suggests that the Soviet conventional capability, though numerically significant, remains qualitatively and technologically inferior to that of NATO.

Soviet nuclear forces

For several years the Soviet Union was engaged in what it saw as catching up with the United States in the field of nuclear weapons. By the early 1970s it claimed to have done so. From a position of clear nuclear inferiority the USSR achieved what it regarded as a suitable 'balance'. This was not taken to mean that the Soviet

Union had achieved strict equality with the US, but signified its perceived ability to deter a nuclear strike by the United States. This state of nuclear balance came to be known as 'parity'.

The conservatives, in opposition and in power after 1980, challenged this concept, redefining parity to mean 'Soviet strategic superiority'. To justify this assertion conservatives pointed to the predominance of Soviet land-based ICBMs, and the fact that Soviet 'megatonnage' was larger than that of the US nuclear force. President Carter was attacked for 'going soft' on the Soviets by agreeing to the terms of SALT II, and indeed he was eventually compelled, as re-election time drew near, to reject it.

SALT II was premised on the view that strategic nuclear parity did not in any way deprive the United States of its historic military superiority. In a speech delivered on 8 February 1977 President Carter stated:

> At the present time, my judgement is that we have superior nuclear capability. The Soviet Union has more throw-weight, larger missiles, larger warheads; we have more missiles, a much higher degree of accuracy, and also, we have three different mechanisms which are each independently adequate to deliver atomic weapons – airplanes, submarines, and intercontinental ballistic missiles. I think that we are roughly equivalent, even though I think we are superior, in that either the Soviet Union or we could destroy a major part of the other nation if a major strike was made.
>
> (Labrie 1979: 419)

In this speech he pointed to the one-sided nature of Soviet strategic forces, identifying the Soviet superiority in land-based missiles as a *disadvantage*. According to this view, talk of superiority at such massive levels of overkill was absurd. 'Parity' was all that each side could hope to achieve, and parity did not deprive the USA of its technological lead (still in the order of five to ten years for the introduction of new strategic systems). Henry Kissinger put it this way to the US Senate Committee on Foreign Relations when Secretary of State in the Nixon administration:

> It is of course very difficult to assess what superiority is when you are dealing with weapons for which there is no operational experience and which are so difficult to relate to political objectives. I think there is, however, common agreement that at

> no time in the post-war period has the Soviet Union had any military superiority over the United States in the strategic field of any significant category. This condition obtains today as well.

The nuclear debate in the 1980s has largely been about new nuclear weapons in the European theatre. The NATO dual-track decision of December 1979 was based upon the assertion of the 'strategically significant superiority' of Soviet nuclear forces in Europe – their 'theatre' weapons, the SS-20 and Backfire bomber. NATO argued that it had no match for these weapons, which constituted a qualitatively new threat. The USA, went the argument, would be unlikely to respond to a conventional or nuclear attack on Europe by escalating to all-out strategic nuclear war, 'sacrificing Chicago for Dusseldorf'. The Soviet Union would be able to blackmail the west into submission in this 'strategically significant' area for the western alliance by exploiting the 'credibility gap' in NATO defences.

However, on 16 October 1983, on the very eve of the Cruise and Pershing II deployments, the *Observer* reported a story which suggested a different reason for the employment of the Soviet threat rationale:

> The Americans, correctly predicting the rise of the peace movement, hoped to avoid the hostile protest which had greeted the plans for the neutron bomb.

In this same article David Owen, Foreign Secretary at a crucial period leading up to the dual-track decision, was reported as saying that 'it was never part of our belief that the new weapons had to match the SS-20s. Later, it began to get political. If you take the view, as I do, that there is such an excess anyhow, you are not worried about the numbers game.'[5]

As in conventional armaments the evidence suggests that Soviet nuclear forces are still technologically inferior and relatively vulnerable to those of the west, as a few basic indicators show: Soviet ICBMs still use notoriously unreliable liquid fuels as opposed to the more advanced solid fuel systems of the Americans; on average Soviet missiles have only a tenth of the accuracy of comparable American weapons (see SIPRI 1983a: 56); their submarines are frequently detected by NATO patrols, while at the time of writing no NATO nuclear submarine had ever been 'caught' on patrol.

Soviet foreign policy

A further bone of contention concerned the nature of the Soviet role in the world. The conservatives portrayed the Soviet Union as an expansionist, imperialistic power with ambitions of global domination. The International Institute for Strategic Studies reported in its *Strategic Survey 1983–84* that such opinions were now entrenched in the top echelons of NATO's government:

> The most eloquent exponent of Reagan's world view, National Security Council Soviet expert Richard Pipes, believed that the Soviet Union was not only militarily superior to the US, but was also driven by a domestic system that inherently generated aggressive outward drives.
>
> (54)

President Reagan himself, in his speech to the United Nations Second Special Session on Disarmament on 17 June 1982, explained why 'we are so concerned about Soviet conduct':

> Since the Second World War, the record of tyranny has included Soviet violation of the Yalta agreements leading to domination of eastern Europe, symbolized by the Berlin Wall – a grim, grey monument to repression that I visited just a week ago. It includes the takeovers of Czechoslovakia, Hungary, and Afghanistan and the ruthless repression of the proud people of Poland. Soviet-sponsored guerrillas are at work in Central and South America, in Africa, the Middle East, in the Caribbean and in Europe, violating human rights and unnerving the world with violence. Communist atrocities in south-east Asia, Afghanistan and elsewhere continue to shock the free world as refugees escape to tell of their horror.

Underpinning the fear of Soviet military strength and Soviet expansionism was a conservative moral repugnance of socialism as a system, typically expressed in a speech made by Ronald Reagan in March 1983:

> Let us pray for the salvation of all those who live in that totalitarian darkness, pray they will discover the joy of knowing God – but until they do let us be aware that while they preach the supremacy of the state ... they are the focus of evil in the world.

The Soviet threat, as invoked by the conservative leaders of the

NATO alliance, was not only military but moral. NATO was said to be defending not merely a collection of national state boundaries but civilization itself from the 'totalitarian darkness' of socialism.

As with conservative assessments of Soviet military strength these views were widely challenged. As reported in *The Times* of 12 August 1983, academics at Lancaster University counted the number of foreign interventions made by various countries between 1945 and 1976, and concluded the following:

> One study showed that the western countries intervened in 64 wars, while the Soviet Union and its allies took part in six. A different analysis looked at foreign intervention in 641 post-war conflicts (defined more broadly this time to include coups and large civil disturbances as well as wars). Western nations intervened on 243 occasions and the communist countries, including North Vietnam, Cuba, China, and the Warsaw Pact nations, only on 20.

Fred Halliday, of the Institute of Policy Studies, challenged the conservative analysis of specific international problems, for example, that the Soviet role in the Middle East – one of the main 'hotspots' of recent years – had been or was now an aggressive, expansionary one:

> They [the USSR] were among the first to recognize the state of Israel ... they have never denied Israel's right to exist. ... Soviet arms supplies have never been such as to give the Arab states overall military superiority ... they have never acceded to Arab requests for nuclear weapons, despite the fact that Israel is known to have an almost immediate nuclear capacity.
>
> (1983: 73)

Jonathan Steele, foreign affairs correspondent of the *Guardian*, has argued that:

> contrary to the conventional wisdom in the west, the Kremlin has always tended to act in the Middle East with restraint. ... The Soviet Union discouraged the three recent Arab–Israeli wars and has imposed limits on its arms deliveries, often at the risk of incurring Arab displeasure. On the central aspect of the Arab–Israeli dispute, the existence of Israel, Moscow has consistently urged the Arabs to recognize the Jewish state.
>
> (1983: 180)

The conservative view of the Soviet threat was contested even by politicians of the right such as Enoch Powell MP. In a speech reported in the *Guardian* of 10 October 1983, Powell referred to:

> a quintessentially American misunderstanding of Soviet Russia as an aggressive power, militaristically and ideologically bent on world domination. ... The notion has no basis in fact; it exists wholly in the realm of the imagination. While the United States, often with some of its allies, has fought two major wars in Asia and intervened with military force in Central America and the Middle East, no Russian soldier stands today an inch beyond where they stood in 1948, with the one solitary exception that proves the rule – Afghanistan, where a backyard war is being fought with the same motives and prospects of failure as it was twice fought by the British Empire in India. If Russia is bent on world domination, she has been remarkably slothful and remarkably unsuccessful.

The historical western superiority in weapons of all kinds, if it has been narrowed in recent years by the Soviet Union, has not been eradicated. Furthermore, as this chapter has attempted to show, the dominant view of the Soviet threat as expressed by the conservatives in power during the 1980s was far from being 'consensual'.

Against this background, Chapter 3 examines the view of the Soviet Union constructed by television news: television's image of 'the enemy'.

Part II

Images of the enemy

3

Reporting the Soviet Union

This chapter examines what television news reports about the USSR: television's image of 'the enemy'.

The analysis refers to three separate samples of news. The first included all news bulletins broadcast by BBC1, BBC2 and ITV – the three then-existing channels – between 1 May and 30 June 1982. The second included the main evening bulletins on BBC1, BBC2, ITV, and Channel 4 between 10 May and 8 June 1983. Seventy-five items in the category of Soviet news were identified over these periods (excluding references to the Soviet Union in the context of arms control talks, which are analysed in a subsequent chapter).

These items were concerned, on the one hand, with coverage of Soviet society (reportage on events going on inside the USSR, or comments on those events from outside the USSR itself) and, on the other, coverage of Soviet foreign policy and events in which the USSR is reported as an actor on the world stage, including Soviet–British relations. Table 3.1 lists these items by story.

The chapter also looks at coverage recorded on the deaths of Soviet leaders Brezhnev, Andropov, and Chernenko between November 1982 and March 1985. These 'special' events saw the Soviet government pass through a period of rapid change. In a political system renowned and in some quarters reviled for its predictable stability, three state and party leaders died in quick succession: Leonid Brezhnev in November 1982, Yuri Andropov in February 1984, and Konstantin Chernenko in March 1985. These events saw the passing of one leadership generation in the USSR and the arrival of another. The leadership changes had an obvious and enormous impact on Soviet and world affairs and were also the occasion of a unique series of *media* events.

Until the death of Leonid Brezhnev television news had never been present at the state funeral of a Soviet leader. The television era arrived too late to record the death of Stalin in 1953, and nearly thirty years passed before another Soviet leader died in office. But following the death of Brezhnev, and indicative of how top-heavy

Table 3.1 *Routine Soviet news for the sample periods May and June 1982, and 10 May–8 June 1983*

Story	*Number of items*
Moscow Peace Committee	1
Bella Korchnoi	1
Anatoly Scharansky	1
Andrei Sakharov	3
Alexander Solzhenitsyn	2
Moscow newsreader, 1983	3
Soviet space programme	5
1982 May Day parade	1
Andropov promotion, 1982	1
Volga river disaster, 1983	6
The Russian system	1
Soviet involvement in Middle East, June 1982	3
Soviet involvement in Middle East, June 1983	5
Soviet involvement in Afghanistan	7
Soviet involvement in the Falklands	13
European gas pipeline	2
US–Soviet grain deal	1
Defence White Paper, 1982	5
Diplock Security report, 1983	4
Geoffrey Prime affair, 1983	8
Computer smuggling, 1983	2
Total	75

with old men the Soviet leadership had become, his two successors survived for only sixteen and thirteen months respectively. Three times in less than three years western journalists marked the passing of a Soviet leader. So used to it did they become that by the time of Konstantin Chernenko's funeral on 13 March 1985, they were describing the ceremony as 'a well-practised ritual' with well-established traditions:

> Then once again, *as tradition now dictates*, the military parade began.
>
> (3 2200 13/3/85)

Had this study been able to include television coverage of one such change in the Soviet leadership it would have been fortuitous.

That there were three within the period of the research was a somewhat bizarre coincidence, providing the opportunity to assemble a unique sample of 'in-depth' coverage of the USSR. This news was more than a simple reporting of the facts about the death of one leader and his succession by another. As background to the basic event journalists constructed long and detailed narratives about the Soviet Union. As such they provide an opportunity to examine what television journalists say about the USSR when they have time and resources to report 'in-depth'.

Selecting Soviet news

The selection of news about the Soviet Union is partly determined, like other categories of output, by routine journalistic news values. Disaster stories, major state occasions, and space flights, for example, are regularly covered. But the major theme in routine news coverage of the USSR is that of dissent – the activities and experiences of groups and individuals opposed to the Soviet system inside the USSR itself (dissidents) and outside (defectors and exiles). In samples of news recorded during 1982 and 1983 this theme occupied the largest proportion of coverage of Soviet society (see Table 3.1).

Dissent and human rights are important themes in coverage of all countries, but the particular emphasis given to them in news coverage of the Soviet Union deserves comment.

Soviet dissent is a form of political activity with little visible support from the general public. Soviet dissident Roy Medvedev, a man who has himself experienced harassment from the Soviet state, writes that in the USSR 'socialism as a system claims the consensus of practically the entire population ... beyond all doubt the vast majority of the population endorses the Soviet Communist party' (1980: 51). The American Sovietologist Marshall Shatz notes that 'Soviet dissent is confined to relatively isolated individuals and circles within the urban educated elite' (1980: 178).

Peter Ruff, who worked as the BBC's radio and television correspondent in Moscow for three years, remarks: 'It's interesting to see just how high a percentage of the people appear to support the leadership.'[1]

Unlike Poland or South Africa, the dissident movement in the USSR is not and has never been a mass movement. And if the treatment of Soviet dissenters at the hands of the state may be harsh and sometimes brutal, this and worse is the case with some countries which receive very little human rights coverage. Britain has itself been found guilty of human rights violations in Northern Ireland by the European Court of Human Rights although, as Hartley notes, British dissidents tend to be reported in rather different terms by the media:

> Of course there are groups and individuals in 'our' society who also act outside the official channels. But they are not seen as dissidents: they are seen as deviants. ... The terms used to characterize strikes, direct action, and other expressions of dissent concentrate on notions of irresponsibility, irrationality, and other mindlessness or bloody-mindedness; there is always the implication of violence.
>
> (1984: 84)

It is in this context that the *particular* newsworthiness of Soviet dissidence is significant. In his study of the north American press, Herman argues that the quantity of news coverage given to dissidence in a given country is generally unrelated to the degree of state-sponsored brutality involved, or to the extent of popular support for the dissident. Rather, the significance imputed to dissent depends on its *political* context. Herman suggests that the dissident who opposes the social system of an ideological 'enemy' tends to be more newsworthy and will be covered more sympathetically than s/he who opposes the social system of an ideological ally:

> The point is strikingly evident in the case of 'martial law' in Poland, which dominated the headlines and aroused the mass media and political leadership to a state of frenzy in early 1981 and 1982. In contrast, martial law imposed in Turkey in 1981–2, accompanied by mass arrests, torture, and executions (which threatened to engulf a good part of the trade union leadership by early 1982) aroused little attention and no indignation. 'Frightful abuse' in the enemy sphere equals a 'return to stability' in the client state.
>
> (1982: 144)

The Glasgow University Media Group refer to an example from BBC's 9 *O'Clock News* of 19 May 1980, of coverage of the Turkish military coup that year which nicely illustrates Herman's point:

> Turkey has a long border with the Soviet Union on the southern flank of NATO, and the west have been watching with gloom the trouble building up there. So putting aside a few crocodile tears about democracy, most western observers are quietly pleased that the region looks *that much more stable tonight* than it did last night.[2]
>
> (1985: 7)

In this case the brutal imposition of martial law by Turkey – a member of NATO and thus an ideological ally – was defined on television news as 'that much more stability'.

The important point to note here is not that television news covers dissent in the Soviet Union. Rather, it is the extent to which dissent dominates the definition of Soviet reality which the news constructs. Television news tends to speak about Soviet society from the perspective of the dissident or the emigré, and to ignore or downplay the experiences of ordinary Soviets. Events of little intrinsic news value in the international arena are routinely defined as newsworthy if they can be employed to signify Soviet dissent.[3]

Conversely, there is little or no coverage of the *presence* of human rights as defined by the Soviets themselves. Such themes as the state's commitment to full employment, the prioritizing of health care and education, or the maintenance of low basic prices are rarely reported, even in items which are specifically addressed to describing Soviet society.

An edition of the children's news programme *Newsround* illustrates this. *Newsround* marked President Reagan's visit to Europe in June 1982 with a special item which set out to show 'what life is like on either side of the Iron Curtain' (1 1715 11/6/82). The item focused on the city of Berlin, the eastern part of which, if not part of the Soviet Union, was unambiguously labelled as 'the Russian system'.

First, President Reagan's visit to Europe was defined in terms of America's 'vital role' as protector of the western countries:

> President Reagan's visit is important because *since the Second World War America has played a vital role of backing countries on the west of the Iron Curtain.* Countries in the east look to the Soviet Union – Russia – for support. America and the west say there's no freedom under the Russian system. The people can't speak out against the government and there are no elections. But the Russians say that under their system – communism – everyone is equal. The difference between the two is clear in Germany.

The account which follows juxtaposes positive images of the west with negative images of the east and 'communism'. For example, both NATO and Warsaw Pact forces occupy Berlin. They have done so since 1945 for complex historical reasons. As this is explained to the audience the journalist makes an important distinction between the military forces on both sides:

> West Berlin is still an occupied city, under the control of the allied forces of Britain, France, and America. And once a year they put on a huge military parade. It's a show of force, a reminder to the Russians on the other side of the Wall, and *a way of assuring the West Berliners who turn up to enjoy the parade that they are well protected.*

In West Berlin military occupation protects and assures people against 'the Russians on the other side'. They 'enjoy' the military presence. East Berlin, however:

> is still as much an occupied city as West Berlin. In theory no East German troops are allowed inside the city boundary. Here, *it's the Russians who rule.*

The differences in language are not merely semantic. To 'protect' from 'the Russians' is one thing, to 'rule' over the Germans is another. The view that the Soviets or the East Berliners might feel themselves in any need of protection is foreclosed. Their forces threaten, while ours protect.

This account can be compared with another, taken from the more authorial form of the television documentary. Documentaries do not claim the neutrality of news journalism, and their authorship – in this case by Jonathan Dimbleby – is often a major attraction of the programme. Nevertheless, Dimbleby's examination of life in East and West Germany illustrates what *might* be said in a comparison. In *Taking Sides*, Part 1 of Dimbleby's series, *The Cold War Game*, he employs the symbol of the military parade to comment on the human rights issue. In the course of this account, the construction of meaning around the image of the military parade is significantly different from that of *Newsround*:

> In Berlin the western allies parade their military might to approval, and to disgust from a small group which turns its back in silence on a military extravaganza which a growing number of

> young West Germans detest. And then, in a city which is said to be a symbol of western democracy, the police move in.

On camera we see the protesters beaten and dragged away as Dimbleby observes that:

> In the cold war game it's only the authorities on the other side who treat their dissidents thus. This was not a question of 'human rights', but a 'minor incident' that was swiftly dealt with.

This account challenges the absoluteness of the concepts of human rights and dissidence, directing the audience to the *possibility* of differing interpretations of the terms. The implied suggestion is that if communists do not have a monopoly on brutality and repression, the west does not have a monopoly on democracy and human rights.

Newsround's account of life on either side of the Wall presented an image of West Berlin as a place of gaiety and affluence:

> West Berlin is like an island of western life in a communist country. The city's main street, the Kurfurstendamm, is busy and lively, full of cafes and luxury hotels. The shops are expensive and they sell the same range of goods as any other western city.

In East Berlin, by contrast:

> what they couldn't get away from were the same problems and shortages which dog the other East bloc nations. The goods may look alright in the windows but they are expensive, the choice is highly restricted, and the quality doesn't match up to the west.

Such an account is internally contradictory. There are expensive shops on both sides, according to the journalist, but only in the east are they defined negatively. One might infer that in the east there are no cafes or luxury hotels, and that in the west there are no shortages or problems. Western problems like unemployment and poverty (from which West Berlin is not exempt) are omitted from the comparison, as are advantages of 'communism' such as full employment and low basic prices for the necessities of life. Throughout the account economic indicators which might construct a negative image of the west, such as unemployment statistics, were excluded, as were those which might have constructed a positive image of the east, such as the fact that with 17 million people East Germany was at this time higher in the league of industrial producers than Britain. It was noted that:

> East Germany is a rigidly controlled society. There's no choice of schooling but it is strongly competitive and for those who don't fit in the possibilities are limited.

There were no references to the 20 million unemployed in western Europe at this time, whose possibilities, from some perspectives, might be regarded as at least equally limited.

Television news is not, of course, a medium with the space to provide a meticulous comparison of every aspect of life in east and west, and no one would expect it to do so. Nevertheless, the selective, comparative approach adopted in this example consistently led to the presentation of 'the Russian system' negatively, and the west as 'an island of life and luxury'.

Dimbleby's report, to which we have already referred, illustrates some of the things that *could* have been said in an account of life in East Germany. He, for example, presents an East German family, whom he describes as average, working and living apparently normal lives. They watch television, drink beer, and go on holidays. For a three-bedroom flat they pay:

> Twenty marks weekly, or roughly £5 from a family income of £100. Food, which is heavily subsidized, costs them about £25 a week. The price of basics like bread, meat, potatoes, and milk has been frozen for twenty years; like fares, gas, and electricity. After paying for all their necessities they have the equivalent of £25 a week which they put in the bank. The family give an appearance of genuine contentment.

Dimbleby's account presents a society 'where there's no freedom' from another perspective. From a different perspective an alternative image can be constructed. In *Newsround*, only the problems of the system and the dislikes of its inhabitants are newsworthy:

> If you asked an East German what he disliked most about his country, he'd probably tell you the restrictions on travel abroad . . . the shortage of housing is serious.

No East German was asked what he *liked* most about his country, nor were there any references to a serious shortage of housing in West Berlin. There were no amendments to the simple east/west, bad/good juxtaposition being constructed in the account. The youthful audience was presented with a selective image of socialist society as seen from the limited perspective of free market values.

Even where there is space for journalists to look at the USSR in greater depth than routine news bulletins allow, coverage of the Soviet economy has also tended to focus on its negative aspects. During news coverage of the death of Leonid Brezhnev, references to the Soviet economy were exclusively negative. One bulletin claimed that:

> The crisis which erupted in Poland in 1980 leading to the emergence of Solidarity revealed *the chronic economic ills of the entire Soviet system.*
>
> (4 1900 11/11/82)

While the Polish crisis of the early 1980s was reported to be symptomatic of 'chronic illness' in 'the entire Soviet system', there were no references to the positive experience of countries like East Germany and Hungary. The Soviet economy was defined only as a series of immense problems:

> Whoever makes it to the top will have to cope with the immense economic problems, which is one legacy Mr Brezhnev has left to his country's workers. His policies of rigid control have made this year's growth rate the worst since the war, while the harvest has been the fourth bad one in a row – worse than in Czarist times.
>
> (1 2100 11/11/82)

> there's a flagging economy and a perennial grain shortage . . . in a flagging economy there's zero economic growth.
>
> (3 2200 11/11/82)

The Soviet economy, of course, has many problems. Compared to the advanced capitalist economies it remains relatively undeveloped. Labour productivity is low. Shortages of labour and materials lead to bottlenecks and the inefficient use of resources. These problems are compounded by corruption and slow-moving bureaucratic machinery.

But the Soviet economy also has a number of positive features. Even by the standards of success of western governments – which are not the only proclaimed goals of a centralized socialist economy – the Soviet Union has not performed disastrously. The prices of basic items are low and stable. Inflation is zero, 'booms and slumps' are unknown, growth is constant, there is full employment and an extensive social welfare system, and standards of living have increased continuously since the Second World War. Such claims could not be made of the British economy. Martin Walker, Moscow correspondent for the *Guardian*, comments on his own surprise at arriving in the USSR and finding western media images of the Soviet economy challenged:

> Staying and working here, it's plain that the dominant theme of most western analyses of the Soviet Union in the 1970s and early 80s – that this place is economically a basket-case, that it's collapsing – is just not true.
>
> It's not collapsing. It's a very stable society. It's one which delivers the goods to its people. Their living standards get a little better every year. Sure there are shortages, gross inefficiencies, gross examples of waste and incompetence, but anybody who knows Scotland or the north of England or southern Italy or large swathes of America knows that we're living in a glass house, and we've got to be careful about the kind of stones we're throwing. I think that came as a shock to me – to discover that the system was not only working better than I had read it was, but it also seemed to be capable of change and improvement within its own terms.

Coverage of other aspects of Soviet life also focuses on problems. ITN's coverage of the death of Brezhnev defined the Soviet Union as a 'huge political and administrative headache' where:

> the Russians themselves are about to become the minority. There are 260 million Soviet citizens. Just 159 million of them live in the Russian republic. The big population explosion is out in Muslim Asia, among the Uzbheks and Kazhaks. That is why the Soviet Union went into Afghanistan.
>
> (3 2200 11/11/82)

In addition to the Islamic problem (asserted without substantiation to be the reason for Soviet involvement in Afghanistan), 'growing urban problems familiar to the west' were also noted in this item, such as 'hooliganism and alcoholism'. There was a reference to the problem of the 'new class' in Soviet society:

> They are privately contemptuous of the political system that deprives them of more than material things. In the history of revolutions it is those who are better off who are the most dangerous.

Images of crisis and impending doom are a familiar feature of Soviet news, and the above passage exemplifies a type of reporting criticized by Patrick Cockburn, Moscow correspondent of the *Financial Times*, in the following terms:

> Journalists tend to have an attitude towards this country. Often if you look at a headline it says 'Soviets face crisis'. It's usually not true. This whole system was designed to avoid crisis. Take Central Asia. There are some indications that there's been a greater popularity of Islamic belief and worship, but there isn't *much* evidence. There's no evidence at all that the Soviets face a crisis because of the Islamic revolution. If you examine any country and see every crack as indicating a current or potential earthquake, you'll produce this caricature. There's a tendency for journalists to dramatize things, but particularly here.

The Soviets abroad

The Soviet Union is frequently mentioned in news coverage of international trouble spots, such as the Middle East or Central America. In such cases accounts and interpretations of the Soviet role tend to reflect dominant western definitions of the problem, as the Middle East crisis of May 1983 illustrates.

One year following its invasion of the Lebanon in 1982, Israel was anxious to withdraw its troops, for pressing domestic reasons. The Americans suggested that this could be achieved equitably by Israel and Syria *both* removing their troops. Syria refused, and a confrontation with Israel began to develop.

To see how the US definition of this problem was preferred on television news, one has first to note that there were competing approaches available at this time.

The US government, in line with the general tendency of the Reagan administration to make sense of international crises in terms of 'Soviet expansionism', held that the problem was related to Soviet influence in the region. In particular, the Soviets were alleged to be building up their military forces in Syria, and urging the Syrian government to reject the US peace plan.

A different perspective on the crisis, and on the Middle East situation in general, appeared in an article by Robert Fisk of *The Times* on 13 May. Fisk reported that Soviet military supplies to Syria were for defensive purposes only. He agreed that 'there are

3,000 Soviet military advisers training the Syrian army. But there are no combat troops in Syria. ... In Lebanon, no independent witness has yet identified Soviet troops.' Fisk went on to point out that Soviet military power in the region was a great deal less impressive than that of NATO:

> The multinational force is not made up of United Nations peacekeepers but of troops from the United States, France, Italy, and Britain. Beirut has over the past eight months been transformed into what is in effect a NATO base, complete with all the logistics and intelligence apparatus that the western allies choose to place at its disposal. The waters off Beirut have become, quite literally, a [US] Sixth Fleet anchorage.

In the *Guardian* of 14 May Jonathan Steele challenged the view that Syria and the Soviets were working closely together:

> President Assad is no Soviet lackey ... [his] government spends more of its time talking to the American Embassy than to officials from the Soviet mission.

This view was reported only once during the sample, on Channel 4 news during an interview with a Middle East expert, Dr Adeed Dawisha:

> Dr Adeed Dawisha: The relation between the Syrians and the Soviet Union is one really of equal allies. This is something which people do not seem to appreciate. The Syrians are not clients of the Soviet Union. They have shown in the past, repeatedly, to be taking independent actions which the Soviets themselves have not agreed to.
>
> (4 1900 17/5/83)

Despite the availability of this framework for interpreting the Soviet role in the crisis, the US definition of the problem was generally favoured by journalists.

Statements by US political leaders asserting a belligerent Soviet role in the crisis were not balanced with statements of competing interpretations:

> Today Mr Schultz [the US Secretary of State] called on the Soviet Union to *get on the side of peace* in Lebanon and to support America's attempts to get all foreign troops out.
>
> (3 2200 10/5/83)

> The American Defence Secretary Mr Caspar Weinberger said in New York that *the Soviet build-up in Syria made agreement more difficult and increased the danger of war between Syria and Israel.*
>
> (3 2200 13/5/83)

Journalists linked 'Syrian war-cries' with actual, or implied, Soviet support:

> Syria has again talked about a new war with Israel over Lebanon. Syria, *which is armed and backed by Russia*, turned down the deal for Israeli troop withdrawal from Lebanon negotiated by the American Secretary of State Mr George Schultz last week.
>
> (3 2200 10/5/83)

> Syria's war-like noises over Lebanon are probably designed to show the Arab world she is a force to be reckoned with again and to try and make life difficult for the Israelis who desperately want to get their troops home from Lebanon. But *even with her new Russian support* it's unlikely Syria really wants another war.
>
> (3 2200 13/5/83)

> Syrian war-cries *are backed by an enormous influx of Soviet military equipment.* Hundreds of T-72 battletanks, artillery pieces, and aircraft have replaced the losses of last year's conflict with Israel.
>
> (1 2100 16/5/83)

An item about US military aid to Israel, by contrast, was couched in very different terms. On 19 May it was reported that President Reagan 'says he's going to announce in the next few days that America will sell 75 F-15 bombers to Israel' (3 2200 19/5/83). Here there were no references to 'an enormous influx of military equipment'. On the contrary, this sale of weapons (to a country which one year before had used similar equipment to kill an estimated 30,000 civilians in Beirut) was explained by an unqualified statement of the official view:

> The US Defence Secretary is worried about the Soviet military build-up in Syria.
>
> (3 2200 19/5/83)

While Soviet supplies to Syria were reported on the news as the *cause* of conflict, those from the US to Israel were reported as a *response* to Soviet build-up.[4]

In an item which appeared on BBC1's 6 *O'Clock News* early in 1987 the BBC's Washington correspondent, Tim Sebastian, referred to Nicaragua as a 'communist country' and 'a Soviet bridgehead'. Both of these terms were in favour with the Reagan administration at the time, and likely to be used as an excuse for invading the country.

Most western observers, including many within the US itself, would dispute that Nicaragua is either a communist country or a Soviet bridgehead. In this item, nevertheless, the labels were taken on and employed without qualification, as if they were neutral descriptions.

Soviet military power

Television news accounts of Soviet military power tend to reflect those views which maximize the Soviet threat and assume 'worst-case' assessments of Soviet capabilities to be true.

In coverage of the death of Leonid Brezhnev, the BBC referred to Soviet military expansion in recent years as 'the biggest military build-up the world has ever seen', contrasting this image with President Brezhnev's advocacy of disarmament:

> President Brezhnev's place in history is assured. The man who advocated disarmament yet presided over the biggest military build-up the world has ever seen.
>
> (1 2100 11/11/82)

A bigger military build-up, one might wrongly infer from this statement, than that initiated by President Reagan after he came to power in 1980. Elsewhere in the same bulletin it was noted that:

> In Brezhnev's final years the Soviet military build-up continued, outstripping NATO in a number of areas.

The item contained no information as to the areas in which NATO is surpassed by the USSR, or their relevance to the overall military balance, or the areas in which NATO outstripped the Soviet Union. There were no references to a NATO military build-up in the narrative, although by November 1982 President Reagan was well advanced in his defence programme. All these factors are important if the viewer is to make an informed appraisal of the 'meaning' of the term 'Soviet military build-up'.

BBC coverage of the Brezhnev funeral picked out Soviet Defence

Minister Marshal Ustinov from the leaders standing on the Lenin Mausoleum and identified him as the man who had 'presided over an unprecedented military build-up' (1 2100 15/11/82).

The BBC, then, presented the viewer with an unqualified, uncontextualized image of a Soviet military build-up which was 'unprecedented', 'the biggest the world has ever seen', and 'outstripping NATO in many areas'.

Channel 4 news coverage of Brezhnev's death, referring to the SALT II arms limitation treaty, stated that it had been signed 'only after five long years of haggling':

> and Russia's military might grew *alarmingly*.
>
> (4 1900 11/11/82)

Soviet military power grew during the 1970s, as did that of the United States. That it grew 'alarmingly' is a question of opinion rather than fact.

ITN's coverage of Brezhnev's death referred twice to Soviet defence spending, entering a debate which, as noted in Chapter 2, is an important area of contention in the wider debate about the Soviet threat. It was shown there that the extent of Soviet defence spending, like Soviet military power in general, can be guessed, calculated, assessed, but not *known* as a fact. Assessments vary. The 'worst-case' assessment, contained in the UK Ministry of Defence 1982–3 *Defence Estimates*, was that:

> Soviet defence expenditure now accounts for some 14–16 per cent of GNP in current prices, over twice the level of any NATO country.
>
> (1983: 20)

In 1984 NATO acknowledged this estimate to be exaggerated by a factor of two. On television news in 1982 it was appearing as a statement of fact, without qualification or identification of its source:

> President Brezhnev was an enthusiastic supporter of detente with the west but under his leadership there was no let up in Soviet military spending. Russia has consistently spent *over one-eighth of its national income on defence, that's about twice the proportion of most western countries.*
>
> (3 2200 11/11/82)

> in a flagging economy there's zero economic growth, lagging technology, and *15 per cent of production spent on defence.*
>
> (3 2200 11/11/82)

These assessments of Soviet defence spending – one-eighth or 15 per cent of GNP, twice the proportion of most western countries – are the same as those found in the official sources quoted in Chapter 2. They were originally produced by the CIA for the US Defence Department under pressure from the conservative Committee on the Present Danger, yet their source was not indicated to the viewer by the preface that 'the British government claims' or 'the CIA estimates'. There was no indication that the figure of '14–16 per cent' was a disputed estimate. There was no reference to the relevant consideration that Soviet GNP is approximately 50 per cent that of the United States ($850 billion as against $1700 billion in 1976), and that for this reason figures for defence spending as a percentage of GNP have to be qualified. The phrase 'spends twice as much as western countries' is particularly evocative, but could be qualified by the fact that, in hard cash, according to western bankers, NATO spent on defence about $200 billion more than the Warsaw Pact in 1982.

As in the earlier BBC example, the information is presented in such a way as to qualify Brezhnev's policy of detente: 'President Brezhnev supported detente but . . .' We might reasonably reconstruct the meaning of the statement in the following way – detente is nice in theory *but* you can't trust him because he spends over twice the amount of western countries on defence.

In the sample of news coverage on which this study is based there were only two occasions when journalists qualified images of Soviet military power by pointing out that the west retains military superiority. In the first example, from coverage of Brezhnev's death, a reference to Soviet military inferiority is included as a brief addendum to an account of what is described as a 'revolution' in Soviet military technology:

> Under the leadership of Brezhnev Russia's armed forces have undergone a technological revolution in recent years. Soviet ground forces in Europe have been considerably strengthened by new weapons like the T-72 tanks on display last week in Moscow, and Russia spent vast sums of money on the development of new weapons in space. Large numbers of navigation and communication satellites have been launched, and new radar satellites which can track NATO ships at sea. And in the past decade the Soviet navy has expanded dramatically, with a new ability to project power worldwide.
>
> (3 2200 11/11/82)

These images of 'dramatic' expansion were contextualized by the observation that Soviet military forces remain inferior to those of the United States:

> Russia's purpose with all this technology is to try to *catch up with the Americans.*

A second counter-example accompanied coverage of Chernenko's death, on the eve of a new round of Geneva arms control talks. One of the major issues at these talks would be the United States' planned 'Star Wars' project, the Strategic Defence Initiative. One bulletin presented this account of the military balance in space weapons:

> The Russians already have killer satellites to knock out American military satellites, and plans for space stations like this which could serve a number of purposes in war. But by and large the Russians' space technology *lags far behind the Americans'.*
>
> (4 1900 11/3/85)

East–west relations

A major theme of coverage of the USSR has been the state of east–west relations. Journalists have tended to concentrate their accounts on two aspects of the problem: the poor state of relations in general, and the fact that no progress had been made in the area of arms control. Coverage has tended to favour the dominant western explanation of the new cold war, i.e. that it is essentially a problem located in some aspect or other of Soviet behaviour. References to the breakdown of detente and the onset of the new cold war have focused blame on Soviet actions and Soviet policies:

> With the Soviet invasion of Afghanistan American–Soviet relations went into irreversible decline.
>
> (4 1900 11/11/82)

> The SALT II treaty was never ratified by Congress. East–west relations were moving into a difficult period, not helped by allegations of Soviet maltreatment of dissidents.
>
> (1 2100 11/11/82)

> They shot [the Korean airliner] out of the sky, bringing world-wide condemnation down on the Kremlin. East–west contacts were shattered.
>
> (1 2100 10/2/84)

These were significant events, but were not in themselves the cause of deteriorating east–west relations. In some respects they were a consequence of that deterioration. The reason given publicly by Presidents Carter and Reagan for the ultimate failure of the SALT II negotiations made no reference to 'Soviet maltreatment of dissidents' but alleged that SALT II would codify Soviet strategic superiority. Similarly, the Korean airliner disaster did not 'shatter' east–west contacts, but confirmed in the view of some commentators the dangers of a situation where high-level contacts were virtually non-existent.

Individual Soviet leaders have been blamed for the crisis. Brezhnev, one journalist remarked, 'never quite managed to convince President Reagan's America that the old men in the Kremlin were genuinely interested in peace, co-operation and detente' (4 1900 11/11/82).

After the death of Andropov, BBC news wondered if his successor would make 'any *real* effort to get the arms talks going again' (1 2100 10/2/84). The implication that Andropov had *not* made such an effort took no account of the views of those such as Denis Healey, who argued after the death of Andropov that:

> It's fair to say that Andropov tried very hard to improve relations both with China and with the west. He failed because neither took the hand offered out.
>
> (3 2200 10/2/84)

When Chernenko died it was reported that under his leadership:

> the United States remained in *Soviet-imposed quarantine* and Mr Reagan in his pre-election campaign could do no right.
>
> (1 2100 11/3/85)

In these accounts blame for the east–west 'problem' is attributed to aspects of Soviet behaviour – Soviet policies, Soviet leaders. This feature of coverage is exemplified in the following report, from coverage of Brezhnev's death:

> In order to stress how deeply the United States wants detente, *despite Mr Brezhnev's harsh words last week*, the administration will probably send its second-highest ranking member Vice-President Bush [to the funeral].
>
> (3 2200 11/11/82)

The United States, we are told, 'deeply wants detente', *despite* what are described as Mr Brezhnev's 'harsh words' (which were not reported). The President's refusal to go to the Brezhnev funeral, and his dispatch of the Vice-President instead are presented as evidence of his sincerity.

Reagan's attitudes to the USSR at this time were not a secret. Nowhere in these bulletins was it noted that he was the first United States President in forty years not to meet his Soviet counterpart, or that his first meeting with any member of the Soviet government had been with Andrei Gromyko only weeks before the Presidential Election of 1984. On the contrary, it was the Soviets who had 'imposed quarantine'.

Statements about east–west relations which appeared after Andropov's death reinforced the argument advanced by the Reagan administration for the fact that relations had not advanced during his brief tenure in office, i.e. that he was unfit and an invalid:

> The feeling in Washington is that with the uncertainty over Mr Andropov's health now over, a major obstacle to ending the present freeze in relations between the two superpowers may have been cleared away.
>
> (4 1900 10/2/84)

> Inside and outside of the administration there's a sense here of a new opening and opportunity for dialogue with the Soviet Union. And whether or not the President goes to Moscow he's likely to grasp at it.
>
> (1 2100 10/2/84)

The US administration is said to be 'grasping' at the opportunity to open a dialogue. Western demands for 'improvements' in Soviet behaviour were reported uncritically, as in the following examples:

> the United States will be looking to the new leadership for some signal of a willingness to ease the present tension.
>
> (1 2100 11/11/82)

> Some western leaders are *starting to demand some kind of sign from the Kremlin* about its promised goodwill. . . . Mrs Thatcher is likely to call *for genuine evidence that the Russians are serious about multilateral disarmament.*
>
> (1 2100 15/11/82)

In the context of the east–west debate it is to be expected that western leaders should have made such statements and attempted to present themselves to their own citizens as sincere peacemakers.

Television news assumed the sincerity of these claims, although alternative analyses, in which the western role would not have been perceived in such a positive way, were available.

Consider the following accounts taken from coverage of the funeral of Leonid Brezhnev:

> For President Reagan the hope of a new start for east–west relations.
>
> (1 2100 11/11/82)

> Mr Andropov said he wanted relations based on full equality, non-interference, mutual respect, and what he called a revitalizing of the international atmosphere.
>
> (3 2200 15/11/82)

Both statements contain expressions of a desire for improved east-west relations. Both are typical examples of the diplomatic style. But there is a subtle difference in their presentation. The first statement presents a *fact* – President Reagan *hopes* for a new start. There is no suggestion that this might be public relations.

Mr Andropov, on the other hand, is reported as *saying* that he wants improvement, a statement which can be 'read' in a number of ways, according to wider assumptions about the credibility of Soviet views. The assumption of good intentions on the part of the US administration is reinforced by the media presentation.

Consider, too, the following account of Mikhail Gorbachov's speech at the funeral of Konstantin Chernenko:

> Mr Gorbachov repeated the *well-oiled formula* about Russia's readiness to maintain neighbourly relations with all countries.
>
> (4 1900 13/11/85)

There were, by contrast, no references to 'well-oiled formulae' in the statements of western leaders such as President Reagan or Mrs Thatcher. Their statements of a desire for detente, of a hope for improved relations with the USSR, were never 'made sense' of in this manner.

As Gorbachov followed Chernenko, relations between east and west were improving to some extent. Coverage accounted for the change in terms of the 'new, younger man in the Kremlin':

> The west will be hoping that in time the fact that there's a younger man in charge now in Moscow, hopefully one who's more receptive to new ideas, and with the prospect of twenty

> years or more at the top with which to carry them out, that that will all lead to a significant improvement in east–west relations.
> (3 2200 13/11/85)

Despite the optimistic tone, and references to a 'younger man with new ideas', journalists are continuing to assume that western leaders are 'hoping for a significant improvement' in relations, an improvement which has been thwarted by recent Soviet leaderships.

The enemy within

In coverage of Soviet relations with Britain the USSR generally appears as a protagonist, a threat, or an enemy. This may be in the context of official statements, such as that of 22 June 1982 when the Conservative government published its annual defence White Paper, setting out the priorities of UK defence policy for the coming year. Following as it did so soon after the conclusion of the Falklands War, the 1982 White Paper was expected to be controversial. Would there be, for example, a review of the government's already announced decision to cut the navy, given its successes in the South Atlantic? Would there be a greater emphasis in the future on conventional as opposed to nuclear weapons? The principal conclusion of the 1982 Defence Paper, notwithstanding these debates, was that 'the main threat to the security of the United Kingdom is from the nuclear and conventional forces of the Soviet Union and her Warsaw Pact allies'.

The White Paper was reported on five bulletins, and while there was some reference to the intra-service debate about the role of the navy, there was no media discussion of this statement of the threat.[5]

> The government's White Paper still treats the Soviet Union as the main threat to Britain.
> (1 1740 22/6/82)

> Today's White Paper reasserts the government's view that the main threat to British security still comes from Russia and her Warsaw Pact allies.
> (3 1715 22/6/82)

On 20 May 1982, the Diplock Commission's report on internal security was published. Its conclusions identified 'left-wing' and Soviet subversion as the main internal threats to national security.

Reported on four bulletins throughout the day, the Commission's conclusions escaped analysis or discussion. The following was typical of their presentation:

> Britain's democratic institutions are under challenge from new subversive groups, mainly on the extreme left, according to the report of the Diplock Commission on security. The report says that at the same time the threat from the Soviet bloc intelligence services remains strong.
>
> (3 1745 20/5/82)

Another kind of story in which the USSR regularly appears is the 'spy scandal'. Sometimes Soviets working in Britain are accused of spying and expelled (see Chapter 8), and sometimes this news is concerned with British citizens alleged to be working for the Soviets or their allies.

Exceptions to these negative images sometimes appear in the context of news about British–Soviet trade. In June 1982 the British and American governments fell out over the US ban on contracts for the Soviet gas pipeline then under construction. The ban threatened to affect companies working in Britain, and was rejected by the Thatcher government.

> The British government said today that the American ban on exports of high technology for the Soviet gas pipeline is unacceptable, so it will protect British companies engaged in such sales. The Trade Minister Mr Peter Rees is in Washington to tell the Americans about the damage they're causing.
>
> (3 2200 30/6/82)

Such stories, when they appear, arguably qualify images of the USSR as a threat by presenting instead a country with whom Britain can work and trade. Following Mrs Thatcher's visit to Moscow in 1987 it might be expected that 'positive' images of the Soviet Union will become more common in the British media as a whole.

The extent to which the assumption that the USSR is an 'enemy' of Britain structures news output can be seen in an item from coverage of the Falklands conflict in 1982.[6] The USSR monitored the conflict by satellites and other means, as did the USA, and for similar reasons. The Falklands War was the first post-war conflict fought at sea, with many new weapons and tactics on display. Both superpowers attended as spectators, and several news items took this as their theme.

The launching of a Soviet satellite on 17 May was covered by BBC and ITN. ITN's coverage initially placed the Soviet satellite in the context of similar monitoring activity by the USA:

> This latest launch *matches the American Big Bird spy satellite put up last Wednesay by the US air force* at a cost of $80 million to keep watch on the Argentine fleet. The Americans have also just changed the orbits of two top secret Keyhole 11 satellites operated by the CIA so that they can cross the Falklands twice a day when the sun is low on the horizon.
>
> (3 1300 17/5/82)

There was, however, a distinct change of emphasis in a later item that day. Gone were references to the US Big Bird satellites, to their cost and to the fact that they preceded the Soviet satellite in their stationing above the Falklands. 'One of the [Soviets'] biggest satellites' became 'a giant spy satellite ... that ... passes low right over the Falkland Islands twice a day' (3 1745 17/5/82) (see Figure 3.1)

Figure 3.1. 'A giant spy satellite ... passes low right over the Falkland Islands twice a day' (3 1745 17/5/82)

4

Making Soviet news

Images of the Soviet Union are the result of a complex process of news production. The factors involved in that process are the subject of this chapter.

The journalists

Broadcast images of the Soviet Union begin with the correspondents on the ground in Moscow, many of whom recognize that their audiences back home are largely ignorant about life in the USSR. They acknowledge their responsibility to address what the BBC's television news correspondent in Moscow, Brian Hanrahan, calls 'the unknown factor' of Soviet life. Hanrahan considers his job as a Moscow correspondent for the BBC to contain two aspects. The first is:

> the political reporting, the stuff you'd get out of any society but that's important here because you're dealing with a country which has a big effect on the world. So there's that, and all the things that have a direct bearing on that, like the economy.

But the second aspect of his job, as he sees it:

> is the unknown factor. We don't know a lot about this country, but because it has a big effect on everybody there's a lot of interest in knowing about it. People want to know a lot about Soviet life, because it's a completely different system in every way: the fact that there are a lot of different cultures here, how they run things, how they make things work, is all a challenge to the rest of the world. Finding out how they do it, how their social organization works, how advanced they are, is all of interest just by itself.

Peter Ruff, the BBC's radio correspondent in Moscow argues that:

resources for covering international news are limited. As a BBC correspondent in Moscow your role is an international role. You're not here as a local news reporter, a feature writer, a ballet critic, or a chess expert. What you have to do is report, first of all, the government's view on east–west relations and regional problems. The bulk of your job is keeping an eye on changes of emphasis, changes of policy towards various countries, and so on.

But another part of the job is to try and describe to people in the west what life is like here, and to explain Soviet policy. What I find most interesting is to leave Moscow and see what life is like in other parts of the Soviet Union.

The *Financial Times*' Moscow correspondent, Patrick Cockburn, finds that:

> western people are interested in Soviet life. If you go anywhere in Britain, people do not want a very long conversation about the Soviet attitude to Star Wars. They are interested in what the Soviets get paid, what their houses are like, what they wear, if they have difficulty in getting clothes, what their education is like, what is it like when they go to a doctor? People in the west are interested in hearing how people live here, and that's an interest correspondents should be able to satisfy.

The previous chapter argued that television news coverage of the Soviet Union does not generally satisfy that interest, in so far as it produces a selectively negative image of the USSR. Many of those who produce news about the Soviet Union concede that this is true. They accept, too, that the nature of Soviet coverage is partly a consequence of the attitudes and ideological assumptions which some journalists bring to their work. As Patrick Cockburn puts it, 'It's evident that there's an ideological bias amongst journalists. That's quite obvious.' This point refers specifically to journalists working in Moscow, but is equally valid for those based in Britain who report on Soviet affairs. Cockburn continues:

> There are people who think that it's a deeply evil society. When you go back to England or America what is deeply shocking is the demonology about the USSR.

Peter Ruff acknowledges that 'A lot of journalists come here with the feeling that this is somewhere special, it's dangerous, it's a threat, and that it must be taken very seriously indeed'.

The existence of such attitudes is often revealed in the language journalists employ in news about the Soviet Union. The BBC's coverage of the 1982 May Day parade in Moscow reported that the party slogans carried by the participants were announced 'weeks in advance every year, and every year they duly and ritualistically appear'. The phrase 'duly and ritualistically' would not appear in coverage of a British state occasion, such as the Queen's Speech. Journalists would not be likely to report that 'the words are written by the government weeks in advance, and every year they duly and ritualistically appear in the mouth of the Queen'.

BBC coverage of the death of Leonid Brezhnev described him as:

> the ruler of Russia ... arguably the most powerful man in the world ... a man who's dominated the communist world for so long ... the man who embraced detente, but made sure democratic stirrings in his own empire were crushed.
>
> (1 2100 11/11/82)

ITN's newscaster stated that Brezhnev 'kept the Soviet Union a garrison state. Under him there was no Russian spring. He had only one answer to the change that threatened his system. Stop it!' (3 2200 11/11/82).

In ITN's coverage of the state funeral of Leonid Brezhnev, the newscaster gave an account of meetings which took place after the funeral between George Bush, Francis Pym (then British Foreign Secretary), and Yuri Andropov, the new General Secretary of the CPSU. There was, he said, 'a long receiving line in the Kremlin, of thirty-two heads of state, fifteen prime ministers, and just about every foreign minister who could get there' (3 2200 15/11/82). Then, over Soviet-supplied film of the funeral procession and the ceremonies afterwards, the following commentary was given:

> Intent on being there were the *Polish puppet* General Jaruzelski, who was among those who queued patiently for their handshake. And also Cuba's bearded Fidel Castro. Their *new master* was holding a party. One of the few non-communist faces Soviet viewers would recognize was Mrs Gandhi, with Afghanistan on her mind. And she bowed to Brezhnev's picture.
>
> They came to Red Square today to bury Brezhnev, and not particularly to praise him. All who were there were there by official invitation. So it is when *dictators* die. Others were there by orders.

> His old friend had come, Indira Gandhi who spoke her mind, and *the clients who didn't – Jaruzelski from Poland, Castro from Cuba, and Yasser Arafat.*
>
> And his widow Victoria, his daughter, and his son said goodbye in *an older ritual than the atheistic state allowed.*

The terms used to describe the principal actors in this drama reflect anti-Soviet, anti-communist stereotypes. As to the validity of the labels, Fidel Castro, explicitly identified as 'a client who doesn't speak his mind', has frequently adopted an independent foreign policy line *vis-à-vis* the Soviet Union. Indeed, he boycotted the later funeral of Konstantin Chernenko because, according to Channel 4 news at the time, 'relations with Moscow' were 'strained over Central America' (4 1900 13/3/85). Yasser Arafat, also included among 'the clients who don't speak their minds', is not even a communist, nor is the PLO a communist organization. On the contrary, the greatest proportion of PLO funds come from the oil-rich, pro-western Arab states.

In coverage of the funeral of Yuri Andropov, BBC2's *Newsnight* reported, in voice-over to shots of the Kremlin reception, that 'after the funeral, Mr Chernenko *held court*, receiving first his European *satraps* Kadar of Hungary, Jaruzselski of Poland, and the others' (2 *Newsnight* 14/2/84).

When Andropov died he was described as 'a hardman as far back as 1956' and 'a former secret police chief' (1 2100 10/2/84), and in another bulletin as 'the KGB hardman ... no friend to dissidents' (4 1900 10/2/84).

This language might be compared with the coverage of US Vice-President George Bush who has never, as far as is known, been described on British television news as 'the CIA hardman', although he was director of the CIA during the Ford administration. Such language 'makes sense' of the relations between the USSR and its allies in terms which might be taken for granted in Conservative Central Office, but are far from 'neutral'.

It should be said, however, that the employment of ideologically loaded language in news coverage of the USSR is not universal. ITN's coverage of the Andropov funeral eschewed negative descriptive labels:

> Pride of place went to the communist leaders of eastern Europe, with Kadar of Hungary, Jaruzelski of Poland, Caesesceau of

> Romania well to the fore. And then Russia's allies around the world like Fidel Castro.
>
> (3 2200 14/2/84)

In this example, the language of 'clients', 'dictators', 'puppets', and 'masters' was replaced by distinctly less evocative terms such as 'allies'. Journalists can and do choose to eschew cold war rhetoric.

Straightforward 'ideological bias' is one explanation for the tendency of television news to reproduce stereotyped images of the USSR, but there are other factors which must be taken into account. Some journalists, as we have seen, acknowledge that such themes as the lifestyle and habits of the ordinary Soviet citizen, as opposed to the dissident/refusenik/dissenter, are newsworthy and should be reported. The fact that they have been neglected in coverage is not, they argue, entirely the responsibility of western journalists. On the contrary, the Soviets themselves have made it difficult for journalists to gather news on the themes of their choice. For example, Brian Hanrahan claims that his ability to produce human interest or 'lifestyle' pieces about the Soviet Union is heavily constrained by the fact that he cannot take pictures without getting official permission:

> What you get at the end of the day in terms of human interest is what the Soviet government deems suitable. So your view of the Soviet Union can be controlled very easily. If I go to a factory, I have no idea whether it's a typical factory or not.

He adds:

> When I have asked officially if I can go somewhere and film something the answer is no, you have no permission to do this. A typical Soviet house is not on the agenda, because they think it will reflect badly on their society, it might not look well to people in the west who are used to a different standard.

Feature-type, human interest stories about the USSR are more difficult for broadcasting journalists to produce than is the case with their press colleagues. The technology and grammar of television (and, to a lesser extent, radio) demands material which the Moscow correspondent cannot always provide. Hanrahan stresses:

> To do human interest stories I must have co-operation, I must have help from the Soviet authorities. On the other hand, I can

do politics, whatever happens, with or without co-operation. The story comes out of your head and you can illustrate it with visual material from some other source, but human interest stories must come out of a camera. I can do politics without help, I can't do human interest without help. I'd like to do both.

According to some journalists the existence of these constraints is at least partly responsible for the tendency of western media coverage to focus on the themes of dissidence and dissent. 'If there was greater access', says John Tusa of the BBC, 'coverage would be better.' It is precisely this reluctance to deal with western journalists which has contributed, Hanrahan believes, to the negative coverage the Soviet Union has received over the years:

> In some ways I don't think the Soviet Union gives itself a fair press. It cuts itself off so much from the world. It doesn't tell about the characteristics of Soviet society that might make it attractive to outsiders. It leaves itself open to all this critical reporting because it won't allow people to come in and see it as it is, with the pluses and the minuses.

To illustrate the effects of Soviet reticence in dealing with the western media journalists point to the preponderance of dissidence stories in coverage of Soviet society. Journalists argue that by creating an 'information gap' in the 1970s and early 1980s refuseniks, dissidents, and other opponents of the Soviet state – almost by default, the argument goes – filled the space. Patrick Cockburn explains it this way:

> The Soviets complain that in the late 1970s and afterwards the foreign media here were obsessed with dissidents and refuseniks, and so forth. To some extent there's some merit in that. You could say that the amount of reporting of these themes gives an exaggerated opinion of the numbers involved in these movements. On the other hand they do exist, and secondly, in a political vacuum this was the only type of activity going on. If you have a wholly inert political leadership the spotlight falls on the only signs of activity.
>
> By placing these obstacles all they've done in the past is to ensure that correspondents often rely on dissidents or whoever for opinions. If you take those blocks [where the journalists, diplomats, and others in the foreign community live] an ordinary Russian can't walk into them without being stopped by the

militiaman. The people who have absolutely no fear of coming in are people who are dissident, because they've got nothing to lose. Ordinary Soviets or members of the party will not want to come here, so automatically it's much easier to have someone who's out of the ordinary anyway come to the office or the flat. That's the way it works.

Martin Walker of the *Guardian* makes a similar point:

I think coverage in the past has been inadequate, and I think a lot of that's been the Soviets' fault. They were such a closed society for so long that in the 1970s coverage became dominated by dissidents.

Thus journalists who are concerned to construct what they believe to be a more balanced image of the USSR, to address the 'unknown factor', have found themselves frustrated by bureaucratic obstructionism and other constraints imposed by the Soviets. Kate Clark, who works for the *Morning Star* in Moscow and is less likely than most to 'rubbish' her hosts, concedes that 'there are constraints on the western journalists here, but I think you have to understand why. After all, this country has seen itself portrayed in this horrible way since the Revolution.'

The constraints also affect journalists based in Britain. Nik Gowing, ITN's Soviet correspondent, described his negotiations with the Soviet authorities for access to the USSR at the time of the 27th congress as an 'enormously long, tortuous path. In true Soviet-style', he added, 'everything has to be done in advance.' Stories which involved travelling outside Moscow could, he stated, take up to nine months to organize.

There are a whole battery of bureaucratic and diplomatic constraints affecting journalists in the Soviet Union which do not exist for foreign correspondents in other countries. The BBC, for example, is tightly restricted in the number of personnel it can have in Moscow. As a consequence, journalistic staff are heavily involved in the day-to-day running of the bureau. Peter Ruff explains:

The number of British correspondents in Moscow is determined by how many Soviet correspondents there are in London. So there is a restriction on the number of personnel you can have. The BBC bureau has one radio and one TV correspondent.

The resident correspondent has to be bureau chief, administrator, psychiatrist, personnel officer, accountant, and everything else, as well as being a journalist. This directs a lot of time away from pure journalism and researching stories.

Other bureaucratic constraints include the requirement that journalists, if they wish to travel more than forty kilometres from the centre of Moscow in order to do a story, must ask for permission two days in advance. 'And when you get there', says Ruff, 'whatever you do will be monitored by Foreign Ministry "minders", as we call them.'

> On a working trip they insist on going with you, and have a sort of veto on what you do and how you do it – not necessarily a political one, but it means that you can only do what they allow you to do. You have to plan a trip weeks in advance, and when the date comes for going there may well be another story keeping you in Moscow.
>
> Another problem we have, as broadcasters particularly, is that as soon as you leave Moscow you're out of touch with your home base. News editors in London are reluctant for you to leave Moscow, because you will then be out of touch. I can't file a story for the radio anywhere but Moscow, effectively. If we travel with a VIP delegation we can get calls to London within about twenty minutes. If you went as a journalist accredited in Moscow that phone call could take two days, because they want to make sure that all the correspondent's material is monitored in Moscow before it's done. We don't have direct dial telephones.

Technical constraints of this kind play havoc with deadlines and schedules back home. In this respect broadcasting journalists are worse off than their press colleagues since they cannot, unlike the latter, substitute telephones with telexes. The voice of the broadcasting journalist must always be heard on the air.

Access to locations for filming, and to news-sources for comment and opinion can also be problematic, although the experiences of journalists appear to vary here. Nik Gowing of ITN, who travelled to the USSR in order to cover the 27th congress of the CPSU, gave his view that access to Soviet citizens for interviewing purposes was relatively easy, provided that they themselves were willing to be questioned. John Tusa of the BBC, on the other hand, who also went to Moscow for the 27th congress, stated that 'you need permission for everything you do'.

The extent to which journalists are constrained from gathering news on the subject of their choice appears to depend on the nature of the request, and on the timing. Most of the journalists interviewed agreed that during the 27th congress facilities for newsgathering were relatively good by comparison with normal Soviet practice. Here again, however, the press correspondent enjoys an advantage. He or she does not require film with which to illustrate stories, in contrast to the needs of the broadcasters. Permission to film is more difficult to obtain than permission to do 'vox pop' or 'stick' interviews on the streets of Moscow, and is rarely given inside public buildings and a range of other locations which might be of interest to television news.

Peter Ruff argues that the structure of Soviet society makes it difficult for him to check stories and verify their accuracy:

> You can't check facts with Soviet people. First of all, because they don't know them as well as you do. Second, they're told to be very careful of foreigners, and westerners in particular. There are always stories in the media about western secret service infiltration of the foreign community.[1] There's also a new law which makes it illegal for a foreigner to be given any official information. The state determines what is official information. The law is now established in the criminal code – you don't pass on any information or give any help to foreigners without official permission.

The potential of this law for limiting the freedom of journalists to gather news is considerable, a point also made by Hanrahan:

> There's a limited area you can gather news from. A lot of the things you can do elsewhere you can't do here. You read the morning papers, you read the evening papers, you watch *Vremya* [the main television news programme in the USSR], you take notes on what is said, and it all comes from officially controlled sources. You very rarely get any first-hand information. Here there is almost nothing as an alternative to government sources. If you go out to try and cross-check stories, you're getting into the realm of espionage.

On the other hand, many western journalists in the USSR do not speak Russian, a self-imposed constraint of no small significance. The BBC, like many western news organizations in Moscow, only functions by employing Russian interpreters to monitor the Soviet press every day. In addition, the Soviet news agency TASS produces English texts of all major stories.

Western journalists in the USSR are isolated from their subject not only by language, but by the fact that they are required to reside, together with diplomats, in special apartment blocks, separated from the Soviet population both physically and in the comparative opulence of their lifestyles. Entry to the blocks for an ordinary Soviet citizen is inhibited by the presence of a policeman.

The degree to which these kinds of constraints affect the journalist clearly depends on the individual's ability and inclination to establish the kinds of contacts necessary for journalistic work in general. Some correspondents learn Russian and acquire a sufficient number of Soviet contacts to construct reasonably accurate and reliable stories. Inevitably, however, some journalists are better at this 'routine' task than others.

Cultural isolation, whether self-imposed or created by the Soviet authorities, is clearly a major constraint on gathering news about the USSR, and its effect on the journalistic tendency to overemphasize the theme of dissent has already been noted. Another consequence of cultural isolation is a routine reliance on western diplomatic sources for comment and information about Soviet-related events. Martin Walker of the *Guardian* observes that:

> many of my western colleagues here are still terribly close to their own Embassies as news-sources, particularly as commentary sources, and the Embassies – certainly the British Embassy these days – tend to follow slavishly the American line, the Reagan–Thatcher line. The dominant mood among the British and the Americans is – this is the enemy, you can't trust these guys an inch, whatever they're up to it's a trap.

While emphasizing that on technical issues Embassy sources were frequently valuable and reliable sources of information, Walker believes that their political commentaries are predictable and biased:

> Before I telephone the British Embassy for a comment, I know what that commentary is going to be. I can almost write it.

A major theme in news about the Soviet Union in recent years has been the war in Afghanistan. The journalists' tendency to rely on official western sources in coverage of this conflict has been particularly pronounced, as Jonathan Steele notes in the *Guardian* of 10 March 1986. Based on his own experiences as a press correspondent in Kabul, Steele criticizes what he calls 'one-sided coverage', and western journalists' uncritical acceptance of anti-Soviet, pro-mujaheddin accounts of the conflict. 'When the enemy is the Soviet Union', he writes, 'distinctions between hard news, soft news, and outright propaganda seem to lose all validity.'

> The result is that week after week the western world is being fed a story of mujaheddin success and Soviet discomfiture which may be far from the truth. The only beneficiaries, at least in the short term, are the mujaheddin and their political and military backers.

The extent to which western journalists rely on western diplomatic sources for commentary and background to stories is clearly a factor in shaping coverage. This reliance may be a matter of the journalists' choice, in which case it reflects a form of 'bias' towards some sources rather than others. On the other hand, it may be a consequence of constraints placed in the path of the journalist by the Soviet authorities. Either way, it inhibits the construction of an 'impartial' or objective image of the USSR.

Defining the issues

Western diplomats are among those who enjoy a *privileged access* to news about the USSR. Other groups who routinely dominate access to news about the Soviet Union include representatives of the western political establishment and members of the academic community – the Sovietologists, or Kremlinologists, who specialize in reading the secretive, elaborate codes of Soviet political life.

By virtue of their access to the media these sources become *primary definers* of Soviet-related events and issues. Their views become privileged views. The authors of *Policing the Crisis* (Hall *et al.* 1978) have shown that the routine structures of news media tend to favour the powerful in society, representatives of the establishment who are assumed to be credible and authoritative sources of information.

While these experts are often authoritative, it cannot be assumed that they always are, an observation which is as true for news about the USSR as in any other category of coverage. From his experience as a Moscow correspondent Patrick Cockburn argues for caution in reporting the USSR. 'Soviet high politics are difficult to report, and

Kremlinology – who's doing what to whom in the Kremlin – is impossible.'

> There's a journalistic tradition in reporting the Soviet Union of not doing the things that are feasible – such as reporting how the society works and what are the various political balances – but instead concentrating on Kremlinology, which really isn't feasible if the information isn't there. You don't know enough about the personalities, and the strengths of the people in the Politburo, or in the apparatus, or in the Central Committee, and most of this Kremlinology is absurd because the sources of information are wholly inadequate.
>
> In most places journalists wouldn't dare to produce long theories based on such inadequate information. When you look back at them, you see that most of it's a load of baloney. If you take any straw in the wind, then you can produce a sort of fantasy construction of life here, but it doesn't have much meaning.

The 'absurdity' of much Kremlinology in western journalism is sometimes evident in British television news, as the following example illustrates. On 24 May 1983 Vladimir Danchev, a Radio Moscow newscaster, in the course of a routine English-language broadcast, 'branded Soviet troops [in Afghanistan] as aggressors and praised the Afghan guerrilla forces for their activity against Soviet forces' (4 1900 24/5/83). According to the Channel 4 correspondent, 'the mystifying broadcasts are short. They started when newsreader Vladimir Danchev made a single unprecedented announcement. Tribal leaders, he said, were appealing for increased anti-Soviet activity.' Excerpts from Mr Danchev's broadcasts were played on the news, such as the following:

> Reports from Kabul say that tribes living in the eastern provinces Nangahar and Baktia have joined the struggle against the Soviet invaders. A decision to give an armed rebuff to the bandits was given at the tribes' meeting.

The correspondent noted that it was 'extraordinary' for:

> the Kremlin's personal mouthpiece to the world to admit publicly that the Russians had invaded Afghanistan. . . . And it wasn't just a slip of the tongue . . . it could surely not have been a mistake or personal deviation.

The report ended by posing the following choice:

> was it a mistake, was it Mr Danchev daydreaming as he read, or was this the first known sabotage of Soviet propaganda broadcasts?

BBC1 reported that 'the propaganda voice of the Kremlin has gone haywire' (1 2100 24/5/83). The correspondent asked if it was 'a signal from the KGB that a change in policy on Afghanistan was coming? Hardly', opined the correspondent. 'The Kremlin would never approve words so shocking to Soviet ears.'

All the more surprising, then, that ITN should have allowed Soviet 'expert' Leo Babedz to make sense of the event in terms of a Kremlin power struggle. *News at Ten* that evening began:

> A series of Moscow Radio broadcasts praising the Afghan rebels who are fighting Russian troops are thought tonight to indicate a power struggle in the Kremlin.
>
> (3 2200 24/5/83).

The evidence for this interpretation came from 'experts on Soviet affairs' who 'have ruled out an unofficial protest. Instead they put it down to disagreement between Soviet leader Mr Andropov and Mr Chernenko, the man he beat for Brezhnev's job.' It was not made clear how Danchev's statements could have been of help to a Soviet leader involved in a 'power struggle', and there was no evidence presented for a connection between Danchev and 'the Kremlin'. The 'power struggle' theory became, nevertheless, the favoured explanation.

> *Correspondent*: Are you saying that this is some kind of back-stabbing operation?
> *Leo Babedz* (Soviet expert): It looks like it, but of course we don't know who is the person who is going to be blamed for it, and whether it has a really high connection.
> *Correspondent*: Presumably it is quite high, otherwise it wouldn't be allowed to happen?
> *Leo Babedz*: Otherwise it wouldn't be allowed to go out, of course.

The journalist has taken on the expert's definition of the problem without question.

The story was never followed up on television news. Three years later the correspondent who covered the story for ITN told the author that Danchev had reportedly been re-employed by Radio Moscow after a brief spell of recuperation in a psychiatric ward. While the explanation that Danchev had suffered a nervous breakdown of some kind was recognized as a possibility in *News at Ten*'s coverage at the time, it was written off in favour of the elaborate conspiracy theory outlined by Babedz which became, for all its lurid quality, the dominant explanation of the event.

Of those who gained access to news coverage of the deaths of the Soviet leaders, the great majority were members of the political establishment, and in particular the political establishment of the United States. Only one reported statement from this group of past and present leaders represented the view that, contrary to the claims of western governments, the west was at least partly responsible for the crisis in east–west relations. This point was made by Denis Healey, former British Defence Secretary, in relation to Yuri Andropov:

> It's fair to say that Andropov tried very hard to improve relations both with China and with the west. He failed because neither took the hand offered out.
>
> (3 2200 10/2/84)

On *Newsnight* one of the academic commentators, Geoffrey Stern of the London School of Economics, echoed Denis Healey's interpretation of the Andropov period by suggesting that it had been the west and not the Soviet Union which had prevented the improvement of east–west relations. According to Stern:

> There were a whole proliferation of proposals on arms control. He warmed to the Chinese. There might have been some movement on Afghanistan. It was only in the end, when he came up against an intransigent world, that he became intransigent too. There was no movement in the west, and therefore no movement in the east either.
>
> (2 *Newsnight* 14/2/84)

Soviet sources were not well-represented in these news programmes. During the sample period main evening bulletins completely excluded Soviet opinion from news about Brezhnev, Andropov, and Chernenko, with one exception which counts for the purposes of this analysis only in so far as a Soviet voice was heard to speak. Politburo member Vladimir Scherbitsky, head of a Soviet delegation visiting the United States when Konstantin Chernenko's death was announced, appeared in one bulletin in the following context:

> *Correspondent*: Not many Russians make it to the Oval Office to talk to President Reagan but when Politburo member Vladimir Scherbitsky did last week his central message was reserved for Star Wars, as he told us afterwards.
> *Scherbitsky*: We tried to prove that this is not worthwhile.
> (3 2200 11/3/85)

This was the only statement by a Soviet source to be broadcast on main evening news at any time during coverage of the deaths of the Soviet leaders. On the minority audience programmes two interviews with Soviet commentators were broadcast: one in ITN's Channel 4 studio with Vladimir Dunaev on the death of Brezhnev, and one with Vladimir Posner after the funeral of Chernenko, via satellite from Moscow.

In the latter case BBC's *Newsnight* invited Posner to discuss the significance of Mikhail Gorbachov's speech at Chernenko's funeral ceremony. Posner speaks fluent English with a disconcertingly accurate North American accent, and has become relatively well-known to the British television viewer.

At this time – March 1985 – NATO leaders were continuing, as we have seen, to present the deterioration of east–west relations to a concerned western public as a Soviet problem, and suggesting that the Soviet Union was to blame for the new cold war. In the interviewing style adopted by the journalist this definition of the issue is taken as a 'given', rather than as one interpretation of the problem among several which were competing in the public domain. The interview began with the journalist enquiring of Posner if 'a more conciliatory approach' could be expected from the new leader:

> *Journalist*: I asked [Posner] if Mr Gorbachov's emphasis today on goodneighbourly relations [in his funeral oration to Konstantin Chernenko] meant that he would adopt *a more conciliatory approach to the west than his predecessors have been doing?*

In assuming that a lack of conciliation on the Soviet side has been a feature of recent east–west relations the journalist closes off alternative definitions of the issue, although Posner refuses to be restricted to this framework:

Posner: You know, I think that if you look back on the people you call his predecessors, to begin with Mr Brezhnev, during his period we had detente in the early 1970s, followed by Mr Andropov who was clearly interested in preserving detente and having good relations with the west, and of course Mr Chernenko who followed the same line. I don't think that what Mr Gorbachov said was anything sensational or surprising. This country, indeed, always wanted and very much desires good, normal, business-like relations with the west.

(2 *Newsnight* 13/3/85)

The reasons for the relative lack of Soviet opinion in Soviet news can be related to two factors. One is the assumption that the Soviets are not legitimate sources of information. This was, apparently, a problem for American broadcasters during the Chernobyl crisis, when the appearance of Soviet commentators on television news coverage prompted the claim from certain political groups that it was not appropriate for these views to be allowed to take part in US political debate.[2]

Another, perhaps more important explanation focuses on the reluctance of the Soviet authorities to provide commentators as and when required by the broadcasters: in short, failures in Soviet news management. Questioned as to the reason for the relative lack of Soviet commentators at periods when their point of view might be of some importance to a fuller understanding of events, John Tusa of BBC news told the author that interviews with them take too long to 'set up' on British television. They could, he said, take up to two days to arrange.

We should note here that the adverse effects of this reluctance to provide commentators for the western media have apparently been recognized by the Soviet leadership which came to power after the death of Chernenko. From the period of the 1985 Geneva summit more Soviet commentators have been appearing on British television news. Their increased availability is in line with the new information policy of *glasnost* which has accompanied the ascension of Mikhail Gorbachov to the leadership of the party, and of which we shall have more to say in Chapter 7.

It should also be noted that the greater degree of access remains largely confined to minority-audience programming. In general, Soviet sources are given more access to minority-audience bulletins than to the main evening bulletins on BBC1 and ITV, a trend which was evident before Gorbachov and continues into the *glasnost* era. Minority-audience programmes are relatively *open* to competing viewpoints when compared with the main evening bulletins, in the sense that 'some types of programming are relatively closed. They operate mainly or wholly within the terms of reference set by the official perspective. But other forms are relatively open in the sense that they provide spaces in which the core assumptions of the official perspective can be interrogated and contested, and in which other perspectives can be presented and examined' (Schlesinger, Murdock, and Elliot 1983: 32). These authors refer to the entire range of televisual forms, including fictional ones, but a similar distinction can be made within news programming.

We shall have occasion to note this feature of news again, and it can be illustrated here with two examples.

Channel 4's coverage of the death of Chernenko counterposed the views of two experts to construct a debate about the nature of the USSR. The journalist set up the debate by making a rare acknowledgement that:

> in the west there's often open disagreement about how the nature of the Soviet system should be perceived.

First, the viewer heard the opinions of Zbigniew Brzezinski, a conservative and a firm believer in the basic illegitimacy and inevitable downfall of the Soviet 'empire':

> *Zbigniew Brzezinski*: The Soviet system is in crisis ... the Soviet empire is nearing the end of its days, and I think it behoves us to find ways of making that end gradual and peaceful rather than explosive.

Brzezinski's views were balanced by those of the British academic, Peter Frank:

> *Peter Frank*: The Soviet Union is not in a state of crisis ... it has very serious problems. I think, however, the same could be said of any major power in the world.
>
> (4 1900 11/3/85)

Another example of an item in which negative perceptions of the Soviet Union were constructed as matters for debate, rather than of fact, fell outside the main sample period.

On 18 October 1983, on the eve of another round of the Geneva INF talks between the superpowers, BBC's *Newsnight* broadcast a report on the debate about the Soviet threat, and how this related to the impending Cruise and Pershing deployments. The item concerned the publication of two new books about the Soviet Union which in different ways criticized perceptions of the Soviet Threat: *The Limits of World Power* by Jonathan Steele, and *The Threat* by Andrew Cockburn. These works became the basis for an item in which 'through the eyes of these authors and with the help of a Soviet general and a leading British expert on Russia, we explore the case for regarding the Russians as perhaps less of a threat than they're sometimes made out to be' (2 *Newsnight* 18/10/83).

The 'leading British expert' was Professor John Erickson of Edinburgh University, and the Soviet general was Lt-Gen. Mikhail Milstein, visiting Britain with the Soviet delegation to the Edinburgh Conversations of 1983.

The presenter began by outlining two competing views of the Soviet Union. First, 'the current perception of the Soviet Union as depicted for us by those at present in charge in Washington and London':

> a very massive and threatening military power, stretching from Central Europe to the extremes of Asia, poised to exploit any opportunities for expansion.

This view was contrasted with another, 'looking from the inside outwards', and of which 'we hear much less these days':

> the view that sees the men in the Kremlin swamped by Russia's own internal problems and encircled by a whole range of external threats to their security. The Chinese in the east, the unsettled Muslims to the south, and the Afghans still unbeaten. Beyond that the Americans deploying massively in the Indian Ocean. To the west, beyond their own recalcitrant allies in eastern Europe, a whole ring of the west's nuclear and conventional systems pointing at them from Turkey around to northern Norway.

The item proceeded with a critical examination of the views of 'those at present in charge'.

Asked by the journalist if western leaders 'exaggerate Soviet military capability', defence expert Andrew Cockburn, giving examples from the Soviet tank forces and navy, replied that 'our general image of Soviet military power doesn't really correspond to the reality when you look at it close up'.

The item then moved on to an interview with the Conservative MP George Walden, who criticized the Thatcher government's attitude to the USSR.

By accessing British and Soviet sources with views different from those of current political leaders, this item created a space in which the dominant Soviet threat framework for making sense of defence and disarmament issues could be contested. It shows that television news *can* be structured so as to be open to radically opposing viewpoints, even on the most basic Soviet threat assumptions. This does not necessitate the inclusion of Soviet sources, since there are many within the establishment who also challenge the perspective of current western leaders. It merely requires a recognition that 'currently dominant views' are open to question, and a readiness to extend access to those who could express alternatives.

5

'Russia condemned': the Korean airliner disaster

Journalist: Could I ask you for the BBC, what do you think of the way that the western press has been handling all of this?
Soviet Foreign Minister, Andrei Gromyko: Essentially not objective.
Journalist: Do you think the situation will be cleared up soon?
Gromyko: I think it is clear now.
Journalist: And do you think the world will just forget about the incident soon?
Gromyko: We are sure that you will forget, now facts are at the disposal of the people.

(1 2100 7/9/83)

In time the Korean airliner disaster *was* forgotten, as the Soviet foreign minister predicted at the Madrid security conference of September 1983. Like all such tragedies, it exploded upon the world for a brief period and was then no longer news, replaced by other more pressing concerns. The Korean airliner disaster was newsworthy for approximately two weeks. Yet the destruction of KAL 007 was perhaps the single most controversial east–west incident since the Cuban missile crisis. Those two short weeks were the occasion of a bitter propaganda war between the west and the Soviet Union, centred on the deaths of 269 civilian passengers and crew. This chapter examines how the competing views of the Soviet and United States governments were reported on British television news.

As a major media event, commanding many hours of television coverage in its initial phase, the KAL tragedy provided a classic opportunity to examine the role of broadcasting journalism in propaganda warfare between the superpowers. There will, it is certain, be further incidents of this kind in the future, and it is of more than passing interest to understand how broadcast news is likely to cover them.

The background

East–west relations were already at a low point in September 1983, and the Korean airliner disaster plunged them even deeper into gloom. A little more than two weeks later, President Reagan would succeed in obtaining from a hitherto reluctant Congress approval on increased defence spending, the manufacture of chemical and nerve gas weapons, and funding for the MX missile system. Few observers doubted that the Korean airliner disaster was a factor in smoothing the paths of these controversial programmes. In Europe the Geneva arms control talks were building up to the arrival of Cruise and Pershing II missiles in December. Western negotiators did not deny that the Korean airline incident affected their approach to the negotiations. Nicholas Ashford in *The Times* of 10 September 1983, expressed clearly the likely effects of the incident when he wrote: 'The sheer horror of the Russian action will undermine those critics who have accused Reagan of following belligerently interventionist foreign and defence policies. For instance, who now will resist the President's plans to deploy the MX missile and modernize the US nuclear weapons when the adversary has shown itself capable of such cynical brutality?' These words were to prove prophetic.

The stark horror of the Korean airliner disaster, and the central facts – that 269 civilian passengers and crew died when their aircraft was shot down by Soviet fighters – were established at an early stage in the crisis. The Soviet news agency TASS first referred to the loss of human life on 2 September 1983, in a statement which 'expressed regret over the loss of human life', and there was no denial in any subsequent statement that actions by Soviet defence forces had led to the aircraft's destruction. The ensuing controversy was concerned not with what had happened to the airliner but with the question of *why* the tragedy had occurred, and who was to blame. In the official United States version of events the aircraft had accidentally strayed into Soviet airspace on a routine commercial flight, where it had been shot down without warning by Soviet fighters. The principal evidence to support this allegation were tape-recorded conversations between Soviet fighter pilots monitored by US and Japanese intelligence services in the region.

It was further alleged that the Soviet fighters had been close enough to the airliner to identify it as a civilian plane, and that the Soviet defence forces had been in possession of this knowledge when they attacked. US officials suggested that the incident proved it was now Soviet policy to shoot down civilian airliners that strayed into Soviet airspace. This version of events was personally championed by the President of the United States, and accepted by US allies and friends around the world.

The Soviet Union's defence became clear by 2 September. A TASS statement issued that day argued:

> The intrusion into the airspace by the mentioned plane cannot be regarded in any other way than as a pre-planned act. It was obviously thought possible to attain special intelligence aims without hindrance by using civilian planes as a cover.
>
> (English translation from *Soviet News*, no.6189)

The 'spy-plane' theory first advanced by the Soviets on 2 September, and to which they adhered thereafter, rested on circumstantial evidence. Gaps in the US account of events, and a number of remarkable coincidences, led the Soviets to conclude that the aircraft's flight-path had not been accidental, and to claim that they had genuinely misidentified the Boeing 747 as a US reconnaissance plane.

The Soviet authorities asked why, for example, if US intelligence had been able to monitor the progress of the KAL flight for several hours, it had not attempted to prevent the disaster taking place by warning the pilot?

On 6 September an official government statement claimed further evidence for the spy-plane theory from the fact that a United States reconnaissance plane, the RC-135, had flown 'in the same area at the same altitude' as the Korean airliner. This statement also noted that the airliner's flight had taken it over sensitive military areas, including one site where a missile test was scheduled for the next day. It was claimed that the airliner had flown without navigation lights, in the dark, and had failed to respond to warnings and internationally agreed procedures for such incidents. For all these reasons, it was claimed, 'the anti-aircraft forces of the area arrived at the conclusion that a reconnaissance aircraft was in the airspace of the USSR'.

At a news conference on 9 September in Moscow Marshal Nikolai Ogarkov, General Chief of Staff of the Soviet Armed Forces, alleged that the Korean airliner had been acting in concert with the RC-135 in a mission designed to test the Soviet defence system:

> The 135 reconnaissance plane was in the area of the violation of Soviet airspace by the South Korean plane with the aim to test the capabilities of the Soviet air defence system. We believe that that was not the only aim. Both planes acted concertedly. Their flights were performed so as to complicate the air situation and to confuse our air defence systems. In addition, the RC-135 must have been controlling the initial stage of the flight of the Boeing 747 and keeping track of the actions of our air defence at that time.
>
> (English translation from *Soviet News*, no. 6190)

During the period of the propaganda war analysed below, these were the 'facts' as both sides presented them. In the United States version the Korean arliner had been an innocent straggler: the Soviet authorities had known precisely what they were doing when they shot it down in an act of cold-blooded 'murder'. The Soviet government continued to insist that an 'unprecedented accident' had occurred. In their account responsibility lay with the United States intelligence services and, ultimately, with the US government itself.

When the Korean airliner crisis had disappeared from the headlines and the war of words was no longer news the arguments continued between commentators and analysts. As time passed the Soviet version began to win support in the west. On 20 September 1983, an article was published in *Pravda* which gave details of a more elaborate intelligence operation than had previously been alleged. The author of the article, Marshal Pyotr Kirsonov, stated that:

> It has been established beyond any doubt that the Boeing 747 had taken off from Anchorage in Alaska forty minutes behind the regular schedule. The airline representative explained the delay by 'the need for an additional checking of the onboard equipment', although no malfunctions had been found. But another thing has now come to light. The delay was needed in order to strictly synchronize in time the plane's approach to the coasts of Kamchatka and Sakhalin with the flight of the American intelligence satellite Ferret-D.

The article alleged that the times of the satellite's passing over Soviet territory coincided exactly with the Korean airliner's two separate entrances into Soviet airspace.

This expanded version of the spy-plane theory received support in an article in the British publication *Defence Attaché*. 'P.Q. Mann', a pseudonym for an anonymous, but reportedly authoritative defence analyst, agreed with the detailed timings of the *Pravda* article and on the alleged role played by the RC-135 aircraft. The article introduced new speculation about a possible role in the operation by the US space shuttle Challenger. Andrew Wilson, defence correspondent of the *Observer*, reported on 17 June 1984 that the article:

> claims to offer new evidence that the civil jet was steered deliberately into Soviet airspace in order to provoke radar and electronic signals that were picked up by a simultaneously orbiting Ferret spy satellite and the space shuttle Challenger. The Russians themselves drew attention to the Ferret's orbiting pattern at the time, but the magazine goes much further. It says the coincident flight of KAL 007 with a US aircraft of similar profile – an RC-135 – within range of Soviet radar less than half an hour before was 'a dummy selling tactic', creating the possibility that a military aircraft was flying in to cross the borders of the Soviet Union.

Alain Jacob, discussing P.Q. Mann's theory in the *Guardian Weekly* of 23 September 1984 noted that 'the space shuttle Challenger, which was fired from Cape Canaveral on 30 August 1983 made three sweeps over the far eastern part of the USSR during and after 007's flight over Kamchatka, the Sea of Okhotsk, and Sakhalin Island':

> If the launch had not been held up for seventeen minutes on account of bad weather, the sweeps would have coincided even more closely with the various stages of the flight.

Other facts emerged.

Boeing 747s are equipped with the Inertial Navigation System. This 'all-but-infallible' system, as Murray Sayle described it in the *Sunday Times* of 27 May 1984, operates by means of three independently functioning computers, which are routinely checked and cross-checked. How, then, had the aircraft strayed off course by more than 300 miles? This question was never resolved. Human error was also considered, and seemed a more likely explanation, although this implied that a major and basic error had been compounded by all three members of the crew, two of whom were experienced military pilots. The captain's reputation for attention to safety and detail when flying had earned him the nickname 'Mr Computer'.

Two of the pilots, including the captain, were known to have had links with the CIA. KAL 007 had carried eighteen extra crew members (twenty-nine instead of the usual eleven) who were not named in the official list of those lost. The Soviet Union alleged that these had been military personnel involved in the intelligence mission. Passengers on previous KAL 007 flights reported that they had been ordered to close their curtains and dim lights for long periods of their journey, strengthening the possibility that the Korean airliner could have been, as the Soviets alleged, flying without lights on. In isolation these points were hardly conclusive, but together they detracted from the official US position that the spy-plane theory was 'preposterous'. Former director of the CIA, Stansfield Turner, had revealed on Channel 4 news on 2 September 1983 that civilian planes could be and were used on military missions by both the USA and the USSR. R.W. Johnson noted in the *Guardian Weekly* of 25 December 1983 that Korean Airlines are closely linked to the Korean CIA, 'set up by the CIA in 1982', and that 'in 1978 a KAL airliner overflew the great Soviet naval base at Murmansk and was fired on by Soviet fighters'.[1]

The spy-plane theory was further supported by the fact that, as Andrew Wilson put it in the article cited above, 'the Soviet electronic activity provoked by Flight 007's intrusion provided western intelligence with its biggest coup for many years'. Whether planned or not, there was no doubt that US intelligence services had reaped a rich harvest of information about Soviet defences from the Korean airliner incident.

On 19 July 1984 the accumulation of evidence supporting the spy-plane theory prompted the *TV Eye* current affairs programme to produce a special investigation of the disaster. The presenter's opening comments acknowledged that the evidence he was about to present had first been revealed by the Soviet Union. They also indicated this journalist's inclination to dismiss 'the Russians' as a reliable source of information:

> Predictably, it was the Russians who first made the charge that Korean Airlines flight 007 was part of a spying mission, but as *TV Eye*'s investigation has disclosed, that charge can no longer be dismissed simply as propaganda.

The half-hour *TV Eye* investigation brought together much of the evidence and interviewed several analysts and former military personnel. The lawyer representing the relatives of the dead passengers, Aaron Broder, set the context of the investigation by explaining that he and his clients were far from satisfied with the US government's account:

> My clients all feel that there has been a cover-up of the real culprits here. My clients feel that there was an intelligence-gathering mission . . . and that there is a great deal more here than a sheer coincidence that an airliner was 450 miles off course and that it was just by sheer accident over that area of the Russian defence network.

Broder argued, on behalf of his clients, that if the Soviet account was shown to be correct:

> There would be an investigation as to why there was a cover-up of this which would exceed anything we saw in the Watergate era. It would be a disgraceful affair that our government from the very first day following the occurrence denied all responsibility and then it turned out that they were responsible, that it was an espionage mission. There's no doubt in my mind that this would go on for years in an effort to get at the heart of this: whether our President was aware of it, what information he had, when he learned of it, and why he failed to disclose it to the American public.

Retired US diplomat, John Kepple, announcing his intention to call for a special Congressional Hearing which would have access to the US government's classified material on the incident, gave his reasons:

> If you look at the mechanics of the flight you cannot believe that it was not intentional . . . there is some kind of stretching of the mind here because it's incredible to use a full airplane full of innocent people who'd paid their money and wanted to go somewhere but I can't personally believe that the flight was not intentional.

Here the presenter interjected with the observation that 'the unthinkable, that lives were deliberately put at risk and lost, is being thought . . .'.

The programme contained detailed interviews with various

experts on specific points. Lufthansa pilot Rudolf Braunberg, who had flown the KAL 007 route many times, testified that in his opinion it was 'impossible' for three such experienced pilots to make an error of such magnitude. Tom Bernard, a former operative on board RC-135s, confirmed that it would have been possible for the US military aircraft in the area on 31 August to have contacted KAL 007 and warned it out of Soviet airspace. He also maintained that it was possible for the RC-135 to report directly to Washington if need be. Ernest Volkman, an American intelligence analyst, outlined the nature of the 'intelligence bonanza' spoken of in the P.Q. Mann article:

> the tragic incident managed to turn on just about every single Soviet electro-magnetic transmission over a period of about four hours and an area of approximately 7,000 square miles ... a Christmas tree lit up, everything you could ever hope for. Now admittedly that's a cynical statement, but we're talking about a cynical business here.

The *TV Eye* programme added to a growing list of articles and publications which contradicted the picture of the Korean airliner disaster initially presented by the US government. By July 1984 the principal points of the Soviet account had been substantiated by numerous independent sources, weakening correspondingly the view that the disaster had been an act of premeditated, cold-blooded murder. One year almost to the day after the disaster the official stance of the Reagan administration itself changed, as the *Guardian* reported on 1 September 1984:

> A senior administration official has said that he believes the Russians shot down the Korean Airlines flight 007 a year ago because they were genuinely convinced it was on an intelligence mission. The comments by one of the State Department's senior Soviet experts on the Soviet Union went further in publicly acknowledging an honest error by the Soviet Union than the administration has done in the past.

One year after the incident a major strand of the Soviet Union's justification for its actions had been conceded by the same authorities who had at first been so adamant in their condemnations: that the aircraft had been confused with an RC-135. Indeed, according to a *Newsnight* report of 8 September 1986, this fact was known to the US government in the first week of the crisis. The item contained an interview with Seymour Hersch, an American journalist and author of a book about the incident. On the programme Hersch stated that 'there's agreement inside the [US] intelligence community that the Russians made a wrong ID. It's unanimous.' According to the correspondent:

> The raw intelligence was available early and persuasively to show that the Russians did not knowingly shoot down a civilian airliner. They did not identify the plane as Korean Airlines 747 but confused its track with that of the earlier reconnaissance flight. Within the Pentagon there was one group, Airforce Intelligence, which reported accurately that the Russians did not know they were shooting down an airliner.

Hersch argued that 'Between day two to day seven of the crisis, we began to get a firm hold on the fact that the Soviets had done nothing other than make a terrible ghastly mistake.' 'Why then', asked the correspondent, 'were these views discounted?' Why did the Americans insist, 'against the best evidence they had, that the Russians had knowingly shot down a civilian airliner?'

> By then the Americans were already embarked on a propaganda offensive. To the administration's ideologues it was the classic case of the evil empire in action.

In Hersch's view, 'The Soviet-haters are here at the top of this government, they truly are, and they went public with the hardest story they could.'

During the period of the propaganda war the US government made statements of revulsion and outrage, launching a campaign of denunciation in which it sought to ostracize the Soviet Union from the international community as a 'state based on the dual principles of callousness and mendacity'. President Reagan and his advisers presented the incident as 'clear justification of their view of the Soviet Union as an evil empire' (2 *Newsnight* 8/9/86).

The administration sought and received backing from its allies in imposing sanctions on cultural and commercial exchanges (though, as quickly became clear, relations between the USA and the USSR were already so poor that little could practically be done to make them worse: banning Aeroflot was suggested, for example, until it was pointed out that Aeroflot *had* no flying rights in the United States). The Soviet Union was unambiguously condemned by the European Parliament, NATO, and professional bodies such as the International Federation of Airline Pilots' Associations.

The US government's main objective during the crisis was to portray the incident as being entirely consistent with Soviet behaviour. The Korean airliner incident was not perceived in this account as an extraordinary event, but one wholly consistent with normal Soviet behaviour. Such a 'heinous act of barbarism', as President Reagan described it on 2 September, was a measure of Soviet brutality, a graphic manifestation of the Soviet threat.

According to this view the lessons to be learned from the Korean airliner disaster were clear. As US Senator Robert Byrd put it, on BBC news of 4 September:

> I would hope that our west European friends would take very close note of this. If they are willing to shoot down an unarmed commercial plane they're certainly willing to shoot down an unarmed European city, one that can't respond.

The linkage drawn between the incident and the nuclear debate in America was not lost on the pro-nuclear lobby in Britain. A *Times* editorial of 6 September noted that:

> This callous regime, which shoots first and asks questions afterwards, has served a timely reminder on the members of the Atlantic Alliance that if they do not hang together they may be hanged separately.

The 'timeliness' of the Korean airliner crisis lay in the scheduled arrival of new American nuclear missiles in Europe by December that year, a controversial deployment which was creating serious political problems for NATO. Western governments used the Korean airliner disaster to legitimize the new deployments and to justify their 'tough' negotiating stance at the INF talks in Geneva.

The likelihood that western negotiators would take a tougher stand at the INF talks, because of the incident, was noted in an ITN report:

> As the two sides met for the first time for two months the atmosphere didn't seem to have worsened. But inside there was little doubt that the actual talks will be even more difficult.
>
> (3 2200 6/9/83)

The reason for this was said to be that: 'The Americans can hardly make any fresh concessions now.'

On 12 September the US Congress reconvened in its first session after the Korean airliner incident. ITN reported that 'as a result of the Korean airliner incident Congress is now more likely to approve President Reagan's planned increase in defence spending, including the deployment of the controversial MX missile' (3 2200 12/9/83).

The very real effects of the Korean airliner incident on east–west relations and on the arms control process were thus shown to be an escalation of the United States' rearmament programme, unfettered by the need to 'make fresh concessions now'.

The Soviets also linked the incident to the coming of Cruise and Pershing II, and the ongoing INF negotiations at Geneva. In the Soviet view the incident was deliberately being exploited in order to discredit the Soviet negotiating position at the Geneva talks. The Soviets went further and suggested that lives had knowingly been put at risk on the Korean airliner with the propaganda potential of the incident in mind. The USSR was 'contemptuous of American hypocrisy, insisting that the 747 was on a spying mission and had deliberately strayed off course' (2 *Newsnight* 8/9/86). A Soviet government statement of 6 September, reproduced in *Soviet News* no. 6189, claimed that 'the plan was to carry out without hitch the intelligence operation but if it was foiled, to turn all this into a major political provocation against the Soviet Union'.

Before examining television news coverage of this 'battle of words' it is important to draw attention to the different approaches of the two countries to information and 'propaganda'. A significant factor in determining how the American and Soviet positions were reported on television news was the inability or refusal of the latter to present its case with the same sensitivity to western public opinion as the Americans. As suggested in the previous chapter, news management and news input have effects on coverage of east–west issues. Coverage of the Korean airliner tragedy cannot be adequately understood without taking this factor into account.

The United States' view of the Korean airliner disaster was immediately communicated to the world, through the mass media, in televised Presidential addresses, news conferences, dramatic presentations of evidence to the United Nations, and a steady flow of commentary which ensured that the US account was highly visible. By contrast, the Soviets released only three short TASS statements in the first seven days.

Given the scale of human tragedy involved in the disaster this was simply inadequate. The first TASS statement, issued on 1

September, said nothing about casualties and failed to confirm that Soviet fighters had shot the aircraft down. These omissions left a gap in Soviet propaganda. Although the statement of 2 September saw the first exposition of a consistent, credible and increasingly detailed Soviet view, the damage was done in so far as a framework for understanding the incident as 'Soviet brutality' had already been established in the media. Peter Ruff was the BBC correspondent in Moscow at the time of the crisis:

> The Korean airliner threw the whole Soviet propaganda military machine into total chaos. For several days they didn't know what to say. They had no idea. First of all, they wouldn't admit that it had happened, and then it all came out in bits and pieces.

Some western analysts who later accepted that the incident itself was explicable without recourse to the concept of Soviet barbarism were nevertheless highly critical of what they interpreted as confusion and indecision on the part of the Soviet authorities in the ensuing propaganda war. One such was Geoffrey Stern, who argued on BBC's *Newsnight* of 2 February 1984, that:

> It's quite conceivable that any government would have shot down an alien intruder that flies over the most sensitive of all your equipment you have. After all, this whole region contains three extremely sensitive areas for the Soviet Union. Therefore, I think whatever happened, there being no communication between the United States and the Soviet Union, the plane would have been shot down. The Israelis shot down a civilian plane when they thought that it constituted a danger to their vital interests. However, I think that the way it was handled after that betrays the way in which things were going in the Kremlin at the moment. They could have been handled in a very different way.

On the same programme, Dr Dimitri Simes of the Carnegie Institute in Washington stated that:

> The Korean airliner was shot because of standard operational procedures. The Soviets honestly were confused, they thought that this was an American spy-plane, but their air defence system did not function well, they did not have much time before the Korean airliner left Soviet airspace. Where I believe the Soviets could handle it differently was not before shooting the plane but after. They performed miserably. It looked like nobody was in

> control, one man did not know what the other was saying, and if Mr Andropov was in better health I assume that the Soviets could put together a more credible show.

In the first few days of intense media coverage there were no direct statements or appearances by Soviet leaders. It was not until the TASS statement of 6 September that the destruction of the airliner was officially confirmed. Things began to improve on 8 September when the Soviet Foreign Minister addressed the Madrid Conference on European Security and Co-operation, the first time that a member of the Soviet government had spoken on the incident. On 9 September the Soviet authorities mounted a special news conference for Soviet and western journalists in which they gave a detailed account of what they claimed had happened to the Korean airliner. In Peter Ruff's view:

> I think a policy decision was taken at the time that someone was going to have to account for this. I equally believe that someone said, why don't we have a full-blown press conference. The decision was taken that it would have to be the military so you suddenly had Ogarkov appearing coast-to-coast live on television. And in their terms it was probably judged a success. In a sense, the Soviet state decided to confront the thing head on, which was something they'd never done before. After an initial period of confusion and obvious political in-fighting, it was decided that they would take on the world and justify what they'd done.

Soviet delay in 'confronting the thing head on' undoubtedly contributed to the way in which television journalists reported the propaganda war. Had the Soviet authorities paid more attention at an early stage to the mechanics of an information war fought on the western media, it is possible that the Soviet version of why the tragedy occurred would have been received differently. On the other hand, it is significant that quantitative media coverage of the incident fell away sharply after the Moscow news conference of 9 September, as it became increasingly likely that the Soviet Union had a credible case to put. As the idea of Soviet 'barbarism' began to lose credibility, western journalists in general seemed to lose interest in the affair.

Nevertheless, it is the contention of this chapter that the Soviets *were* putting a case after 1 September. The following analysis shows how it was received, *vis-à-vis* the slicker, but no more 'truthful' account of the Korean airliner disaster offered by the Reagan administration and its western allies.

The American view

News bulletins on Friday 2 September established an explanatory framework which would dominate coverage throughout the Korean airliner crisis. BBC news dispensed with headlines and led with an excerpt from a statement made by President Reagan in California that day:

> *Ronald Reagan*: What can we think of a regime that so broadly trumpets its vision of peace and global disarmament, and yet so callously and quickly commits a terrorist act to sacrifice the lives of innocent human beings?
> *Newscaster*: President Reagan, condemning the Soviet Union for shooting down the Korean airliner. Tonight Moscow apologized, and changed its version. The fighters did open fire, but the Jumbo was spying.
>
> (1 2100 2/9/83)

This introduction was typical of the pattern of privileged access extended to the US government's account of the disaster during the crisis. In the section of the speech chosen for transmission the President did not state a fact, or make an announcement, or express an opinion. Rather, he posed a rhetorical question: what can *we* think of such a regime? His assumption that a terrorist act had been committed and innocent lives sacrificed by the Soviet Union was allowed to set the agenda immediately, while at the same time instructing the audience to make the link between this behaviour and Soviet intentions on arms control. This definition of the event was legitimized thus:

> tonight Moscow apologized, and changed its version.

Although the implication of the journalist's comment is that the Soviet Union has conceded responsibility and changed its story neither the statement of 1 September nor that of the 2nd accepted responsibility for the incident. ITN's main evening bulletin retained headlines:

> Mr Andropov regrets the deaths in the Korean airliner.
> Mr Reagan says – how can you trust such people?
>
> (3 2200 2/9/83)

From the way in which the respective positions of the two sides are set out a framework for understanding the issue is established which shares the basic assumptions inherent in the President's statement. No indication is given to the viewer that assumptions *are* being made, or what these are. By the nature of introductory presentations it is difficult to portray the complexity of the issue, but in the lengthier reports which followed on both bulletins the same assumptions were present. The President's interpretation of the Korean airliner disaster set the terms of the propaganda war from the outset of the crisis, quickly becoming the preferred reading of the incident on television news.

President Reagan's speech on 2 September was open to varying interpretations. In general terms the assumptions made in it, and its linking of the Korean airliner incident to wider issues of east–west relations, were an obvious extension of his conception of the Soviet threat:

> *Reagan*: In the wake of the barbaric act committed yesterday by the Soviet regime against a commercial jet liner, the United States and many other countries of the world made clear and compelling statements that expressed not only our outrage but also our demand for a truthful accounting of the facts. Our first emotions are anger, disbelief, and profound sadness.
>
> While events in Afghanistan and elsewhere have left few illusions about the willingness of the Soviet Union to advance its interests through violence and intimidation, all of us had hoped that certain irreducible standards of civilized behaviour none the less obtained, but this event shocks the sensibilities of people everywhere. The tradition in the civilized world has always been to offer help to mariners and pilots who are lost or in distress on the sea or in the air. Where human life is valued, extraordinary efforts are extended to preserve and protect it, and it's essential that as civilized societies we ask searching questions about the nature of regimes where such standards do not apply.
>
> Beyond these emotions the world notes the stark contrast that exists between Soviet words and deeds. What can we think of a regime that so broadly trumpets its vision of peace and global disarmament and yet so callously and quickly commits a terrorist act to sacrifice the lives of human beings? What can be said about Soviet credibility when they so flagrantly lie about such a heinous act? What can be the scope of legitimate mutual discourse with a

> state whose values permit such atrocities? And what are we to make of a regime which establishes one set of standards for itself, and another for the rest of humankind?
>
> (1 2100 2/9/83)

As is clear, the speech does not focus on the airliner incident itself, but concentrates on drawing out appropriate lessons. The language of the speech – 'flagrant liars', 'barbarism', 'atrocities' – seeks to expose the Soviet Union as a regime with whom there can be no 'legitimate mutual discourse', whose arms control proposals are by implication bogus, which is capable of horrendous acts of violence. It is taken for granted not only that an act of barbarism has been committed but that this is a normal expression of Soviet values. These claims had ideological roots in the conservatism of the Reagan administration, yet correspondents on television news at no point challenged them and indeed reinforced them by their own commentaries.

ITN portrayed the President as a defender of the free world against the Soviet threat, whenever and wherever it occurred:

> When the Soviets act in a way which angers the western world, as in Poland or Afghanistan, that world turns to the United States to carry the banner of protest, and it is precisely to discuss the options open to him that the President is returning to the White House.
>
> (3 2200 2/9/83)

Having informed the viewer that: (*a*) the west is angry with the Soviet Union, (*b*) the Korean airliner incident is just like Poland and Afghanistan, the reporter concludes that (*c*) the United States carries the 'banner of protest' for us all. The first of these assertions could be described as a fact. The others express only the opinion of the journalist that President Reagan had in this case both right and might on his side. Subsequent discussions of options open to the President underlined the extent to which the US account of the incident had already been established as the 'consensus'. ITN's report ended with speculation on the dilemma facing the President. How could he make them pay?

> Whatever sanctions President Reagan takes against the Soviet Union, sooner or later he will have to lift them, and the Soviet slate will in a sense be wiped clean and so the President is certain to ensure that the memory of what the Soviet Union has done lives long beyond whatever action he takes against them.

By this stage in the bulletin no evidence of any kind had been presented to confirm or deny precisely what it was that the Soviets had done. Journalists nevertheless assumed that the Soviet Union was capable of and had in fact deliberately destroyed a civilian airliner. President Reagan's speech was taken as the starting point for an 'impartial' account of the incident, rather than being seen as itself part of the propaganda war and the 'battle of words' which was developing. The only controversy systematically analysed in subsequent discussion was the question of the severity of sanctions.

BBC news followed its report of President Reagan's speech with a report from the United Nations building in New York where an emergency session of the Security Council was about to begin. In the course of the item one Senator questioned the value of the United Nations, challenging it to respond 'effectively' to this latest instance of Soviet barbarism:

> *Senator Alphonse D'Amato*: It's about time that the free world came together. We've had too much rhetoric, not enough action, we've had condemnations in the past, we've had allies not act in concert. Number one we should convene the world body, the UN, let's see if it is more than a debating society.

The speaker assumes that the Korean airliner incident is a matter for 'action' as opposed to 'rhetoric', and states his belief that action against the Soviet Union is long overdue. The correspondent follows on with a commentary on the role of the United Nations which takes on Mr D'Amato's remarks and appears to accept their basic validity:

> *Journalist*: There are many people of course who do regard the United Nations as little more than a debating society. Even if enough delegates voted for a resolution to condemn the Russians the Soviet Union still has a right of veto. It is at best a safety valve, an opportunity to express indignation without getting any really tangible results.

This commentary is informed by a particular reading of the Korean airliner disaster, that of right wingers in the US government. This account had become the basis of the interpretative framework used by journalists to make sense of the incident, while the questions of what actually happened to the airliner and who was responsible were bypassed.

This pattern was evident throughout the crisis. Speakers appeared on the news, presented the US account of the incident as fact, and proceeded to condemn the Soviet Union accordingly:

> *Journalist*: American officials insist that the action was not just a simple and terrible mistake.
> *Assistant Secretary of State Richard Burt*: This was certainly not the action of a rogue fighter pilot. We know for a fact that this fighter pilot was in continuous contact with his ground control and that ground control exercised authority over his actions. We have yet to find any convincing evidence that that airliner received any warning from the Soviets.
> *Journalist*: Though Congress is not sitting the toughest demands for retaliatory action of some kind have come from Capitol Hill where there's outrage particularly at the death of Congressman Larry Macdonald, an arch-conservative from Georgia.
> *Senator Daniel P. Moynihan*: First of all the President should call the Congress back into session to let the world and the Soviet Union know how serious this is, they have murdered an American Congressman. Two, we should go to the Security Council. Three, we should go to the World Court and ask every other country in the world who is signatory to the Chicago Civil Air Convention of which the Soviets are a party to go to the court with us and get damages and a condemnation.
>
> (1 2100 2/9/83)

The uncritical reporting of statements which agreed with the dominant interpretation of the crisis became a typical feature of news coverage:

> *Henry Kissinger*: The first thing I would do now is to suspend the meeting between Gromyko and Secretary of State Schultz until there is a satisfactory explanation.
> *Zbigniew Brzezinski*: Thus we mustn't make it into an American–Soviet affair. The United States should join the international community, hopefully the international community will react equally strongly, in condemning the Soviet Union.
>
> (3 2200 2/9/83)

Even after 4 September, when major gaps in the administration's evidence began to be noted by such figures as Democratic Congressional leader Jim Wright, challenges to the dominant interpretation of events were limited to two items, both on BBC2's *Newsnight*, and both written by Charles Wheeler, the BBC's Washington correspondent at that time. The content of these items and the fact that they both appeared on minority-audience programmes illustrates once again the distinction which can be made between the relatively 'closed' main news bulletins and the relatively 'open' minority-audience programming.

By 4 September it was becoming clear not only that the United States' account was curiously silent on major points – such as the failure of US and Japanese monitoring facilities to warn KAL 007 of impending disaster – but that some of the Soviet assertions were true. BBC1's main news that day reported a claim by Soviet General Romanov that 'the Jumbo looked like an American reconnaissance plane, the RC-135. He said the Jumbo was flying without any lights, and the outline resembled that of the RC-135, a military version of the Boeing 707. American officials admitted tonight that there was an American spy-plane in the vicinity of the Korean Airlines flight.'

Some evidence strengthening the Soviet account emerged from a Presidential briefing session on 4 September. The Democratic Congressional leader Jim Wright, who was present at the briefing, told reporters that from the evidence of the tapes of the incident made by US and Japanese intelligence it was *not* clear that the Soviet fighter pilot had recognized KAL 007 to be a civilian airliner, contrary to the assurances of the Reagan administration. In fact, said the Congressman, he had twice heard the Soviet pilot refer to the aircraft as an RC-135.

On 5 September ITN reported a statement by Congressman Wright that, according to his hearing of the administration's tapes of the incident 'there wasn't any clear definition of the aircraft [by the Soviet pilot]. It was referred to on those tapes as "it" or "the plane" or "the target". The question arises as to how high was the level of understanding that this was an unarmed commercial civilian airplane' (3 2200 5/9/83).

Main evening bulletins never developed the implications of this statement, which clearly undermined the Reagan administration's position that there was no possibility of a mistake having been made. Indeed, main evening bulletins constructed no critical or sceptical readings of the administration's account at any time during their coverage. Only one journalist – Charles Wheeler of *Newsnight* – developed the available evidence and drew conclusions which seriously challenged the US account.

We reproduce at some length here one of Wheeler's reports, in which the evidence about the RC-135 was employed to legitimize the Soviet account. Broadcast by *Newsnight* on 5 September, the item began by pointing out 'undue selectivity' in the American account of the incident:

> *Wheeler*: In advance of the President's speech [a reference to the speech made by President Reagan on American television on 5 September] what chiefly intrigues people here is how Mr Reagan will handle the accidental disclosure yesterday of a possible pertinent fact that the administration was keeping to itself, that an American military reconnaissance plane was flying just outside Soviet airspace but in the same area while Soviet fighter planes were tracking the Korean airliner they later shot down. In the minds of some this revelation not only reinforces what seems to be shaping up as the Soviet case for the defence – that the Russian fighter pilots mistook the 747 for an American spy-plane – it also suggests that Washington is being unduly selective in its presentation of the evidence.
>
> The story of the American reconnaissance plane, an RC-135, surfaced on Sunday morning . . . .
>
> Eventually a reluctant White House spokesman Larry Speakes conceded that yes, there was evidence that the Russians at one time thought they were tracking an RC-135 and yes, a plane of that type had been flying a mission over Soviet territory. The RC-135 is a military version of the Boeing 707. It has a specially extended nose. It is far smaller than a 747. It does not have that characteristic Jumbo hump and a competent Soviet pilot ought to be able to tell one from the other, especially in the light of a three-quarter moon. But the presence of not one but two unidentified planes, one of them just outside and the other well inside Soviet airspace may well have created confusion and should surely have been disclosed along with all the other evidence. Nobody here is condoning the shooting down of that Korean aircraft but there is criticism of the way the Reagan administration has handled the crisis.

The item now leads into an interview with Dimitri Simes, an emigré Soviet academic at the Carnegie Institute, Washington, and consultant to the US government on Soviet affairs:

> *Wheeler*: Do you regard it as significant that there was an American reconnaissance plane, an RC-135, in the area?

Dimitri Simes: Definitely significant because it adds at least some element of credibility to the first Soviet explanation ... it does not look like a flagrant lie as it appeared after the statement was issued and totally rejected by the State Department.

This example illustrates the nature of the questions being asked of the United States' account, even at this early stage, and the availability of an alternative version of the incident. The item raises the *possibility* that the Soviet account is not, after all, a 'flagrant lie'. This alternative framework is arrived at by the simple device of examining the available evidence, including Congressman Wright's testimony that, according to the US tape of the incident, the Soviet fighter pilot who shot down KAL 007 actually referred to an RC-135 on two occasions. On main bulletins the disclosure of the presence in the area of an RC-135 was reported by journalists, in line with American claims, as coincidence:

> American officials admitted tonight that there was an American spy-plane in the vicinity of the Korean Airlines flight but it was well outside Soviet airspace and one-and-a-half hours before the airliner was shot down. The spy-plane was on a routine reconnaissance flight, they say, and by the time the Jumbo was shot down the Soviet pilots should have known without a doubt that it was a civilian plane.
>
> (1 2000 4/9/83)

The next day, 5 September, President Reagan gave a major televised statement on the incident which was covered extensively on British television news. By this stage in the propaganda war it was being openly speculated that there would be no 'serious sanctions' (3 2200 5/9/83). The reasons for this, it was reported, were disagreements among the allies as to the effectiveness of sanctions, and the disclosure that, in line with the Soviet account, there had indeed been an American RC-135 spy-plane in the vicinity of the Korean airliner. This, as we have seen, had emerged on Sunday 4 September, after a briefing session between President Reagan and Congressional leaders at the White House.

Partly for this reason, it was predicted that there would be a drawing-back from the 'tough line against the Russians'. Reports of the speech portrayed it as moderate. 'A mild speech' one journalist called it (3 2200 6/9/83). 'President Reagan failed to apply any strong sanctions,' remarked another on the same bulletin, 'and the

White House today received scores of telegrams protesting at the lack of real action.' The BBC reported the President's own description of his sanctions as 'a calm and measured response' (1 2100 6/9/83).

Alternatives to the view that the speech was a 'calm and measured response' were not reported on the main evening bulletins. Again, however, Charles Wheeler on *Newsnight* challenged this reading. In his *Newsnight* item of 6 September the Reagan speech was employed as an example of the President's 'simple and comprehensible' style, and used too in a wider analysis of the reasons for his popularity:

> For people who still wonder how it was that the actor Ronald Reagan became President of the United States, and for those who wonder if he'll be re-elected if next year he runs for a second term, his speech last night provides the answer. America found in Reagan a leader with a simple comprehensible philosophy, and an exceptional ability to put his case across. He was always good at television. Last night he was matchless. Three years in office have made Reagan the master of his role. His popularity and his power have given his actor's talent an edge that wasn't there before. He was helped of course by the nature of the issue. A civil airliner packed with innocent people sent to their deaths by a Soviet missile. A simple case, he said, not merely of murder. As though it were a feature film he gave the tragedy a title – the Korean Airline Massacre, and he called it that five times.

After a lengthy excerpt from the President's speech, the journalist comes back in to contextualize it, not as a calm and measured response, but as 'demagoguery':

> President Reagan addressing the nation. Reactions here vary widely. From the left to the political centre there is clearly relief that the actions the President has called for are strictly limited. 'The White House avoids flamboyance' says the *New York Times*, and from CBS, 'the speech of a statesman'. At the other end of the political spectrum, the far right, it is being called a 'namby-pamby speech that won't wash with the American people because it is too soft' and that has been the reaction clearly anticipated by the President's aides. At a White House briefing they stressed that the restraint he showed does not mean any softening in his attitude to the Russians, and in private conversations duly put into print today they added that the appearance

of restraint was crucial to Mr Reagan for foreign and political reasons. Well restraint it seems is in the eye of the beholder. Perhaps it can be said that in this observer's view Mr Reagan came closer last night than John Kennedy, or Lyndon Johnson, or Richard Nixon ever did, to being a demagogue.

In this example the Reagan administration's viewpoint is reported as 'propaganda'. The President is not presented here as a moderate and sensible statesman making a calm and measured response to grave provocation, but as an 'actor', a 'demagogue', complimented on his ability to manipulate emotions with 'simple, comprehensible philosophies'. This reading of the speech, or of the official US viewpoint throughout the crisis, was never echoed on the main evening news bulletins.

It was not only the Reagan administration which publicly professed its outrage at Soviet 'terrorism'. The majority of NATO governments joined in the condemnations. They, too, received uncritical coverage. The British Foreign Secretary, for example, remarked on 2 September that:

> the world is bound to reflect on what kind of government and what kind of society it is that allows this kind of thing to happen.
> (1 2100 2/9/83)

Echoing closely the sentiments expressed earlier in the day by President Reagan, the central assumption was again one of Soviet barbarism. The journalist reported the statement as moderate and conciliatory, under the circumstances:

> But in spite of all this condemnation it's been noticeable today that no one in power has actually suggested cutting off any links with the Russians. Quite the opposite, in fact. Sir Geoffrey, like the State Department in Washington, is saying that the real need is to keep on talking to the Russians, to persuade them that they shouldn't behave like this.

The administration's account of the incident had been established as reasonable and consensual, although no such assumption could have been made on the evidence alone.

At the end of the sample period the British Defence Secretary visited Washington. As the Foreign Secretary had done, Michael Heseltine used the Korean airliner incident to portray himself as moderate and conciliatory in the context of the Soviet threat. These elements were neatly merged in his support for a policy of 'negotiating from strength' (3 2200 14/9/83). Mr Heseltine's visit to Washington was closely linked to the impending arrival of Cruise missiles in Britain, and his statements during the visit illustrate how western politicians frequently used the Korean airliner disaster to justify and legitimate their defence policies in terms of the Soviet threat. Such usage was reinforced by television news:

> Mr Heseltine has told the Americans that the shooting down of the Korean plane reinforced the need for the west to pursue arms control talks. The incident, he said, said nothing new about Russian behaviour but because the Soviet Union was capable of such acts it was imperative to go on talking to them about nuclear weapons.
>
> (1 2100 14/9/83)

The opinion that there was 'nothing new' in the Korean airline disaster appeared without qualification or comment, as it did in ITN's report:

> The Defence Secretary Mr Heseltine has said the Korean jet incident has made arms talks with Russia even more important. He said in Washington the west must still look for a dialogue simply because the Soviets are capable of doing such things, and he warned against a rhetoric of confrontation.
>
> (3 2200 14/9/83)

This was followed by news of more criticism of the USSR from President Reagan: 'but President Reagan kept up his fierce criticism of Moscow tonight. He said we cannot allow such a brutal regime to militarily dominate this planet.'

Journalists did not merely report images of a 'brutal regime out to militarily dominate this planet': they frequently appeared to share the assumptions on which such rhetoric was based. This was borne out on one of the few occasions when a view which dissented from the dominant interpretation (other than those from Soviet sources) was reported.

On 12 September a summit meeting of the Foreign Ministers of the European Economic Community was held in Athens, under the chairmanship of the Greek Foreign Minister. An attempt was made at the meeting to secure a resounding condemnation of the Soviet Union for shooting down the Korean airliner. The Greeks, however, disagreed with this approach. ITN reported that:

> Nine of the Common Market countries are angry with the tenth, Greece, for blocking a united condemnation of the Soviet Union. The Community Foreign Ministers could *only* agree to issue a statement *simply* regretting the loss of life.
>
> (3 2200 12/9/83)

The language of the report – they could 'only' issue a statement, 'simply' regretting the loss of life – reveals the underlying assumption that more should have been said. As the report continues, Greece is held responsible for 'a weak compromise cobbled together' which 'merely expressed deep emotion and agreed to a full investigation'.

There is no obvious reason why expressions of regret and calls for a full investigation should be dismissed as a 'weak compromise', unless the assumption had already been made that no investigation was required. The BBC report took a similarly dim view of the Greeks:

> Europe's Foreign Ministers failed to show a united front today.
>
> (1 2100 12/9/83)

The journalist's description of the Foreign Ministers' statement was remarkably similar to that of the ITN report:

> Eventually there was a bland, compromise statement expressing sympathy for the victims of the disaster, but the Greek Foreign Minister was still the most unpopular man at his own meeting and the statement did not condemn the Russians.

In so far as the statement failed to condemn 'the Russians' it was a 'bland compromise'. In neither bulletin was any attempt made to view the 'bland compromise' position from the Greek perspective, and to explain why the Greeks felt it to be valid. The viewer, however, was reminded that Greece had a 'left-wing government'.

The story was followed up three days later when the European Parliament met in Strasbourg. Here, as the BBC reported, there was no 'weak, bland compromise':

> Brutal and despicable. That was how the European Parliament condemned the shooting down of the South Korean airliner when it met in Strasbourg today. In its resolution the Parliament spoke of its deep indignation at the incident, calling it cold-blooded murder, assassination and execution, but it wasn't only the

> Russians who came in for criticism. The Greek government was censured for refusing earlier this week to agree to an outright condemnation of the Soviet attack.
>
> (1 2100 14/9/83)

With its accusations of cold-blooded murder, assassination, and execution, this statement received a distinctly more sympathetic response than had the earlier 'bland compromise'. It was quickly endorsed by the correspondent as redressing the perceived inadequacies of the Athens statement:

> It's taken fourteen days for Europe to pull together its collective act. Fourteen days before it bypassed its own bureaucracy and condemned Russia's attack. This was the day the sleeping Parliament in Strasbourg woke up, with Greece in its sights.

While congratulating the Parliament for at last pulling together, we were offered a belated and brief account of *why* the Greek representatives had behaved in the way that they did:

> The Greeks said their stand had been prompted by a need to preserve detente and not risk peace, but that argument was rejected by others who voted to condemn Russia by name.

In this manner, those who challenged the official reading of the Korean airliner disaster were implicitly censured by journalists. On the opening day of the 1983 TUC conference in Blackpool the BBC reported that the General Council had passed an emergency motion condemning the Soviet Union. This was followed by the news that:

> Tonight Tony Benn in a wide-ranging speech *attacking the west* said the truth hadn't come out in the first instance, that there was a reconnaissance plane accompanying the Korean airliner over Soviet territory.
>
> (1 2100 5/9/83)

Mr Benn's statement that the Reagan administration had been withholding important information from the public was contextualized by the qualification that he was 'attacking the west'. This hardly seems relevant to the subject of the Korean airliner, unless to connect in the eyes of the audience Mr Benn's views on the subject to an 'anti-west' position.

The Soviet view

Soviet accounts of the circumstances surrounding the incident were not ignored, but they were consistently reported within a framework which interpreted the spy-plane theory as a 'cover-up' rather than a credible explanation. The assumption of Soviet culpability structured coverage throughout.

As the propaganda war developed Soviet statements were consistently reported as admissions of guilt, although responsibility for the civilian deaths was blamed by the USSR throughout on the United States. At the same time, the main case for the Soviet defence, that the aircraft had been mistaken for a spy-plane, was routinely juxtaposed with 'balancing' statements by representatives of western governments. Statements from official western sources were not subject to critical analysis or challenge by journalists, and when used to 'balance' the debate they tended to be juxtaposed as 'truth' to Soviet 'propaganda'.

As we saw, the initial statement made by President Reagan received uncritical coverage. The speech set the tone and established the interpretative framework which dominated subsequent coverage. Soviet statements reported at this time were immediately contradicted by reference to the Reagan speech and by the opinions of privileged 'others'. The BBC's statement that 'non-communist leaders say the Soviet version is inadequate' was followed by a lengthy list of condemnations:

> The Foreign Secretary Geoffrey Howe summoned the Soviet ambassador to the Foreign Office and told him of Britain's horror and revulsion. Other nations west and east have spoken too. France called the incident 'cruel and intolerable'. West Germany, 'despicable, brutal, and unparalleled'. Italy called it a 'mad gesture of war'. China said she was shocked. So too did the Pope.

ITN balanced the Soviet statement with President Reagan's accusation of 'flagrant lying'. Then:

> America insists that a Soviet fighter shot the plane down, killing the 269 people on board.

As noted in the introduction, Soviet statements initially failed to confirm the fact that the aircraft had been destroyed by a Soviet fighter. But the 2 September statement, expressing 'regret' over the loss of life and condemning those who 'allowed' it was not a denial of that fact. In the above report of the propaganda exchange it is implied that such a denial has taken place. The Soviets are implied to be covering up, while the US State Department and President Reagan are staunchly insisting on the 'truth'. The debate at this point was not about whether the aircraft had been shot down, but *why*. Was it the consequence of a typical act of Soviet brutality or the accidental byproduct of a US intelligence operation? The statements released by both sides on 2 September made this clear. On television news the debate was shifted on to different terrain, away from the doubts surrounding the American account of the incident.

The TASS statement was also interpreted by journalists as a 'coming clean' or a movement 'in the direction demanded by western governments', although it was a clear condemnation, both of the United States for causing the tragedy, and of western leaders in general for exploiting it. That the statement did not contain an admission of responsibility for the deaths was clear from news accounts, and was explained by one journalist as being due to the fact that 'the Soviet Union never apologizes'.

> The Foreign Secretary summoned the Soviet ambassador, told him the earlier Soviet explanation was totally inadequate and presented him with a list of demands. ...
>
> Tonight the Russians have moved a little of the way in the direction Sir Geoffrey and the Americans are demanding. It came like this on Moscow Radio's account of the affair, broadcast in English and it was brief in the extreme. [Radio Moscow broadcast follows.]
>
> The leading circles that are expressing their regret can only be the political leadership in the Kremlin, headed by President Andropov. It's a less than half acceptance of responsibility and a less than half apology, but in the usual way the Soviet Union never apologizes for what it does and is even less willing to admit it was wrong than most western countries are and that brief sentence dropped into an elaborate defence of what happened must represent the minimum of what Mr Andropov and his colleagues feel that the west will accept.
>
> (1 2100 2/9/83)

Coverage of the 2 September TASS statement illustrated a number of contradictory themes. On the one hand, the Soviets were reported to be coming clean in response to western condemnation; on the other, that they were engaged in a cover-up to deny the obvious fact that they had shot down a civilian airliner; the Soviet exposition of the spy-plane theory was contextualized as part of this cover-up, and discredited accordingly.

These contradictions continued to appear in coverage. On 5 September British television news picked up on a Soviet television commentator's remarks about the incident, which were almost as vitriolic in their attack on the United States as Mr Reagan's comments about the Soviet Union had been. The BBC report began by pointing to some 'movement' in the Soviet position:

> Tonight the Russians came the closest they've come yet to admitting responsibility. A Soviet commentator said on television their defence forces had fulfilled their duty in protecting the country's security. But there was no apology from Moscow tonight. The television commentator accused the Americans of being 'worse than the Nazis, sacrificing lives for their own ends'.
>
> (1 2100 5/9/83)

> On Soviet television's main news tonight the commentator said the incident was all part of an American plan to gain nuclear superiority in Europe. He said the innocent passengers on the plane had been sacrificed just as Hitler's troops forced women and children to go in front when they were attacked. The commentator came close to admitting that Soviet fighters shot down the plane.
>
> (3 2200 5/9/83)

To say that one has 'fulfilled one's duty' is not the same thing as admitting responsibility. A major TASS statement was released the next day which expanded further on the statement of 2 September and referred directly to the RC-135 spy-plane. The statement also contained the first official reference to the destruction of the airliner by Soviet fighters and was interpreted by journalists as the admission of guilt 'everyone has been waiting for'.

> Good evening. Six days after the destruction of the Korean airliner the Soviet government have finally owned up. ... That admission came less than twenty-four hours after President Reagan had gone on television to appeal for international action against the Soviet Union.
>
> This statement, carrying with it the full authority of the Soviet

> leadership, is an admission that a Soviet interceptor brought down the Jumbo jet. Coming as it does with the full authority of the Kremlin this is the acknowledgement that everyone has been waiting for.
>
> (1 2100 6/9/83)

ITN interpreted the statement as a response to President Reagan's 'mild speech' of the previous evening. Again, ITN avoided the basic issue of *why* the airliner had been shot down and, like the BBC, concentrated on reading the Soviet statement as an admission of guilt:

> Good evening. The Soviet Union admitted tonight for the first time that it did shoot down the Korean airliner last week, and it came near to saying it was sorry.
>
> (3 2200 6/9/83)

Balance was achieved by juxtaposing the Soviet claim with a straight denial by the United States government:

> The statement, expressly by the Soviet government, was rejected by the American Embassy in Moscow as inadequate, too little, too late but in saying the airliner's flight had been terminated by the Soviet air defences, President Andropov may have reasserted his civilian control over the Soviet military who've been insisting they did nothing wrong. Mr Andropov was away on holiday when the airliner was brought down. He may also have responded to Mr Reagan's mild speech last night which called for little more than a Soviet apology and compensation for the victims.
>
> (3 2200 6/9/83)

Later in the bulletin we are told:

> White House officials are still studying the reports from Moscow but a spokesman said, 'if it's true, it will be about time too'. It'll certainly be welcome news for President Reagan who throughout has tried to avert a full-scale confrontation with Moscow in the hopes that the arms control negotiations with the Russians would not come to a grinding halt.

The implications of these comments are clear. The Soviet Union, having confessed its guilt, will have pleased President Reagan who has never sought a confrontation over the incident. At the same time, it is 'too little, too late'. The presentation of the statements and opinions of the principal actors in the drama is principally determined by the assumption that one side is guilty of the accusations being made against it by the other side. The United States appears in the account as flexible, anxious to avoid conflict, prepared to forgive the crime which has been committed. President Reagan is portrayed as 'trying to avert a full-scale conflict' rather than as the cold war ideologue which some felt the Korean airliner incident confirmed him to be. Soviet 'guilt' was read into a succession of statements which claimed the opposite.

Television news covered subsequent Soviet inputs into the propaganda war by concentrating on its alleged refusal to apologize or compensate for the crime. Yet, from 1 September, the Soviet Union repeatedly stressed its 'regret' for the deaths of innocent people in the disaster, while refusing to accept responsibility. The distinction between these positions was not reflected in coverage.

On 8 September the Soviet Foreign Minister Andrei Gromyko attended the Madrid Security Conference on Security and Co-operation. In the course of his speech to the conference he reiterated the Soviet position and stressed that 'we have expressed regret over the loss of human lives' (English text from *Soviet News*, no. 6190). Journalists disagreed:

> Mr Gromyko, the Soviet Foreign Minister, showed no remorse. On the contrary, when he spoke at the European Security Conference in Madrid he accused the United States of sending the plane across Soviet territory on a spying mission.
>
> (1 2100 8/9/83)

> In his speech Mr Gromyko offered not a hint of regret or apology.
>
> (3 2200 8/9/83)

Mr Gromyko did express his government's regret, while blaming the tragedy on the actions of the United States intelligence services. The journalist excluded this from the account and contradicted Gromyko's accusations with statements by the British Foreign Secretary and the US Secretary of State:

> Sir Geoffrey Howe told him 'Your explanation is still not credible'.
>
> (1 2100 8/9/83)

> *Journalist*: Mr Schultz reacted angrily to what he'd heard.
> *George Schultz*: I would have to say that from the very beginning we have heard nothing but falsehoods from the Soviet Union, and it is disappointing for me to sit in that hall at a conference that is dedicated to human rights, to truth, and hear the Foreign Minister of the Soviet Union continue to state the same falsehoods.
> (3 2200 8/9/83)

It had become clear by this time that several aspects of the Soviet position were not 'falsehoods'. As we have seen, as early as 4 September the *possibility* that the Korean airliner had been mistaken for a US RC-135 spy-plane had been made available as an explanation for the incident. If, as Seymour Hersch argued above, the US administration already knew beyond doubt by 9 September that this explanation was the correct one, it is clear that the public in general (and television news journalists) did not. Only the *possibility* had been established, although this might have been viewed as enough to justify qualification or even criticism of the dismissive statements of western leaders about Soviet claims. With the exceptions of the Wheeler items mentioned in the previous section there were none. The assumed incredibility of Soviet claims appeared to render unnecessary their serious examination. The apparent consensus which had been established around the theme of Soviet barbarism meant that those who alleged it to be true did not have to substantiate their claims.

A notable feature of the propaganda war was the relative dearth of evidence produced by the US government in support of its account. The only piece of hard evidence used was a tape-recorded conversation between Soviet pilots and ground control. These tapes, however, proved only that the airliner had been attacked and destroyed by the Soviet fighters. They did not prove the main thrust of the US position, that a deliberate act of murder had taken place. If anything, as Congressman Wright had observed, they lent support to the Soviet claims that a genuine mistake had been made. Yet the US account remained the favoured one on television news. Journalists showed zeal in reporting anything which appeared to confirm the 'cold-blooded murder' scenario. As balance to the Gromyko speech on 8 September, ITN reported that:

> The White House said it had further, almost irrefutable evidence that the Soviet authorities knew the airliner was an unarmed civilian plane. The White House claims that it has further

> information which proves that the Russians knew full well that they were about to shoot down a civilian airliner. It's believed this evidence is contained in a series of yet to be released tape-recordings of conversations between the Soviet jet fighters and their controller on the ground.
>
> (3 2200 8/9/83)

Such evidence would, of course, have fundamentally weakened the Soviet position on the incident. However, as the correspondent went on to reveal in the next sentence, there was no new information available:

> But tonight President Reagan's spokesman denied the report. One possible reason is that it's a highly delicate issue because questions could be asked as to whether the Americans were using a spy-plane to obtain this evidence.

The most detailed and 'media-conscious' presentation of the Soviet version came on 9 September at a special news conference staged in Moscow. The spy-plane theory remained essentially the same as that first expounded on 2 September, but was further elaborated with diagrams, maps, and specific allegations relating to the role played by the RC-135 aircraft.

As noted in the introduction to this chapter, this conference can be seen as something of a turning point for the Soviet authorities, both in relation to the Korean airliner tragedy and to their information policy as a whole. This was reflected in coverage, which emphasized the unusual staginess of the event:

> Good evening. The Russians took an unusual step today in their attempts to explain why they shot down the Korean airliner. They rarely put their generals on display but today one of them was allowed to answer questions from western journalists.
>
> (1 2100 9/9/83)

Then:

> But the message was as defiant as ever.
>
> ITN reported that:
>
> The press conference lasting two hours is thought to have been unprecedented in the Soviet Union, both in allowing journalists to ask real questions and in the seniority of the Soviet spokesmen answering them.
>
> (3 2200 9/9/83)

This was followed by the news that:

They were unrepentant.

The elaborate Soviet account of the flight of the Korean airliner, its deviation and rendezvous with an RC-135, the extent of its course deviation, and the sensitivity of the military areas over which it flew, were dismissed by reference to a throwaway comment from a United States' source:

> The United States remains unimpressed. Where's the evidence, they're asking tonight? The Soviet Union still owes the world answers.
>
> (1 2100 9/9/83)

Despite the confident tone of these comments, the United States had as yet produced no evidence for its *own* version of events. Neither the USA nor the USSR had proven the accuracy of their respective accounts. The United States' denial of the Soviet account, entirely predictable within the context of a fierce propaganda war, was favoured none the less by the space given it in the bulletin to balance and discredit the Soviet version. No comparable emphasis was ever put on the opposite situation:

> 'The Soviet Union remains unimpressed. Where's the evidence, they're asking tonight? The United States still owes the world answers.'

Such an aggressive presentation, as inconceivable as it seems in the Soviet case, was routine for coverage of US statements:

> *Journalist*: It was left to a State Department official to contemptuously dismiss today's Soviet version of what happened.
>
> *US State Department official*: The Soviet Union still owes the world answers and assurances that civil aviation will not be targeted in the future. It is interesting to note what the Soviets did not do today. They offered no evidence to support their assertion that the plane was on a reconnaissance mission. They offered no evidence to support the claim that they attempted to identify or force down the KAL plane.
>
> (1 2100 9/9/83)

ITN reported that:

> at the State Department officials were discounting the latest

> claims from Moscow charging that the Russians were engaged in a cover-up.
>
> (3 2200 9/9/83)

Reports painted a picture of a 'defiant message' 'contemptuously dismissed' as a 'cover-up'. One journalist returned to the theme of the Soviets 'coming clean'. To most observers it was by now clear that the Soviets were not going to admit responsibility for the disaster, or accept Mr Reagan's accusations against them. ITN's correspondent nevertheless chose to give exactly the opposite impression:

> It's taken the Russians nine days to agree with the outline of events originally presented by America.
>
> (3 2200 9/9/83)

As the Moscow news conference was going on a memorial service for the victims of the incident was taking place in Washington, after which President Reagan made a public appeal for a national day of mourning to be held the following Sunday. The service, in which Soviet barbarism was again emphasized by the Bishop of Washington, served further to contextualize the Moscow news conference. The content of the Bishop of Washington's speech neatly framed reports from Moscow, while in ITN's bulletin they received headline status.

Coverage of the Moscow news conference was consistent with the pattern for reporting Soviet statements in the Korean airliner crisis. Balancing, framing, and contextualizing Soviet 'propaganda' in terms of an assumed consensus around the basic issue of 'what happened', the Soviet account was constructed as a less favoured one on the news. Ironically, perhaps, one of the BBC's correspondents noted on 9 September: 'The Americans are sure they're winning the propaganda war.' Given the nature of the coverage examined here, this hardly seems surprising.

What happened?

This section examines how the various theories about what befell KAL 007 were reported on the news. Although the US State Department never changed its position that the airliner had accidentally strayed into Soviet airspace there were, as we have seen, major question marks over the claim. First to point out these doubts were the Soviet authorities themselves in the TASS statement of 2 September. That evening, the BBC announced that it would 'report on why the Boeing went so far off course, and why it wasn't warned' (1 2100 2/9/83). Later in the bulletin it was reported that:

> Demands for explanations about how it happened have been directed at Moscow but, as Moscow's pointed out, it's not only the Russians who have to come up with some answers.

ITN commented that 'Mr Reagan has some explaining of his own to do' (3 2200 2/9/83).

These reports reflected the view that there were valid doubts about the US version of events. But subsequent discussions side-stepped the implications of these opening remarks and assumed the correctness of the Americans' account. The peculiarities 'pointed out by Moscow' were resolved by journalists without serious consideration of the central Soviet allegation that the Korean airliner had been involved in an intelligence mission. This account was beyond the parameters of legitimacy. The spy-plane theory was referred to only in the context of 'what the Soviets say', i.e. as 'propaganda'. The failure to include the spy-plane theory in their accounts of what *might* have happened reflected the journalists' refusal to grant the Soviet account credibility.

The question of what happened to the Korean airliner was raised in four main evening bulletins throughout the sample period. None of these reports included the Soviet account in their speculation about the mystery of KAL 007. The BBC report of 2 September set out one of the problems in the US account:

> If American and Japanese military authorities knew the Korean jet was out of bounds, why didn't anyone tell the crew? American monitoring stations had listened to Russian air defence controllers scrambling the first interceptors two hours before the plane was shot down. Japanese controllers spotted the Russian fighters on their long-range military radar. There's no doubt American forces based in Japan were getting the same picture. The aircraft called Tokyo with a routine request to climb eleven minutes before being destroyed. At that time it was well inside Russian airspace, with Sukoy Flaggers flying alongside, yet Tokyo control didn't mention it to the captain.

What comes next was typical of the way in which journalists resolved the question of what happened. Excluding the possibility of a planned espionage mission, marginalizing it to the realm of the incredible, journalists had no recourse but to speculate freely on the possible accidents that could have occurred. Accounting for the failure of the Japanese or US authorities to warn the airliner, when they had by their own admission monitored the entire flight, one journalist concluded:

> It's all beginning to point to a disastrous lack of communication between military and civilian authorities.

This could have been the case, although there was no more evidence to support this explanation than there was for the Soviet account. Indeed, US intelligence sources later revealed that communications in the region were extremely sophisticated, a fact made embarrassingly clear by the ease with which the entire incident was recorded by the US. Nevertheless, 'a disastrous lack of communications' is introduced as an authoritative suggestion, and indeed the *only* one, while the possibility of a 'pre-planned mission' is not raised. ITN's correspondent chose not to propose any specific theory on the subject:

> The Americans now say that they have a very clear picture of how the Russians shot down the South Korean plane. But when did the Americans have that information? If they knew what was going on while it was happening why did they not intervene directly, perhaps using the Washington–Moscow hotline? It's one of the many questions still surrounding the last hours of the South Korean plane.
>
> (3 2200 2/9/83)

The issue was again covered on 16 September:

> The Japanese have released a tape-recording of the last exchanges between the aircraft and Tokyo ground control. The pilot sounds calm, the flight appears to be proceeding as scheduled, then comes the realization that something is wrong.
>
> The recordings do nothing to clear up the mystery. The Japanese air traffic controllers monitoring their radar screens should have realized the plane was off course and warned it. If the Russians did fire warning tracer shots the Korean aircrew should have seen them. But four minutes from disaster air traffic controller and pilot were chatting about a routine change of altitude.
>
> (1 2100 16/9/83)

This report concedes that the US account is not entirely satisfactory, but the Soviet explanation is again excluded from the list of possible explanations for what happened.

The question of how the airliner had deviated so far from its course was also discussed, but within a similarly limited range of possibilities. The only explanations included on the news were those which assumed that the Korean flight's course deviation was accidental. Debate was not permitted to include the possibility of an intentional 'error' and the viewer was not given any background as to the actual likelihood of the various possibilities that *were* raised:

> Why was the jet so far off course? The fact that the pilot thought he was on track suggests a wrong reading on the plane's inertial navigation system. That could only happen if there'd been a mistake in setting the original co-ordinates for latitude and longitude. One degree equals sixty nautical miles, and any error would be compounded in the long haul across the Pacific. The routine check calls to Japanese trans-oceanic control reported the airliner as on a correct heading. It wouldn't have been until the Jumbo came within radar range that the true position became clear.
>
> (1 2100 2/9/83)

No indication was given of how unlikely such an error would have been. ITN constructed an experiment with a flight simulator and came up with an entirely different, if equally unsubstantiated scenario:

> One possibility that's being considered is a total electrical failure. ... This kind of problem has occurred before on passenger-carrying jets and tonight it's being considered as an explanation for the Korean plane being so far off course.
>
> (3 2200 2/9/83)

There were many possible explanations as to why the aircraft had made such a disastrous error. 'Total electrical failure' was no less likely than the majority of those proposed. Of interest to us here is the fact that no explanation *other* than that of accidental error was considered in these accounts. The Soviet explanation, with its implications for the United States role in the incident, was excluded. News programmes on BBC2 and Channel 4 (with the exception noted above) reported these problems within the same basic assumption: that the spy-plane theory was not credible. On 2 September Channel 4 news interviewed Admiral Stansfield Turner, a former Director of the CIA, who gave *his* opinion that the spy-plane theory was a possibility, if an unlikely one:

> *Journalist*: Admiral Turner, the Russians are now apparently saying that that plane, a civilian plane, could have been on some kind of reconnaissance flight. Is that possible?
>
> *Turner*: Of course it's possible. Any plane can conduct reconnaissance. I think it's highly improbable. It's a very ineffective and risky way to conduct intelligence.
>
> *Journalist*: Is there any record at all, in your experience, of any country using civilian planes as a cover for intelligence-gathering?
>
> *Turner*: Well, any intelligence officer has to answer that question with a 'no comment'. ... If the answer is yes and I say 'no comment' you'll know what I'm trying to do.
>
> (4 1900 2/9/83)

Admiral Turner, while unable to confirm that the Korean airliner *was* spying, continued by stressing the circumstances surrounding the incident which might have made the Soviet Union 'overreact'.

> *Turner*: Without apologizing for the Soviets, looking at it from their point of view, this is the second instance when it's a Korean airliner, a civilian airplane that has penetrated deeply into their country. So, with their normal paranoia you can understand their getting excited. That doesn't justify the degree of their response, which was disproportionate to the threat.
>
> *Journalist*: But you would say they had good reasons to be awfully suspicious?
>
> *Turner*: I didn't say good reasons. I say a paranoid person, having two instances like this by the same airplane, gets suspicious, easily in the Soviet Union.

Admiral Turner clearly took the sky-plane theory more seriously than other speakers on the news, but his opinion was not reflected in Channel 4's own appraisal of 'how it happened':

> It's still far from clear what really happened to Korean Airlines flight 007.

Three theories were then introduced:

> The first suggests a computer failure in the plane's navigational equipment, but 747s carry sophisticated navigational systems with three computers that continuously check each other. If the computers fail, a light warns the pilot. Human error in programming the navigation computers is much more likely. ... The 'Marie Celeste' theory is also possible. It suggests that pressure of oxygen in the aircraft dropped suddenly, rendering crew and passengers unconscious and the plane out of control. The trouble with this theory is that the plane actually turned into Soviet airspace and didn't just drift rudderless into restricted zones. But the theory is attractive because it suggests an answer to the second major unanswered question. Why didn't the crew respond to warnings from the Russian jet buzzing it? If the crew were unconscious, they'd be unable to.

From 'computer failure' to 'Marie Celeste' these theories were as speculative as any proposed on the main evening bulletins, though the journalist sought to present them as superior to the Soviet explanation:

> The new Russian suggestion, that the plane was on a spying mission, sounds as amazing as science fiction.

No more amazing than the 'Marie Celeste' theory, it might be thought. News programmes generally failed to break away from the assumption that the Korean airliner had accidentally strayed into Soviet airspace.

As late as 15 September BBC's *Newsnight* concluded after a lengthy report that there was 'only one *plausible* explanation' for the flight of KAL 007, this being 'navigational error'. According to pilots who have flown the KAL 007 flight, such a major deviation from course is impossible. On this programme it was reported to be 'a regular occurrence'.

The inadequacy of the Soviet public relations machine, alluded to in the introduction to this chapter, cannot be held to account entirely for the fact that the Reagan administration won the key issues in the propaganda war at the time when it most mattered. Given that the Soviet Union did not 'use' the western media with the same facility as their protagonists in the propaganda war, they did nevertheless present *a* version of events which on the evidence available was no less credible than any other account making the news.

Official western accounts presented the Korean airliner disaster as confirmation and vindication of the Soviet threat. This framework was rarely challenged on the news, although evidence supporting the Soviet account was available as early as 3 September. We have given examples of occasions as early as 5 and 6 September when the dominant framework *was* challenged, and these are extremely important to the overall picture, but they were far from being representative. One final counter-example further confirms that critical approaches to official US propaganda were available. The programme was Channel 4's *Friday Alternative*, now defunct. On 17 September it compared the response of the Reagan administration to the Korean airliner incident with the response of President Nixon ten years earlier to a similar tragedy:

> Ten years ago Israel shot down a Libyan airliner which had strayed into its airspace. For the victims the Israelis, unlike the Russians, offered compensation. But their explanations for the events were strikingly similar. Both countries have emphasized similar criteria for shooting down a civilian airliner. But ten years ago US President Nixon simply expressed regret. There were no flags at half-mast, no sanctions, no change in US–Israeli relations. How can two such similar tragedies provoke two such different reactions? In the diplomacy game it all depends on who is in the firing line.

In this major international crisis with potentially dangerous consequences for Britain (as a host country for US nuclear weapons), broadcasting journalists on the whole showed themselves unwilling or unable to maintain a critical distance from the propaganda campaign mounted by one side against the other. At the time of writing it is clear that the United States' account of the incident was based on ideology rather than facts, and that accusations of barbarism and murder directed at the USSR were politically motivated.

On *Newsnight* of 10 September 1986, Seymour Hersch warned that 'our inability to back off and tell the truth about [the Korean airliner disaster] is very ominous. ... The lesson the Russians had better glean from this is that in a crisis we aren't willing to tell the truth about what we know.'

6

The superpower dialogue

The Korean airliner disaster was a special case, with unusual features. A less explosive, but in many ways more important, debate surrounded the issue of arms control.

The arms control negotiations took place partly in response to the development of the defence debate and to rising public concern about the arms race. The collapse of detente, the acceleration of the arms race, and apparent changes in NATO war-fighting strategy produced a wave of popular opposition to nuclear weapons, as well as dissent in the ranks of NATO governments. This was a major factor inducing the Reagan administration to open arms control dialogue with the Soviet Union. The dialogue, when it came, occupied the centre stage in international politics. The issues were complex, the figures and categories of weapons confusing even to seasoned observers, and television's role in reporting and explaining the talks was crucial.

Ronald Reagan came to power in the United States at the head of a conservative coalition whose members took up key positions in his first administration. As noted in Chapter 2, they argued that the Soviet Union was a threatening, expansionary power and that it had established military superiority as a consequence of the policies of previous administrations.[1] For this newly elected group arms control talks with the USSR were counterproductive to the aim of containing the Soviet threat. Ronald Reagan's own record of opposition to nuclear arms control agreements made with the Soviet Union included the Atmospheric Test Ban Treaty, SALTs I and II,[2] and his entry into arms control talks after 1980 was widely perceived as less the consequence of a belief in the intrinsic value of arms control than a political response to public concerns about the administration's attitudes. Talbott (1983) notes that:

> by the end of 1981 political pressures ... induced Reagan to offer an initiative on strategic weapons. But the prevailing approach in the administration to arms control and defence policies

> still seems to be guided by [the following] rather remarkable proposition. . . . If forced by political expediency to make proposals and engage in negotiations, the US must insist on drastic cutbacks in the most modern, potent Soviet weapons . . . no comparable reductions are required, or should be considered, in existing American forces.

Soviet leaders, on the other hand, claimed to be sincerely interested in arms control because, they argued, they had no reason to pursue an arms race, and wished to reduce military expenditure and increase standards of living in their already hard-pressed economy. They would, they said, agree to any level of arms reduction compatible with the maintenance of 'strategic parity' with the USA. The two sides thus approached arms control negotiations not only with conflicting estimates of their respective military strengths but with arguably different attitudes to the principle of arms control itself. This was the context in which negotiations took place after 1980.

Defence and disarmament news covered the dialogue extensively. This involved coverage of the arms control and disarmament initiatives that emerged periodically from both sides; attempts by both sides to go over the heads of normal diplomatic procedures and appeal directly through the media to the populations of the western countries; and the efforts of each side respectively to blame the other for the evident failure of the arms control process. The following discussion examines some key events in this coverage from the Zero Option of November 1981 to the eve of the breakdown of the talks in 1983.

American proposals: the Zero Option and START

On 18 November 1981, in his National Press Club speech, the 'Zero Option' was unveiled before the world with the words of President Reagan that it would be 'like the first step on the moon, an historic step for mankind'. The Zero Option was to form the basis of the United States negotiating position at the Intermediate Nuclear Force (INF) talks with the Soviet Union in Geneva. It set out the United States' willingness to cancel its planned deployment of Cruise and Pershing II missiles (according to the dual-track decision of 12 December 1979) if the Soviet Union would withdraw and dismantle its intermediate range theatre nuclear weapons in

Europe: the SS-4, SS-5, and SS-20 missiles (this demand was later revised to include those theatre weapons stationed in Soviet Asia). The following discussion refers to coverage of the Zero Option on two main evening news bulletins of 18 November 1981.

Western opinion on the Zero Option fell into two categories. Officially, it was a serious arms control proposal with a reasonable chance of success. However, an alternative view dismissed it as an exercise in public relations and 'Alliance management' and therefore worthless in arms control terms. Three weeks *before* Ronald Reagan's speech to the National Press Club, on 28 October, the *New York Times* reported that:

> Many European officials would be disappointed if Moscow accepted the Zero Option approach. ... The adoption of the Zero Option at the beginning of the coming talks is a *necessary public relations move. They hoped it would link in the minds of their uneasy constituents the long-range US nuclear-tipped missiles with the Russian SS-20s.*

Some observers, including people close to the administration, suggested that the Zero Option had been formulated because of growing concern among governments and public in the countries of the NATO alliance about President Reagan's attitude to arms control. Dr William Kincaide, a prominent US defence analyst and consultant to the US government, said of the Zero Option on a BBC *Horizon* documentary that:

> it seemed to strike a chord of sanity across Europe and the United States. Taken alone the proposal seemed equitable, but it ignored many critical factors in the balance of nuclear weapons in Europe. It took no account of aircraft capable of carrying nuclear weapons, nor of how the French and British nuclear forces were to be treated. And it made no sense whatsoever when the superpowers had set no limits on the number of their ICBMs. With all these other issues left out of the talks the Zero Option stood no chance. Nevertheless the proposal drew applause on both sides of the Atlantic, as it was meant to, for in the words of one official at the time, 'it's not arms control we're engaged in, it's Alliance management'. One of the reasons for its rejection is that it was largely a public gesture.

The proposal began from the premise that Cruise and Pershing II missiles were a response to the existing Soviet SS-20s. The removal of this new Soviet threat (new in quantitative and qualitative terms, according to NATO) would thus remove the necessity for the United States to deploy its new weapons. If there were no land-based Soviet missiles in Europe, no American equivalents would need to be deployed. The term 'Zero Option' was intended to signify the administration's goal of the complete abolition of this class of nuclear weapon in Europe.

The Reagan administration's estimate of the European theatre nuclear balance indicated massive Soviet superiority but excluded two major categories of nuclear weapon: the British and French nuclear forces and the United States forward-based systems on aircraft and at sea. Excluded from the INF talks under the terms of the Zero Option these weapons would have remained in operation after the Soviet Union had dismantled its entire theatre nuclear force. It was no secret that the Soviet leadership would not discount these weapons, and when indeed it rejected the Zero Option as a serious basis for negotiations few observers inside or out of the Reagan administration were surprised. *The Times* on 19 November 1981 reported the privately expressed view of Reagan administration officials 'that the chances of gaining Soviet acceptance were slim'.

In an effort to secure maximum publicity the Reagan administration paid for the National Press Club speech to be broadcast live by satellite to western Europe.

Talbott notes that 'the place and the time had been chosen to assure the maximum audience in western Europe. He began speaking at 10 am. It was late afternoon across the Atlantic; Europeans coming home from work would be switching on their television sets. The US International Communication Agency paid for live satellite transmission to the European Broadcasting Union' (1984: 80).

In so far as the proposal received extensive television news coverage, the administration's media strategy was conspicuously successful in Britain's case.

The headlining item on BBC1's early evening bulletin described the proposal as 'significant for the reduction of nuclear and conventional arms in Europe', and 'what the White House said it was, a message to the world'. It was referred to as 'the President's peace offensive', and 'a demonstration to the European allies that the administration is serious in its search for arms control'. The correspondent reported President Reagan's view of the proposal as 'a big offer, and he expected the Russians to take it seriously'.

The only qualification to this interpretation of the proposal which this item reported was contained in a reference to the Soviet viewpoint. This, however, was 'made sense of' entirely within the terms set by the President. To counter the Soviet view that a rough equivalence already existed in intermediate-range weapons in Europe the President employed a bar chart which excluded from the European nuclear balance all British and French nuclear weapons, and all American forward-based systems. This graphic visual image of overwhelming Soviet superiority (see Figure 6.1) received no contextualization or qualification from the correspondent:

> *Correspondent*: And the President countered the Soviet claim that a rough equivalence in these weapons exists.
>
> *Reagan*: Red is the Soviet build-up, blue is our own, that is 1975, and that is 1981.

Reference was made to the fact that the timing of the Zero Option was related to the rise of the peace movements in Europe,

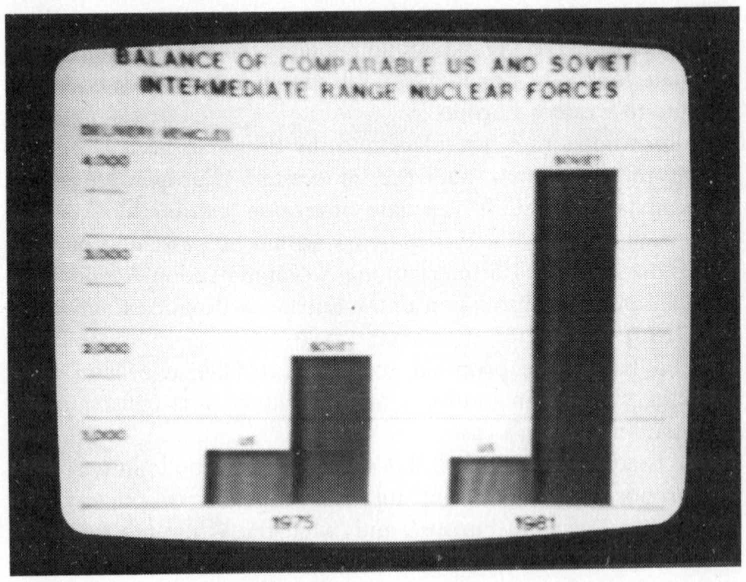

Figure 6.1 'Red is the Soviet build-up, blue is our own. That is 1975, and that is 1981' (1 1740 18/11/81)

and to the bad press created by the Reagan administration's 'conflicting signals' on issues of war and peace. However, acknowledgement of the proposal's public relations function did not lead to a critical interpretation of its value as an *arms control* proposal:

> Now the timing of this is all very important. The administration had become deeply concerned about the peace movements in Europe, and the confusion created by the conflicting signals put out from here on European nuclear policy. The administration now hopes that confusion is at an end and the Europeans have a clearer idea of United States arms control objectives, a policy to coalesce around and present a united and positive front to the Soviet Union.

On the one hand, we are told that the proposal is a 'demonstration of seriousness', while on the other it is said to be a product of the administration's 'deep concern' about its image. These contradictory themes were not resolved.

Likely Soviet reaction to the proposal was contextualized by a reference to 'Kremlin propagandists' and 'the assiduously cultivated Soviet peace-making image'. There were no comparable references to 'White House propagandists' or to the 'assiduously cultivated peace-making image' of the Reagan administration:

> Bearing in mind Mr Brezhnev's talks in West Germany next week, plus the assiduously cultivated Soviet peace-making image, Kremlin propagandists are probably aware they can't afford any peremptory dismissal of the American proposals.

ITN's report on *News at Ten* differed in having to accommodate the fact of a Soviet rejection of the proposal. The newscaster's introduction set out the main content of the proposal, referred to the Soviet interpretation of it as 'a propaganda exercise' and then broadcast the relevant section of the Reagan speech.

As with BBC news, ITN's correspondent acknowledged the public relations function of the proposal, reporting that the Zero Option was intended to counter what were described as the President's 'unfortunate remarks about nuclear war in Europe'.[3] The statement that President Reagan 'wasn't allowed to answer any questions today' acknowledged the presence of criticism about his public stance. It was also noted that:

> One reason for Mr Reagan's statement today was to try and upstage Mr Brezhnev who is visiting West Germany next week,

> and who will present himself as the leader really seeking nuclear disarmament.
>
> The other major reason for the Reagan statement was to try and counter the way the anti-nuclear movement in Europe has portrayed the Americans as the bad guys more so than the Russians.

The correspondent then reported 'speculation' (from unnamed sources) that the effect of the anti-nuclear movement would be to help the Soviets 'spin out' the Geneva talks:

> The peace rallies have delighted Moscow because they are seriously undermining the resolve of the West German government to have the NATO missiles on their soil. And it's speculated the Soviets might try to spin out the Geneva talks in the hope that the NATO plans for new missiles might fall apart under democratic pressure. And then in the end Russia wouldn't have to give up any of her missiles at all.

As in the BBC's account, ITN produced no critical 'reading' of the Zero Option, although ITN's account of the INF debate qualified Mr Reagan's use of the bar chart with an acknowledgement that views on the nuclear balance in Europe 'depend on what type of weapons you include'.

> To the Russians it seems that President Reagan is asking them to remove about 1,000 warheads while NATO keeps its forces as they are. The talks starting in a fortnight in Geneva are about nuclear weapons aimed at targets in Europe, and Mr Reagan used a coloured chart to illustrate his view of the massive Soviet nuclear advantage in Europe, an advantage the Russians deny.
>
> The talks will be extremely complicated. NATO says the Russians have a big nuclear advantage with their SS-20 missiles, but the Russians say there is a rough balance of nuclear forces in Europe. It all depends on what type of weapons you include, and the first big problem in the talks will be to find common ground. The Americans just want to talk about missiles, but the Russians want to include American aircraft which carry nuclear bombs.

While its 'public relations' background was reported, neither the BBC nor ITN items contested the dominant definition of the Zero Option as a serious arms control proposal.

Coverage of the Zero Option was not an isolated example of

television news' approach to US proposals, as coverage of the START talks illustrates.

In the National Press Club speech President Reagan had announced a proposal to open negotiations with the Soviet Union on the reduction of strategic nuclear weapons. Unlike the Strategic Arms Limitation Talks, said the President, the objective of these talks would be not merely to limit nuclear weapons but to reduce them.

On 31 May 1982 the President announced that the negotiations would begin less than one month later, on 29 June. Television news reports noted the political expediency of these talks for the President:

> It was a speech quite clearly adjusted to the politics of his trip to Europe.
>
> (1 2100 31/5/82)

It was widely anticipated that President Reagan's intended 'good-will' trip to Europe in June 1982 would meet with mass opposition from the peace movements. The new proposal was designed at least in part to head off this opposition, as television news reported:

> It was a speech directed at a wider audience, in western Europe particularly and intended to show the President to them as a friend of the Alliance and a spokesman for peace. There are strong fears that what should be an easy popularity-building trip for the President may be soured by the anti-nuclear movement in Europe.
>
> (1 2100 31/5/82)

> trying to defuse some of his critics from the anti-nuclear movement the President said his goal was peace. President Reagan pledged to do his utmost so that no other generation of young men will have to sacrifice their lives.
>
> (3 1300 31/5/82)

As in the INF talks, the proposals brought by each side to the START talks reflected very different views of the nuclear balance. Proceeding from its assumption of 'strategic parity' with the United States, the Soviet Union advocated an immediate freeze on the development and deployment of all strategic nuclear weapons. The United States, concerned with what it argued to be a Soviet strategic superiority in land-based intercontinental missiles (ICBMs) proposed a reduction in sea and land-based missiles to 850 on each side, with a warhead limit of 5,000. Of these only half could be land-based.

US Arms Control and Disarmament Agency Director Eugene Rostow stated before the Senate Foreign Relations Committee on 13 May that this proposal gave 'priority to the acute threat to peace and stability posed by the massive build-up of Soviet ballistic missile forces, particularly ICBM capabilities'.

Like the Zero Option, there were two basic western responses to the US START proposal. The official US view, as expressed by Rostow on 13 May, stated that the proposal was 'sound and equitable', a 'practical, two-stage approach to strategic arms reduction'. Alternatively it was viewed, not as a practical step towards arms reduction, but further confirmation of the Reagan administration's unwillingness to enter into arms control with the Soviet Union. According to this interpretation the proposal would ensure the failure of talks rather than their progress.

The strategic nuclear forces of the United States and the USSR differ qualitatively and in their 'structure' (see Chapter 2). Soviet forces are concentrated on land, with a smaller proportion of sea-based systems and a virtual absence of air-launched weapons. The USA has a predominantly sea-based force with roughly equal proportions of its strength based on land and in the air. The US START proposal excluded the US bomber force, the significance of which can be seen in the fact that by 1984, according to an *Observer* report of 5 January 1985, the US had 3,740 bomber-based strategic nuclear warheads, compared to 372 on the Soviet side. The potential for expansion of this arm of the US 'strategic triad' led the USSR to demand its inclusion in estimates of the nuclear balance.

Of further importance from the Soviet point of view, the US proposal implied a drastic and far-reaching restructuring of the Soviet nuclear force without any corresponding concession from the United States. Had the Soviet Union accepted the demand that only half of its 5,000 permissible warheads could be deployed on land, it would have had to scrap *all* of its 1,398 land-based missiles, with the exception of 250 SS-18s (each of which carries ten warheads). By contrast the US, with relatively few of its warheads on land, would have been able to continue modernizing its land-based ICBMs with the new MX and Minuteman III systems, yet remain within the agreed warhead limit. The North Atlantic Assembly's Special Committee on Nuclear Weapons in Europe concluded that:

> Because of the differing force structures of the two sides, the proposal means greater reductions by the Soviet Union ... the Soviet Union is required to make major concessions both in numbers and in land-based systems. This ... is compounded by the absence of bombers and Cruise missiles from the limitations, both of which represent areas of American advantage.[4]
>
> (Cartwright and Critchley 1983: 31)

Four news items covered the START talks as they commenced on 29 June 1982. Three of these adopted the administration's framework for interpreting the nuclear debate and assessing the value of the START proposal.

For example, journalists presented selective accounts of the nuclear balance which reinforced the logic of the administration's proposal and assumed the basic legitimacy of the administration's arms control objectives.

BBC1's main evening news included an account of 'how the talks came about' (1 2100 29/6/82), which made no reference to the political pressures on the President but simply repeated the official line on Soviet superiority:

> The START talks are designed to replace Jimmy Carter's Strategic Arms Limitation Treaty, SALT II, which was agreed with Leonid Brezhnev three years ago. President Reagan and Congress refused to accept it on the grounds that Mr Carter had permitted the Russians to take advantage of him. Opponents pointed out that ten years ago the United States had slightly more warheads and intercontinental ballistic missiles than the Russians. Today they say the Soviet Union has a superiority of three to one.

One small but relevant detail was omitted from this account of the failure of SALT II. Those who opposed it argued that SALT II codified Soviet superiority in what they claimed were the most dangerous and destabilizing weapons, *land-based* ICBMs. The Reagan administration held to this view in the START talks, defending its focus on land-based ICBMs with the assertion that, as Rostow put it to the Senate Foreign Relations Committee, 'the Soviets have a lead in this *crucial* area of approximately three to one'.

The broadcaster's account also refers to a 'three to one' superiority, but in 'warheads and intercontinental ballistic missiles', a significantly wider category than land-based ICBMs alone.

This is important because it was *only* in the latter, more restricted category that a Soviet superiority existed, offset by US superiority in the other legs of the so-called 'strategic triad'. The United States had more warheads overall, the Soviet Union more launchers; the US had more sea- and air-launched weapons, the USSR superiority on land. The statement of a *general* three to one Soviet superiority was accounted for by reference to the SS-18 missile, claimed by the journalist to carry 'up to thirty' warheads:

> The reason is the continued Russian production of heavy missiles such as the SS-18 which can carry up to thirty independently targetable warheads. By contrast, the American Minuteman has only three warheads.

The statement that SS-18s carry thirty warheads is factually incorrect. They carry ten, as the US Defence Department points out when it states that MIRVed SS-18s carry 'eight or ten re-entry vehicles' (1983: 56).

Furthermore, this account of the nuclear balance excluded all the categories of weapon which favoured the US and did not refer to factors such as the quality and technological sophistication of weapons, areas in which the United States leads the Soviet Union. The item went on to stress the degree of reduction in armaments proposed in the US START negotiating position:

> So President Reagan's speech five weeks ago produced a new way of reducing arms. Instead of counting missiles he wants to count warheads. ... Such a plan would mean reducing the size of the American nuclear arsenal, *in particular its bombers* and Trident submarines. That would mean big savings for the defence budget. It would also mean economic relief for the Soviet Union.

This positive reading of START was qualified with a reference to its 'many problems' of which only one was specifically mentioned: 'The Russians demand that British and French weapons be included in any agreement.' This objection to the proposal was not developed.

The US proposal was also said to involve 'reducing the nuclear arsenal'. However, it was not reported that the Reagan administration's attraction to counting warheads as opposed to delivery vehicles (missiles) stemmed from the increasing adoption of *single-warhead* missiles in the US strategic force. Previously, one could limit missiles but increase firepower by 'MIRVing' (putting more warheads onto each missile). The move towards single-warhead systems such as Minuteman III changed negotiating priorities: one had now to ensure that the number of missiles could be increased while the number of warheads was limited. The number of *new* warheads could still be increased by phasing out obsolete multi-warhead systems. Thus it could have been argued that the intention of the US START proposal was to limit Soviet systems while permitting the US to continue its own strategic programme. This point was crucial to an assessment of START.

The item was also incorrect in stating that 'in particular, bombers' would be reduced under the terms of the US START proposal. Bombers and the Cruise missiles they had the potential to carry were specifically excluded from the negotiations. That the US arsenal would be 'reduced' referred only to outdated nuclear systems. The administration stressed publicly throughout these negotiations that planned modernizations of the US strategic force, such as MX and Minuteman III, would go ahead irrespective of agreements at Geneva.

In both ITN bulletins of 29 June the asymmetrical nature of the two sides' strategic nuclear forces was pointed out. References to Soviet superiority on land were balanced with references to US superiority at sea although there was no reference to the balance in the air, an area of major US advantage:

> There's an imbalance in the type of weapons each side has. The most accurate missiles are land-based. Russia has so many more of these than America, and the US fears her missiles could be destroyed on the ground. America has more of her weapons in submarines and because these ships can hide in the ocean and the missiles cannot easily be destroyed before firing Russia thinks this gives America an edge. Seventy per cent of Russian warheads are land-based though just 20 per cent of American ones are on land. But 50 per cent of American warheads are under the sea and only 20 per cent of Russian ones are in submarines.
>
> (3 1300 29/6/82)

The START talks were said to have arisen because 'the conclusions of the SALT talks are now considered out of date'. The Reagan administration considered SALT to be out of date, but many western governments and defence analysts – and indeed the USSR – did not. In June 1985 pressure from NATO governments compelled the Reagan administration to continue to observe the limitations of SALT II, with the result that a

Poseidon nuclear submarine was scrapped. *News at Ten* reported that:

> The old agreement limiting these weapons was called SALT, standing for Strategic Arms Limitation Talks, *but President Reagan thinks limitation is not enough*, so he coined the word START for the new talks. The letters stand for Strategic Arms Reduction Talks and substantial reductions are what the Americans say they want.
>
> (3 2200 26/6/82)

There was no reference to the view that the US proposed 'substantial reductions' only in the most powerful Soviet weapons, while permitting continued development and production of new US weapons. In the same passage the Soviet START proposal was inferred to be inferior to that of the US, and qualified in the following manner:

> So far Russia has *just called for a freeze* on weapons at existing levels and a freeze on new deployments.

The lunchtime bulletin also referred to the Soviet freeze proposal, and American rejection of it: 'America says the freeze would preserve the Russian advantage, and doesn't want to stop development work on two new missiles.' No comment was made on these justifications.

These examples have been analysed in some detail because they show how the basic assumptions of the Reagan administration in the superpower dialogue inform television news coverage. The simplifications and distortions of complex issues which they display, plus the throwaway attitude to Soviet proposals, are inadequate to a full understanding of the debate.

However, if these examples show a general acceptance by journalists of the Reagan administration's definition of the issues, an important counter-example illustrates the availability at this time of an alternative framework for making sense of START, and the fact that some television journalists are prepared to employ that framework in constructing accounts of the debate. The item, which appeared on *Newsnight*, contextualized US arms control policy in terms of President Reagan's statements on the subject, and related the START talks to political pressures on the administration as opposed to a genuine desire for arms control. By this method, which any television journalist might have adopted, the Reagan administration's arms control policy was interpreted in an entirely different way from that favoured by television news coverage in general.

A brief historical resumé of the background to START (the failure of SALT II to check the arms race and the refusal of the US Congress to ratify the treaty) led the journalist to pose the following question:

> How far is President Reagan consistent in agreeing to these talks, and how far have they been forced on a slightly unwilling President?
>
> (2 *Newsnight* 28/6/82)

This question immediately constructs a framework for understanding US arms control policy which is absent from the other items referred to, and it is answered via Ronald Reagan's own words on arms control, detente, and related matters:

> *Journalist*: According to Mr Reagan the rules of detente have allowed the Soviet Union to achieve clear nuclear superiority, an imbalance he was determined to reverse. Once in power Reagan took the position that America should not pursue arms control talks until the Soviet Union mended its aggressive ways.

Consequently:

> The President's critics here in Washington simply don't believe in his conversion to the cause of arms control. They say he was acting under pressure, both domestic and foreign. They think that if he'd resisted talking to the Russians about arms control much longer the Atlantic alliance would have come apart, as his former Secretary of State Alexander Haig apparently kept reminding him. But it's one thing to be willing to sit down with the Russians and quite another to make the concessions necessary if there's ever to be an arms control agreement, and on that the European governments who don't have a place at the table may have to keep up the pressure.

This item presented a major extension to the range of views reported in the majority of coverage: a critical reading of START which, in marked contrast to other coverage, became the preferred reading. US arms control policy was contextualized in terms of what was *known* in June 1982 about the administration's attitudes.

During the election campaign of 1983 Channel 4 news presented an item in which a critical reading of the administration's arms control objectives was constructed. This counter-example used the imminent reopening of the Geneva INF talks as an angle around which to present a report on the activities of the American Arms Control Agency (AACA). The fortunes of the AACA under the Reagan administration were the starting point for a critical analysis of the seriousness of the latter's arms control objectives. Having explained that the AACA was an independent, advisory body within the US government, set up in 1961 to assist in drafting the US–Soviet Test Ban Treaty, the correspondent turned to a recent controversy within the agency provoked by the appointment of Kenneth Adelman as Director:

> He was viewed by some as a lightweight. The choice of Mr Adelman was seen as evidence that Mr Reagan had little interest in the Arms Control Agency. Questioned at his Senate confirmation hearings Mr Adelman seemed lacking in some of the necessary background information for the job.
>
> (4 1900 13/5/83)

Opinions on the significance of Adelman's appointment were sought from AACA officials (who assured the journalist that he was 'a man of wide experience and great interest in the field'), Eugene Rostow the previous Director, and Paul Warnke, a former US arms control negotiator. Warnke claimed that 'for the President to appoint Mr Adelman confirmed the view of many Americans that he was not serious about arms control'. The item concluded by reporting that:

> at one point it seemed as if President Reagan would disband the entire Arms Control Agency, but that won't happen now. Firstly, because the American Congress won't allow it, and secondly because President Reagan wants to project the image of being very much in favour of verifiable arms control.

In reporting the view that the Reagan administration's interest in arms reduction was *image* rather than substance, this item, like the *Newsnight* example of a year earlier quoted above, was exceptional, and again illustrative of the increased 'openness' of minority-audience news programmes to a wider range of views and assessments of the nuclear issues.

Nuclear freeze and no first use – the Soviet case

US proposals are one side of the superpower dialogue. Soviet proposals are the other. From what has previously been said about television news coverage of the USSR, one can hypothesize that the Soviet case in the dialogue is likely to be subordinate in television news accounts, and this is indeed what coverage of the nuclear freeze and no-first-use proposals suggests.

The first difference between coverage of US arms control proposals and those of the Soviet Union is *quantitative*. In contrast to the routinely headline-grabbing power of US proposals the Soviet case in the disarmament dialogue has a relatively low priority on the television news agenda and tends to be reported in brief items lacking in background or analysis. This can be explained in part by the differing approaches to public relations and propaganda taken by the two sides. Prior to the emergence of Gorbachov Soviet disarmament proposals were poorly presented in comparison with the techniques routinely employed by the Reagan administration. The bumbling, hesitant speeches of such leaders as Brezhnev, Andropov, and Chernenko, given in Russian, were not as attractive to the western media as President Reagan's photogenic displays at the National Press Club. This may account in part for the relative lack of coverage given to Soviet proposals during this period.

But Soviet proposals are also reported within a *qualitatively* different set of *a priori* assumptions. The privileged access of US leaders in presenting their own proposals has its converse in their privileged access to dismiss Soviet ones. The Soviet case is not 'excluded', but the USSR does not take part in the superpower propaganda war as the equal partner in an impartial debate.

On television news during the sample period Soviet proposals tended to be 'made sense' of by reference to the views of western leaders and in the absence of Soviet commentators. In one of the examples quoted above a journalist was heard to describe the Soviet position on strategic weapons as 'just calling for a freeze'. The initial statement of the Soviet nuclear freeze initiative was contained in a speech made by Leonid Brezhnev in Moscow on 18 May 1982. Brezhnev called for a moratorium on the development, production, and deployment of all strategic nuclear weapons while the START talks were taking place. Seven television news bulletins reported the Brezhnev freeze proposal. In five of these the US government was reported as rejecting the proposal on the grounds that the Soviets had a strategic nuclear superiority. The following examples illustrate the contrast between typical coverage of a Soviet arms control proposal and that of US proposals examined in the previous section. Items began with an account of the Soviet proposal:

> In the latest move in the disarmament dialogue between the Soviet Union and America President Brezhnev has said the two countries should stop deploying strategic nuclear weapons.
>
> (1 2100 18/5/82)

Followed by an account of the US rejection:

> President Reagan rejected the idea but said he's ready to discuss reducing nuclear arms. The American Secretary of State Alexander Haig said the proposal would leave his country at a nuclear disadvantage but the Soviet willingness to negotiate was positive.
>
> According to ITN:
>
> President Brezhnev has said he'll put an immediate freeze on nuclear weapons if the United States does the same. ... The US President said tonight the speech indicated Mr Brezhnev was willing to hold talks on a new treaty to reduce nuclear weapons, but he couldn't give a date, though his Secretary of State Mr Haig reacted more coolly. He said an arms freeze would leave America at a nuclear disadvantage.
>
> (3 2200 18/5/82)

Coverage generally took this form: a brief account of the proposal followed with reports of its rejection by the United States government. The Reagan administration, while cautiously 'welcoming' the freeze, rejected it on the grounds that it would perpetuate Soviet nuclear superiority. This logic was consistent with the administration's own position on arms control but contradicted assessments of the strategic balance made by independent sources. And although this was the only reported opinion, no bulletin developed its validity or examined the possible significance of a nuclear freeze.

We noted earlier references to a possible 'peremptory dismissal' of the US Zero Option by Soviet 'propagandists'. No comparable interpretation was made by journalists of the US response to the freeze proposal. On the contrary, bulletins emphasized the 'welcome' extended by the President to the idea. ITN even implied that

President Reagan had been enthusiastic by contrasting his response with that of Alexander Haig who had 'reacted more coolly'.

A little less than one month later, at the United Nations Second Special Session on Disarmament the USSR announced its adoption of a 'no-first-use' policy – a commitment never to use nuclear weapons first. Support for the policy of no-first-use came not only from the Soviet Union. There was a substantial body of opinion in favour of NATO adopting a similar stance, including present and former NATO leaders. From their point of view the policy was perceived as important for NATO's survival, as argued by former US Defence Secretary Robert McNamara in the *Foreign Affairs* article cited on p. 13:

> The basic argument for a no-first-use policy can be stated in strictly military terms: that any other course involves unacceptable risks to the national life that military forces exist to defend.

Television news reported the announcement, made on behalf of Leonid Brezhnev by Soviet Foreign Minister Andrei Gromyko, in three news bulletins on 15 June. Coverage was sparse, even compared to that given the freeze proposal. Just how brief can be seen by a word count. *News at Ten* on ITN devoted forty-two words to the story. Earlier in the month the same programme had used seventy-three words to cover a story about the wife of exiled Soviet chess player Victor Korchnoi. BBC1 reported the declaration in fifty-eight words. It is not suggested that major significance can be drawn from the number of words devoted to a story, but these figures do reveal how little news value was accredited the 'no-first-use' declaration by BBC and ITV:

> The Soviet Union today pledged that it would not be the first to use nuclear weapons. The promise came from the Soviet leader President Brezhnev in a message to a special UN session on disarmament. Mr Brezhnev said that the Soviet Union wanted to do all in its power to deliver people from the threat of nuclear devastation.
>
> (1 2100 15/6/82)

> President Brezhnev has said that the Soviet Union will not be the first to use nuclear weapons. The promise was read out for him at the Special Session of the United Nations on Disarmament by the Soviet Foreign Minister, Mr Andrei Gromyko.
>
> (3 2200 15/6/82)

News at Ten's report was immediately followed by a report on the Soviet military intervention in Afghanistan. A Soviet arms control proposal was juxtaposed with a story about Soviet military aggression:

> From Afghanistan *though* there are reports of a big Soviet victory against guerrilla forces in the Panshar Valley sixty miles north-east of the capital Kabul. The Panshar has long been the centre of resistance to Soviet occupation.

The brevity of these items clearly contrasts with coverage of US arms control proposals.

It could be argued that one explanation for the relative lack of newsworthiness accorded Soviet proposals is the context in which they are made. Soviet proposals start off with a disadvantage (as Soviet statements did in the Korean Airlines disaster) because speeches delivered in Russian at party congresses and other official occasions are less attractive media events than President Reagan's statements, broadcast to Europe live by satellite with the White House paying the bills. Nevertheless, Moscow is a great deal closer to Britain than Washington, and coverage of Soviet statements is not impeded by special technical problems. Another possible explanation is the journalists' apparent assumption that Soviet proposals are predictable propaganda exercises from 'peace-loving propagandists' in the Kremlin.

We refer to one final example. In September 1983 the USSR announced that it would dismantle all of its SS-20s removed from the European theatre, rather than simply move them elsewhere in the Soviet Union. This offer was made in response to demands by President Reagan, after the Soviet Union had agreed to reduce its SS-20s to the level of British and French independent forces in Europe. One news bulletin reported the offer in the following terms:

> He [Andropov] claimed that Russian disarmament proposals were not merely good intentions. Well, our defence correspondent says it's merely another attempt to drive a wedge between America and Europe over Cruise and Pershing.
>
> (3 1740 20/9/83)

Talking about the press, Keeble has argued that 'one subtle way in which Fleet Street discredits the Soviet Union is by describing its peace proposals as "propaganda" while the west's initiatives are presented as genuine' (Curran *et al.* 1986: 53). We would suggest that this feature can also be observed in British television news.

We have examined here television news coverage of some of the most important initiatives made by both sides in the early 1980s. The debate continues, and it is not argued that the dominant tendency to 'prefer' US accounts of the issues is a fixed one unamenable to change. The counter-examples discussed in this chapter show that the Reagan administration's arms control policies can be and are criticized in some news accounts. But there can be little doubt that television news' accounts of the superpower dialogue have tended to reflect *a priori* assumptions about the credibility of the two sides, rather than 'impartial' assessments of the relative worth of their respective proposals.

7

Gorbachov, *glasnost*, and Chernobyl

Previous chapters have suggested that the largely negative images of the Soviet Union which appear on television news are accountable in part by the Soviets' historic inability to compete with the west in news management and public relations techniques. However, with the departure of the 'old guard' in the Soviet leadership – Brezhnev, Andropov, and Chernenko – the USSR began to develop a new approach to propaganda and information policy, and to use the western media more effectively for the propagation of Soviet viewpoints. These changes had significant effects on images of the Soviet Union in the west. This chapter examines those changes, and how they have affected coverage of the Soviet Union on British television.

Glasnost – 'Speaking out loud as a policy'

Journalists who specialize in reporting the Soviet Union differ in their opinions as to when Soviet information policy began to change from that of, as Patrick Cockburn puts it, 'say nothing, but if you must say something say as little as possible'. This approach to information, we have argued in previous chapters, was in part responsible for the Soviet failure to compete successfully in propaganda warfare with the west, and for many of the negative images of 'the enemy' discussed throughout this book. According to Martin Walker of the *Guardian*, the change 'began with the 1980 Olympic Games, when [the Soviets] built themselves the press centre and for the first time played host to several hundred western journalists'.

John Tusa of the BBC suggests: 'They tried out the new information policy at Helsinki [the 1985 European Conference on Human Rights], and at the Geneva summit, and discovered that they could compete with the Americans.'

Most correspondents, however, date the change from the crisis surrounding the Korean airliner incident of 1983, discussed in

Chapter 5 and particularly the news conference held in Moscow on 9 September when Marshall Nikolai Ogarkov outlined the Soviet version of what had happened to KAL 007. This event saw the Soviets for the first time 'confront things head on'.

The new information policy first took shape after the death of Brezhnev, under the leadership group headed by Yuri Andropov and later by Mikhail Gorbachov. This group overturned the Brezhnevian information regime and began to play the news management game according to the rules of the western media.

The new policy was part of a much deeper process of change taking place within the USSR: a process which the Soviets call *perestroika* (reconstruction). *Perestroika* aims to equip and refit the Soviet economy to make it competitive in the race with the west. New technology, new management techniques, and a restructuring of industry are all seen as essential if the USSR is to keep up with and eventually overtake the advanced capitalist countries in productivity and technological sophistication. But successful reconstruction, believe Soviet planners, requires a struggle with the 'inertia' which permeates Soviet society. It is here that the policy of *glasnost* comes in.

Soviet journalist Vladimir Posner explains: '"*Glasnost*" is translated into English as "openness", but that's not quite correct. In old Russian, "*glas*" means voice; and the suffix "*nost*" is like the English "ness". So the word "*glasnost*" means "voiceness". It means speaking out loud as a policy.'[1]

Glasnost is the ideological powerhouse of the drive for reform. The party's plans for the period up to the year 2000 call for a 50 per cent increase in GNP. So radical an improvement of the Soviet economy cannot be achieved without, as Soviet theorists put it, 'transforming the psychology of the masses'. *Glasnost* is intended to assist in this by opening Soviet society up to public scrutiny and peeling away the layers of bureaucracy and secrecy which have dogged it since Stalin's time. *Glasnost*, as a *Pravda* editorial put it on 18 April 1986, 'will allow each of us in turn to feel in practice like true masters of our country. Without *glasnost* there is no possibility of democracy, of political creativity among the masses, or of their participation in management. *Glasnost* is the starting point for reconstruction (*perestroika*).'

Although it had begun with Andropov the new policy was most closely identified with the photogenic figure of Mikhail Gorbachov. As John Tusa sees it: 'Gorbachov is a man they can project.' As the youngest Soviet leader since Stalin, Gorbachov presented a formidable public relations challenge to the US administration. Patrick Cockburn argues that the impact of Gorbachov's personality was crucial:

> For years they had extremely old leaders, who had difficulty in attending Politburo meetings, so there was no particular incentive to show them off to the world's press. Up until the last months of Chernenko they spent most of their time batting away questions about the leader's health, that sort of thing. They had every reason to conceal what was happening to the leader. Now the reverse is true. With Gorbachov they have something to show, and they want to get maximum publicity. What's made the real difference in terms of propaganda is Gorbachov on television. The Soviet leader appears to be human, prepared to discuss problems, prepared to handle questions, and not somebody who looks and behaves like a member of the Mafia.

Martin Walker also emphasizes the importance of the 'Gorbachov factor' in giving *glasnost* substance:

> The very fact that they've got a man who can stand and walk unaided is a change. Soviet officials are very frank about the sense of shame they felt at the succession of elderly invalids in the Kremlin, who couldn't read a speech without losing their way, couldn't stand up without being helped. They think that now they've got a reasonably attractive, energetic young leader. There's never been a Soviet leader quite like him in his sense of relaxation and readiness. He comes across as a nice guy.

Gorbachov's 'nice guy' image was reflected in the western media, including British television news. Following the death of Chernenko and Gorbachov's election to the General Secretaryship television news, as described in Chapter 3, reminded viewers of Mrs Thatcher's reference to him as 'a man we can do business with'. He was recognized from the outset to be different from 'the old, grey, predictable style of Kremlin leadership':

> Just before Christmas when he paid a visit to Britain he established himself as a man who was human, when we rather expected Soviet leaders to be tough and brutal, and capable of cracking jokes when we expected them to be humourless. ... He helped to change our prejudices.
>
> (1 2100 11/3/85)

Brezhnev had been called a 'dictator' and 'the ruler of an empire'. Gorbachov, by contrast, was said to have 'a lively, flexible manner, firm but not at all unreasonable'. Andropov had been referred to as the 'KGB hardman'. Gorbachov, his protégé and far from being a wet liberal, was seen as 'a young man with new ideas'. The richly furred figure of Gorbachov's wife Raisa became a familiar sight to viewers of British television news.

The new leadership not only looked better than the old one. Gorbachov and his supporters came to power, as Cockburn views it, 'conscious that Reagan was scoring points against them, even when he had a very poor case. They were very conscious of Reagan's ability to communicate.' The new Soviet leaders were conscious, too, of the importance of western media images of the USSR on western public opinion. Cockburn continues:

> People like Arbatov[2] regard the general popular attitude to the Soviet Union in the west to be just as significant as the diplomatic attitude. From the Soviet point of view, a decreasing desire on the part of American voters, Congress and senators to vote for large defence budgets is just as significant as the Soviet Union trying to negotiate an arms deal with the US. They saw that they needed to have a platform so that even if the various initiatives produced by Gorbachov on arms control have not produced any diplomatic dividends they feel that they've achieved something if they look good and people in the west feel they're trying; if people don't feel that the Soviets are going to murder them in their beds.

This increased awareness of the importance of public relations was largely the product of campaigning behind the scenes by academics and politicians who had studied the western media, had perhaps spent time in western countries, and who understood something of western-style news management. Alexei Pankin, a Soviet specialist in western media at the Institute for USA–Canada Studies in Moscow, typifies this thinking when he says that 'we'd been trying for some time to persuade the Foreign Ministry and other bodies that it is important for them to work with the media, to inform them, to fill the information-void. We argued that if we don't do it ourselves, somebody else will.' In the leadership group which emerged after Brezhnev's death, such views found a sympathetic ear. Pankin continues: 'In the post-Revolutionary period, the cold war and after, there was very great suspicion of the western media. A great number of Soviets wrote them off, not without reason. But now we realize that without information the western media try to guess things. Now we realize the importance of giving information, and we discuss things in public that were never discussed before.'

In Peter Ruff's view: 'Andropov decided that the west could improve its image by using publicity, and Gorbachov is taking that one step further. Gorbachov saw that the only way to tackle the western propaganda machine, as he would call it, was head on. You decide what your policy is, you announce it officially, you brief on it officially.'

Izvestia commentator Stanislav Kondrashov remarks that 'it's a permanent change. It's the result of a conscious decision to give more information, both to our own people and to the west. The slogan of *glasnost* is being put into practice.'

Glasnost gave the green light to the idea of dealing with the capitalist media on its own terms: feeding information rather than denying it, satisfying the journalists' need for 'scoops',[3] and presenting the party's positions on international issues in a manner attractive to the western audience. As a consequence, major changes took place in the organization of Soviet news management. Martin Walker describes how the Soviets 'learnt the ropes of the modern media age':

> In late 1984 they appointed Vladimir Lomeiko as head of the press department of the Foreign Ministry. He'd worked as a journalist in Bonn. He'd been in charge of the Novosti[4] operation there, so he knew what press conferences and press briefings were, and he made a serious point of organizing a weekly press briefing. It began in a small room with maybe eight, ten, or a dozen journalists and it's now a full-scale briefing. What's more, he's on the record, which is often not the case with briefings in London.
>
> You can ask him anything, on any topic on foreign affairs, and he'll give you a reply. It's probably not a good reply, but it's a reply, and now they've worked out that their main audience is the American prime-time news programmes. They time their briefings for them, they lay on translations, and they do it in a very professional way.
>
> We saw it at the Geneva summit. The press operation there was unprecedented for the Russians. They got there a week before the Americans did, and were holding daily press conferences, daily

briefings. If you wanted to talk to a Soviet expert on Star Wars, no problem. If you wanted to speak with a Soviet military man, step forward General Chernov. They just laid it all on. There were an awful lot of journalists who got there before the summit, and before the White House press corps came in and the big American publicity machine got rolling, so the Russians were all over them. And then at the end of the summit Gorbachov gave us his own two-hour news conference, a televised spectacular, so the version of the summit that went out immediately afterwards was very much the Gorbachov one.

The mechanics of things like press conferences are transformed out of all recognition. At the 27th party congress for the first time we were having daily briefings on what was happening, daily analysis of what was going on, regular chances to interview people who are normally like gold dust to see. I was called up at home by a First Secretary of one of the big regions whom I'd met, and he said 'hello, I'm in Moscow, come and have some coffee'. I found myself having a two-hour private conversation with a member of the Central Committee, speaking openly about anything I wanted to talk about. You don't get that kind of access in Britain all the time.

A similar approach was evident at the Reykjavik summit in October 1986. Again, daily briefings were provided by prominent experts such as Arbatov and Velikov, and at the end of the summit Gorbachov addressed journalists for over an hour.

The new approach has begun to pay dividends for the Soviets in propaganda terms. One journalist at the UPI bureau in Moscow sees 'a complete turning of the tables. Nowadays we get the official Kremlin line given to us at briefings, which means that we no longer have to interpret the line on the basis of whatever information we have. And there's an unprecedentedly open discussion of issues and problems in the press. All of which makes it easier to do good reports. In fact, these days we get more information about the Soviet point of view than we do of the Americans'.'

Peter Ruff believes that, as a result of these changes, 'people in the west are now more aware of what Soviet policy is, particularly on arms control, than they have ever been before'. Ruff also notes the concern of some western officials that this should be the case. Talking about the reaction of US Embassy officials in Moscow, he continues:

the new policy has infuriated the Americans because Soviet spokesmen are constantly on the record. They can be quoted. The Americans, meanwhile, and to some extent the British, cling on to the old idea of background briefings. When you put sets of information up against each other a set of information that has a name to it is always better than this weird formula of 'I understand', or 'sources tell me', or 'a senior diplomat said'. So the Americans have taken to attacking western correspondents, including their own, for reporting the Soviet spokesmen, and that is a serious problem behind the scenes.

Glasnost has also affected the newsgathering operation of correspondents based in Moscow. Chapter 4 showed that some of the inadequacies in western coverage of the Soviet Union were due to constraints placed upon routine newsgathering work by the Soviet authorities. *Glasnost* has reduced these constraints. Western journalists in Moscow now enjoy greater freedom and flexibility to make news and current affairs programmes about the USSR. As a result, both the quantity and quality of western coverage of the USSR has changed for the better.

In 1986 the BBC broadcast *Comrades*, a series of documentaries about life and work in the Soviet Union. In the summer of that year Richard Denton, the producer of *Comrades*, returned to the USSR to make *Caviar and Cornflakes*, a film about British citizens working in Moscow. Mrs Thatcher's visit to the Soviet Union in March 1987 was accompanied by a flurry of television programmes about the country, many of which involved an unprecedented degree of co-operation between British journalists, their counterparts in the USSR, and the Soviet authorities. An edition of BBC2's *Thinking Aloud* came direct from the Telecentre in Moscow and was entirely devoted to a debate in English, chaired by Michael Ignatieff, between Soviet experts about the reforms taking place in the USSR. On 26 March 1987, ITV's *This Week* reported from Moscow, and on 25 March Channel 4's *Diverse Reports* presented a film by Soviet journalist Vladimir Posner. On Monday, 6 April 1987 BBC's *Panorama* broadcast a Soviet-produced documentary about Chernobyl.

As western journalists find the USSR a better place in which to work, the number of resident correspondents based in Moscow has increased. Before *glasnost* there were approximately 300 foreign correspondents working in Moscow, of whom about half were from the fraternal socialist countries. Of the other half, a substantial proportion were not journalists at all, but technicians and support staff. As of May 1986 there were only about forty western journalists working in Moscow, as compared with the 4,000 accredited correspondents based in Washington.

But as *glasnost* has taken hold, news organizations with no permanent representation in Moscow, such as ITN, are sending out correspondents. In Patrick Cockburn's view, the reason for this is simple:

> The USSR is now much more saleable for press and television, so there are more correspondents around, British and others. The more interesting it is here, and the better you can operate as a journalist, the better the journalists you get. In 1984 I was told by one member of a news agency here that when they applied for this job there was nobody else within their organization – which is very big – who was applying for it. But now they know eight people who can speak Russian within their organization who've already applied for the next opening. The knowledge that you can do things means you can attract more and better people.

Nik Gowing of ITN suggests: 'There is so much going on in the Soviet Union at the moment, and thus so much more to report.'

To the extent that we rely on the media for information about the Soviet Union 'more and better people' in the USSR can only be good news. The increased openness of Soviet society has generated western interest in the USSR and also given western news organizations the space to satisfy that interest more fully. The cold war stereotypes of the first half of the 1980s will be increasingly difficult to sustain.

But there are clearly limits to this process. The experience of one group of Soviets invited to contribute to a British current affairs programme suggests that *glasnost* and a willingness to speak to the western media is no guarantee in itself that the Soviet view will be presented 'impartially' on British television.

On the eve of the 1985 Geneva summit BBC's *Panorama* programme invited some Soviet experts to discuss the issues. Among them was Alexei Pankin:

> We think they did a very good job. It's just their mindset. Through their editing of our contributions they made us conform to their mindset. Our own impression is that the message we tried

to give in numerous interviews was somewhat different from the message we gave on the air.

First of all we had each to give a short presentation, speaking for about ten minutes on the subject of the United States, speaking about our views on its values, its achievements, how we feel, and I would say we were very positive. But certainly, each of us also said something to balance that, some negative comments. They cut the positive comments in general, and put as background over our negative comments Soviet military parades in Red Square, Soviet troops entering Afghanistan, so that it formed a rather sinister impression – over pictures of Soviet troops entering Afghanistan we were heard speaking of America as a country of joblessness, of poverty, lack of spiritual values, and so on.

In April 1986, even as this interview was being given to the author in Moscow, an event was taking place which threatened to throw the process described in this section into reverse, confirming once again the intrinsic relationship between western media images of the USSR and Soviet information policy. That event, and news coverage of it in east and west, is the subject of the next section.

Heroes and villains: reporting Chernobyl

At 1.23 am on Saturday 26 April 1986, a Soviet nuclear reactor overheated and exploded, opening what the Soviets refer to as 'the Chernobyl era'. The catastrophic consequences of the accident for the Soviet economy and environment, and its effects on the other European countries over which the radioactive cloud passed, are well known.[5] Here, we are concerned with news coverage of the crisis, both in the Soviet Union where it presented the first real challenge to Gorbachov's *glasnost* policy, and in Britain, where it seemed to confirm that deep-rooted structural and ideological biases continue to shape coverage of the USSR.

The Soviet response to Chernobyl was in stark contrast to the new information policy outlined in the previous section, although by April 1986 the radical transformation of Soviet society initiated by Gorbachov and his supporters was well under way. The policy of *glasnost* was being implemented.

In domestic terms the *glasnost* campaign was largely a call for frankness and sincerity in the news media, and for more and better information on all aspects of party policy. It was accompanied by officially sponsored criticisms of the Soviet media, such as the following remarks made by Gorbachov during his political report to the 27th congress, where he began with some faint praise (a common method by which Soviet politicians prepare their audience for harsh words to come):

> Our television and radio networks are developing rapidly. Changes for the better have appeared: television and radio programmes have become more diversified and interesting, and there is a visible aspiration to surmount established stereotypes, to take various interests of the audience into account more fully.[6]

Then he put the full force of his weighty boot in:

> But can it be said that our mass media and propaganda are using all their opportunities? For the time being, no. There is still much dullness, inertia has not been overcome, and deafness to the new has not been cured. People are dissatisfied with the inadequate promptness in the reporting of news, with the superficial coverage of the effort to introduce all that is new and advanced into practice.

In the USSR, popular dissatisfaction is most frequently expressed through the medium of readers' letters to newspapers. Before Chernobyl gave the issue unprecedented urgency, many readers' letters contained criticism of the self-congratulatory, clichéd content of Soviet news, and such features as the absence of disaster stories and other 'bad news' items. The latter point was eloquently made in the following letter, published in *Literaturnaya Gazeta* of January 1986: 'This silence strikes me as reflecting an entirely unjustified distrust of readers and viewers. . . . It is necessary to have the courage to inform people about unexpected or negative events . . . the ideological losses resulting from incomplete or delayed information are simply too great.'[7]

After Chernobyl, on 17 May 1986, a *Pravda* commentator invoked readers' letters to criticize *Vremya*, the main television news programme in the USSR: 'Readers of *Pravda* write that they still find in *Vremya* shallow subject-matter, excessive praise [of Soviet life], and repetitive reports and interviews . . . all this is reminiscent of the old approach to information. It will not permit a reconstruction of social consciousness in the spirit of the new demands made by life.'

In response to such criticisms, and in accordance with the party line on *glasnost* the Soviet news media were by April 1986 becoming increasingly 'open' and self-critical in their coverage of events at home and abroad. Soviet journalists had begun to report domestic disasters and other 'bad news' stories. Yet Chernobyl itself seemed to produce a return to the 'bureaucratism and inertia' so vigorously condemned at the 27th congress.

The explosion at Chernobyl occurred in the early morning of 26 April, but it was nearly seventy-two hours before the first reference to the disaster appeared in the Soviet media. That reference, when it came in the afternoon edition of *Izvestia* on 29 April, was brief in the extreme, recalling the Soviet government's initial reaction to the Korean Airlines tragedy:

> An accident has taken place at the Chernobyl power station, and one of the reactors was damaged. Measures are being taken to eliminate the consequences of the accident. Those affected by it are being given assistance. A government commission has been set up.

This government statement was the first in a series of announcements which for the first ten days of the crisis constituted the only source of authorized information available to the Soviet people. Details of what had happened were sparse, and in tone the statements were reassuring to the point of complacency. Radiation levels, it was frequently pointed out, were 'stabilizing' or 'decreasing'; only two had died, while those who had been injured were receiving essential medical help; populations at risk were being evacuated; work to 'liquidate the effects of the accident' (as if radioactive contamination could so easily be dealt with) was said to be going on. Eschewing *glasnost* – the policy of 'speaking out loud' – the Soviet media fell back on a variety of techniques aimed at discrediting western accounts of the disaster, which were entering the country through the BBC World Service, Voice of America, and other foreign sources. The need to reply to these accounts, and the images of megadeath and huge destruction which they contained, appeared to be the only concern of Soviet media coverage as the crisis deepened.

Patrick Cockburn notes:

> the initial phase was very much a caricature of Soviet policy as it was under Brezhnev. The first news, on Monday evening after an

emergency Politburo meeting, was a three-line statement. This was combined with very much penny-in-the-slot propaganda mentioning all the nuclear accidents that had occurred in other countries, generally downplaying Chernobyl, and blaming a lot of it on the foreign press. The general impression was given to *Vremya* viewers that it was all got up by foreigners.

The Soviet media were filled with images of the Ukrainian population centres at work and play. Coverage of the May Day celebrations was dominated by reports from Kiev, Minsk, and Gomel – the three cities most immediately at risk from radioactive fallout. None of these items referred to Chernobyl directly, but they indirectly addressed rumours of major catastrophe and large-scale loss of life by showing the inhabitants enjoying the holiday and participating fully in the May Day demonstration. From Kiev on 2 May, *Pravda* reported that 'the joyful sounds of orchestras greeted the hero city of the Dnieper on May Day'.

Some western commentators blamed the Chernobyl incident on the alleged backwardness of Soviet nuclear technology. In response to this, Soviet news media began to give unusual prominence to coverage of nuclear accidents in the west, especially in the USA. On 5 May *Pravda* reported that 'about 20,000 different kinds of accidents and defects have occurred at US atomic power stations since 1979'. The source for this figure was 'the American organization Public Citizen. The facts testify that the number of such incidents in America grows from year to year. Thus, in 1979 at 68 stations in the USA, 2,310 incidents occurred … a serious incident occurs at an American nuclear power station nearly every day. This report is published at a time when they are undertaking an unbridled anti-Soviet campaign around the Chernobyl incident, based on the thesis that such things can't happen here. The facts produced in this document speak to the contrary.'

The Soviet media enlisted the views of foreigners in the USSR who disagreed with the western authorities about the seriousness of the Chernobyl incident, and shared the Soviet view that western accounts were 'provocative'. An item broadcast by *Vremya* on 2 May contained an interview with two British tourists in Red Square, Moscow. Both were travelling with Thomson Holidays, and had been informed by their tour guide that the holiday would be cut short because of the accident at Chernobyl. From this, the following report was constructed:

Newscaster: Western mass media are broadcasting slanderous lies about the Chernobyl atomic power station. Some countries are insulting the Soviet Union and its citizens.
Correspondent: We met with British tourists from the Intourist Hotel during the May Day festival. Railway dispatcher from Glasgow Jim Tweedie and Devon businessman John Smith were completing their holiday in our country, organized by the tourist company Thomson Holidays. They are talking about how their group of seventy people visited Leningrad, then Novosibirsk and Irkutsk, and a few days at Lake Baikal.
John Smith: We've had a very good, pleasant holiday which none of us will forget. Everything was wonderful until we arrived in Moscow yesterday.
Correspondent: Let me ask you, what was the reason for your unexpected return?
John Smith: Very unexpectedly the official representative of Thomson Holidays told us that a nuclear explosion had allegedly taken place in the Soviet Union. She told us that Kiev is being evacuated, that many people were killed and thousands injured. 'Your lives are at risk', she told us, 'we must quickly leave Moscow.'
Correspondent: It's not true. In Kiev the situation is normal. The people there are celebrating May Day the same as here in Moscow.
John Smith: I don't know exactly, but we were told that a special aircraft was coming from Britain to evacuate British citizens from Moscow and Leningrad.
Correspondent: What's your opinion about this?
Jim Tweedie: I am very perturbed, we are all perturbed to have to leave Moscow. Thousands of Muscovites are walking the streets for May Day. We can see that there's no real danger such as we're being led to believe.
John Smith: I've asked the Thomson's representative about this, but they just can't explain. It seems that they're the only ones who are anxious about leaving.
Correspondent: I think it's a campaign of provocation.
John Smith: I'm convinced of it.

Next, the correspondent travelled out to Sheretmetyevo, Moscow's main international airport, where he was able to interview a group of foreign students, postgraduates, and teachers being hurriedly evacuated from the USSR on the advice of their respective governments. The evacuees had been in the cities of Kiev and Minsk when Chernobyl exploded, and were now about to leave on a British Airways 737 specially flown in for the purpose. For the interview, the correspondent succeeded in persuading some of the evacuees to come out of the aircraft and answer his questions. Those who did so, and whose comments were included in the item, were unanimous in complaining about the pressure being applied on them to leave, arguing that it was unnecessary and 'an example of western propaganda':

> *Correspondent*: Many of the students and postgraduates who have been sent urgently to Sheretmetyevo understand that the order to leave is in no way dictated by considerations of health. They well understand that they are being made use of. Here, for example [over film] they stand in the English aircraft rather obviously changing their radioactive clothing. We weren't allowed to film inside the aircraft, and I didn't compel them to give an interview for Soviet television, but of course they came out. What happened?
> *1st British student*: They [the flight crew] persistently demanded that we take off our clothes and they gave us this costume. Thus, I am being used to create the kind of sensation they are writing about in London.
> *2nd British student*: I was studying Slavonic languages in Minsk.
> *Correspondent*: Why are you leaving?
> *2nd British student*: Our Embassy insisted categorically that we leave.
> *French student*: I was studying in Kiev. I think that the western press is using the accident for propaganda purposes. It very quickly became political propaganda. We are sad, and very embarrassed before our Soviet friends. I like your country, I have been here five times already, and I don't want this incident to be used to spoil relations between east and west.
> *Canadian Student*: I too was studying in Kiev. I was strongly opposed to this departure. I would like to be in Kiev now. Our Soviet friends wouldn't allow any danger to our health. If there had been a danger to health people would have been evacuated from Kiev. The children would have left Kiev. It's an example of western propaganda. They reported that 2,000 were dead, and it's only two. That's how it was, in actual fact.

A third report was filmed at the university in Kiev itself, featuring interviews with a group of students from Mali. Their spokesman assured viewers that 'we live in Kiev and we feel nothing. People here are living normally, and there are no problems. Everything [the western press] are saying is lies, in my opinion.'

The views of Soviet citizens themselves were widely reported. In the following item, broadcast by *Vremya* on 3 May, Muscovites were asked what they thought of the western propaganda campaign:

> *Muscovite*: Of course, it's a completely astonishing reaction. Recently there was the Challenger incident, the horror of which was felt by our people. Yet the reaction of the USA and its western allies is surely natural when their policy towards us is based on the premise of 'the worse for us, the better for them'.

Articles in the western press which agreed with the official Soviet position on the incident were frequently reported, as in the following TASS report of 3 May published in *Pravda*:

> The French newspaper *L'Humanité* has been sharply critical of the anti-Soviet campaign taken up by the French mass media in connection with the Chernobyl accident.

If filling the media with material of this sort was not enough to convince the Soviet audience of the unreliability of western accounts of the disaster, the point was hammered home in a number of commentary items which appeared in the press and on television. All shared a common objective: analysing and countering what were variously described as the 'slanders', 'lies', and 'fairy-tales' of western accounts.

The first film from the scene of the disaster was not shown until 4 May. Shot from a helicopter, the film clearly showed the white reactor building, partially damaged. These images were employed on *Vremya* to cast further doubt on the credibility of western accounts of the accident:

> *Correspondent* [over film]: Here you see the area of the Chernobyl atomic power station. ... And here is the reactor building itself. As you can see, the huge destruction talked about by the western mass media doesn't exist. Only the core has been damaged. Everything is satisfactory with the structure, the neighbouring buildings, and the electricity generator as a whole.

This pattern of coverage, if such it can be called, continued until 6 May, ten days after the explosion at Chernobyl. That day two events signalled a change in Soviet information policy, and a reassertion of *glasnost*. The first was the appearance in *Pravda* of a feature article describing the situation at Chernobyl. The second was a major news conference at the press section of the Foreign Ministry on Smolensky Square, addressed by Deputy Foreign Minister Korolyev, and Deputy Chairman of the Council of Ministers Sherbina. Though heavily qualified by attacks on the west the news conference saw the Soviet authorities break their comparative silence on the accident and present for the first time in public a detailed account of what had happened at Chernobyl. Patrick Cockburn recalls:

> The change was evident on 6 May, with the article in *Pravda* and the press conference. From then on you had quite a lot of critical, uncontrolled stuff. It was certainly a watershed in Soviet information policy. Before Chernobyl they'd never been really open about something important and rather damaging. To admit that they had made mistakes, not last year, or ten years ago, but last week, is something that hasn't happened before.

The 6 May news conference was covered extensively on *Vremya* that evening. Following the news, a special programme on Soviet TV's Channel 1 broadcast the ministers' statements in full, and texts were printed in the press the next day. From this point on the release of reliable, official information by the Soviet authorities was unprecedented in the context of a domestic disaster.

The feature article which appeared in *Pravda* was significant in being the first press item to report in depth from the scene of the disaster. The article, by special correspondents Gubaryev and Odinyetz,[8] was also the first to break with the bland officialese of previous Chernobyl coverage by attempting to convey a sense of the human and social consequences of the accident. This was the first of several articles on Chernobyl by Gubaryev and Odinyetz. Their apparent freedom to report what they saw and heard confirmed that an approach to information more consistent with the policy of *glasnost* had been adopted by the Soviet authorities.

'Frank' discussion and self-criticism became a regular feature of these articles. On 9 May, for example, the correspondents took up the theme of rumour-mongering, accompanied by criticism of the authorities for having contributed to creating a situation in which rumours could arise. 'Maybe the inhabitants of Kiev didn't have sufficiently full information at first about what had taken place, or about the state of affairs in their city. This laid the ground for every conceivable rumour – rumours which were, incidentally, actively taken up by a variety of western "sources".'

Criticism of another type came on 12 May, in an article giving an account of meetings of the Pripyat Communist party 'buro'. These included disciplinary sessions directed against party members who failed to perform adequately during the crisis. It was reported that the leaders of one collective, Sichkarenko and Shapoval, 'essentially did nothing [during the emergency evacuation] to help place or manage people, or to guarantee that they would have work to do. Wages weren't paid in good time, clothes weren't provided, and the legal requests of evacuees were ignored. Shapoval appeared indifferent to the fortunes of people who had found themselves in a difficult situation. Political immaturity', continued the report, 'ineffectiveness and poor understanding of a complicated situation cost the collective dearly.'

It was reported that the Pripyat 'buro' had decided to expel Shapoval from membership of the Communist party for 'lack of will, and for exempting himself from the carrying out of his duties. Sichkarenko received a strict reprimand and was demoted to candidate membership of the party.' It was also reported that 'punishment has been passed on to the secretary of the [Pripyat] party organization, Gubsko, who failed to give a timely appraisal of what had happened'. The article acknowledged that in 'an unusual and complicated situation ... a few leaders showed themselves psychologically unprepared to work in the conditions existing after the accident', while emphasizing that 'what happened with these leaders was the exception ... the buro heard much about the selfless, courageous conduct of communist leaders, who worked in difficult conditions to display the qualities of organization and personal courage'. The article quoted the first secretary of the Kiev oblast: 'Cowardice was shown, and there are those who simply ran away.'

An article of 13 May titled 'The struggle continues' reported that the situation at Chernobyl had become 'a little easier', and revealed that 'ten days after the accident there was still a threat that the reactor could have exploded' (i.e. up until 6 May the danger of melt-down still existed). The article described the difficult operation of covering the leaking reactor from above with insulating material, while at the same time preventing the hot fuel crystals from making contact with the water-reservoir beneath the reactor. Academic

Velikov told the correspondents: 'No one in the world has ever been placed in such a difficult position ... it was necessary to appraise the situation very precisely, and not make a single mistake.' Readers were informed that although 'the main danger has been eliminated' it would take 'a very long time, possibly even months, for the decontamination of the area around the reactor to be completed'.

Eventually, 'openness' was extended to discussion of the media coverage itself. In *Literaturnaya Gazeta* of 4 June 1986 Yuri Sherbak wrote that:

> one of the lessons of the first month of the 'Chernobyl era' concerns the mass media – a few of them still haven't reshaped their work in the spirit of the decisions of the 27th congress. ... I am speaking about the quantity and quality of information. After several days when information was extremely sparse articles appeared in newspapers, and television began to transmit speeches by specialists. In these articles and statements much was correct and intelligent. But in a few publications and tele-broadcasts there was a tone of ungrounded cheerfulness and complacency, as if they weren't talking about a massive tragedy but about an academic example or a fireman's exercise.

The pattern of coverage from 6 May onwards strongly suggested that the struggle for *glasnost* in the field of information policy had been resolved in favour of the General Secretary.

British correspondents in Moscow during the crisis also noted the change. Brian Hanrahan notes that 'at first, there was virtually nothing' from the Soviet authorities about the accident. 'There was far more information coming back in from outside. I could have sat here and written you a very good account of what was happening based on sources in Sweden, America, and Britain, but I couldn't actually back it up from here.'

Hanrahan identifies three phases of coverage:

> At first, it looked as though they were trying different ways of responding. Initially, very little was said.
>
> The next stage saw the west being attacked for sensationalizing it. The first offer made by Soviet television to Eurovision was film of British tourists attacking their government for encouraging them to go home. But that wasn't reporting the disaster. Then there was the very odd statement concerning the two members of

the Politburo who went down there.[9] Why on earth did they go down if there was nothing to be concerned about? Very quickly from then on there began to be a flow of information.

When the information started to come, it came in that way you get after any big disaster: contradictions, uncertainties, defensiveness by key officials. Public health warnings started to come out. But all this was taking place with a time-lag of one week. The whole pattern was what you would have expected if the disaster had occurred seven days later. In the third week the papers were beginning to put out information and criticizing officials for not doing the right thing.

Peter Ruff observes: 'Once they'd got their act together, after a week, the flow of information by Soviet standards was incredible.'

Nevertheless, during the first ten days of the crisis Soviet information policy exemplified the Brezhnevian tradition of secrecy and defensiveness in dealing with controversial crisis situations. Soviet news coverage of the Chernobyl crisis was more concerned with discrediting western accounts than with providing a full and accurate Soviet version of events.

The western response

Western media accounts of the Chernobyl disaster were based on two main groups of sources. On the one hand, unofficial, usually anonymous Soviet sources; on the other, official western sources such as the CIA and the US Defence Department. Accounts based on these sources tended to be exaggerated and distorted.

For example, the official Soviet figure for casualties in the initial explosion – subsequently confirmed – was two dead. On 29 April the Moscow bureau of the American news agency United Press International (UPI) filed a report based on an unidentified telephone caller from Kiev which claimed 2,000 deaths. On 30 April *The Times* constructed a report based on this source which read:

> Eighty people died immediately and some 2,000 people died on their way to hospitals, according to the Kiev source. The whole October hospital in Kiev is packed with people who suffer from radiation sickness. The dead were not buried in ordinary cemeteries but in the village of Pigarov, where radioactive wastes are usually buried.

Christopher Walker, *The Times'* own correspondent in Moscow, reported subsequently that 'Miss Rhona Branson, a Scottish teacher in Kiev throughout the disaster period, *confirmed* reports of a possible high death toll. She had heard from local contacts in the Energy Ministry that up to 300 people may have died in the accident.' However, on her return to Moscow with other British citizens at the request of the British Embassy there, Rhona Branson gave a statement to TASS refuting this account of her remarks to the correspondent. Her statement, which was released by TASS on 9 May, said that 'the western press grossly exaggerated what I told them. I insisted that life was continuing perfectly normally in Kiev.'

Television news also found the official Soviet figures for casualties hard to accept. On Tuesday, 29 April Annis Koffman, a Dutch amateur radio enthusiast, picked up a transmission from someone who claimed to be in the region of the disaster. According to *Time* magazine of 12 May the message referred to 'hundreds of dead and wounded':

> We heard many explosions. You can't imagine what's happening here, with all the deaths and fire. I'm here twenty miles from it, and in fact I don't know what to do. I don't know if our leaders know what to do because this is a real disaster. Please tell the world to help us.

ITN's *News at One* introduced this account by first qualifying the official Soviet figure:

> *Newscaster*: The Russians are still giving little away. Officially they say two died and there have been evacuations. But an amateur radio broadcast from Kiev monitored in Holland paints a very different picture. The operator, speaking in English, said many hundreds were dead and wounded, two reactors had melted down and were still burning, and thousands of people were moving south with their children and cattle.
>
> (3 1300 29/4/86)

This preference for anonymous sources, and the underlying assumption that the Soviet authorities were lying about casualties, was condemned by some journalists. Brian Hanrahan, the BBC correspondent in Moscow throughout the crisis, accepts that:

> there were a couple of bad errors made, primarily because of bad journalism, not checking things through, and accepting rumours and hearsay before they were confirmed.

> A lot of journalism is reporting the right thing at the right time ... you listen to rumours, but you don't accept them unless enough rumours all point in the same direction, fit together in a pattern, when one can use one's experience and say – this is a rumour *worth* reporting, *as a rumour*, but you don't report everything you hear because that way you fall prey to all sorts of silly rumours, and the one about the numbers dead – you know, I've never been near any major disaster where rumours of deaths and casualties have not flowed freely all the time, and casualties are the most easily exaggerated things going. You must check them. You do not refer casually to hundreds dead, thousands dead, scores dead or dozens dead. You find out how many dead, and if you don't know, you say there is no death toll. You do not just accept what people say unless they have some reason that it's true. I think the UPI report simply said 'someone knew that there were' [2,000 dead]. It did not say why they knew, who they were, or why they should know. There was no substance to back the report.

Another preferred source of information for journalists were western 'experts' and 'intelligence sources'. Official Soviet accounts of the disaster which contradicted these sources were routinely dismissed.

An example of this from British television news concerned the use of satellite photographs which purported to show a second reactor on fire at Chernobyl.

Tom Gervasi of the New York Centre for Military Research and Analysis points out in the *Alerdinct Tribune* of November 1986 that the Landsat satellite which took the picture could not have been used to support such a claim since it has 'insufficient ground resolution to determine whether it was observing two sources of heat or one'. This was not mentioned in the following item from Channel 4's main bulletin on 29 April. The item contrasts the official Soviet account given on *Vremya* earlier that evening with the image of 'two melt-downs' suggested by 'experts' on the basis of the satellite photograph. Referring to a photograph of the damaged reactor building shown on *Vremya*, Channel 4's science correspondent reported that:

> The picture shows extensive damage and confirmed western intelligence reports that the roof had been blown off a section of the reactor building. The [Soviet] reporter said that levels of

> radioactive contamination were declining near the plant. He said there was no fire and no gigantic disruption, *but these satellite pictures do, according to satellite experts, show that two reactors are in trouble and have probably suffered melt-downs.*
>
> (4 1900 29/4/86)

Subsequently, the Soviet claim that only one reactor had been damaged and that no melt-down had occurred was confirmed.

Some journalists blamed the tendency for the western media to reproduce and reinforce exaggerated and lurid accounts of the disaster on the Soviet 'failure to inform' about what was really going on at Chernobyl during the initial phase of the crisis. If, went the argument, western journalists fell back on official western sources, or anonymous telephone callers and radio hams, this was the Soviets' own fault. Patrick Cockburn argues that:

> If you have a vacuum of information about a topic on which there's enormous public concern, then I think it's naïve to say the least for the Soviets to complain that the vacuum, which they've created themselves, is being filled by rumour and speculation. This doesn't mean that a lot of the speculation wasn't silly, or maligning, or politically motivated. It just means that this is going to happen and it's the Soviets' fault that it happened.

Brian Hanrahan makes a similar point: 'Information stops rumours. You can't say there are thousands dead if there is firm information to the contrary. Even if there isn't firm information, you can put in information which suggests that the rumours are unlikely to be true. The trouble in this case was that there was no information whatsoever.'

As we have seen, the initial Soviet response to Chernobyl gives some justification to these remarks, although it should also be noted that, contrary to the tone of much western media coverage, the Soviets were at no time in breach of the International Atomic Energy Authority (IAEA) agreement which governs the provision of information on nuclear accidents. This agreement 'only expects countries to submit reports [on nuclear accidents] after they have themselves analysed what went wrong'.[10] In an interview on Channel 4 news Foreign Office minister Timothy Eggar confirmed this, despite the attempts of the journalist to extract a statement that in some way the USSR was in breach of international law:

> *Newscaster*: When this is all finished what will be the implications for the deep reticence of the Soviet Union to come clean on a matter of such profound international safety and significance?
> *Eggar*: Well it's obviously of world-wide concern, this attitude. ... We are disappointed that they haven't lived with the spirit of the [IAEA] agreement.
> *Newscaster*: There appears to be *no indication they've even lived with the agreement at all.*
> *Eggar*: Well, strictly speaking, there is doubt as to whether they have a clear obligation as at this moment to provide information under the terms of that agreement.
> *Newscaster*: But within a few days is it your understanding *they will* be in breach of that agreement?
> *Eggar*: Well, I wouldn't go that far.
>
> (4 1900 29/4/86)

Furthermore, the Soviets' 'deep reticence to come clean' about the disaster echoed the behaviour of western authorities in similar situations. The *New Scientist* of 8 May 1986 drew attention to the inconsistency of western protests about the Soviet 'failure to inform':

> The Soviet Union was wrong not to tell the world about the accident at the Chernobyl power station as soon as possible. But that is the limit of its failure to inform.
>
> There is one good reason why the Soviet authorities did not shoot off their mouths about the sequence of events at Chernobyl. It is unlikely that they knew exactly what had happened within the reactor. The people demanding intimate details of what went on within the Soviet reactor would do well to look back to the accident at Three Mile Island. Such was the confusion surrounding events within that particular core that various 'experts' were left to theorize – and to scare the wits out of the local people in the process. It was days, if not weeks, before anyone could paint a reasonably clear picture of what happened.

Tom Gervasi lists occasions when nuclear incidents in the United States were not reported at all, or reported days, weeks, or even months after they had occurred: 'After Three Mile Island's reactor began releasing Iodine 131 and other radioactive materials over the area, it took forty-eight hours before Pennsylvania's governor ordered the evacuation of pregnant women and small children.' He quotes from a *New York Times* report of 3 June 1979:

> The crisis at the Three Mile Island power plant was in its third day before officials began to say publicly how serious it was, and it was not until last week that some details of the reasons for the nation's worst nuclear accident began to emerge in hearings by a Presidential commission.

The commission, notes Gervasi, did not make public its report until 25 October 1979, seven months after the accident.

Soviet defensiveness and secrecy around the events at Chernobyl, though contradicting the 'openness' of Gorbachov's new information policy, was not qualitatively different to that of other nuclear states in similar circumstances. It contributed, nevertheless, to a western media image of the crisis which, as with the Korean airliner incident three years earlier, reflected the views, assumptions, and often erroneous claims of dominant groups in the west.

If any good can have come out of Chernobyl for the Soviet Union, it may be that it reinforced the lesson that, in the global village we now share, there is no alternative to frankness and honesty in crises of this kind.

Part III

The domestic debate

8

Peace movement news

The intensifying nuclear debate was further expressed in the bitter public dialogue which developed between western governments and their own citizens.

The anti-nuclear protest movement constituted a visible and vocal opposition to dominant views on nuclear defence and was partly responsible for exerting the political pressures which led the Reagan administration to enter arms control talks with the Soviet Union. While attempting to assuage popular concerns over peace with the Zero Option and START proposals, western governments also engaged the peace movements in a dialogue which paralleled that going on with the USSR. Television news coverage of that dialogue and the activities of the peace movements are the subjects of this chapter.[1]

The discussion refers mainly to the two routine news samples of 1 May to 30 June 1982, and 10 May to 8 June 1983. Fifty-four items of 'peace movement news' were identified over these sample periods (see Table 8.1).

The analysis also looks in detail at three days of news coverage over the Easter weekend of 1983, when CND activists and members of the Greenham Common peace camp demonstrated at the nuclear establishments in Burghfield, Aldermaston, and Greenham Common – Nuclear Valley, as it had become known to the peace movement.

Peace movement news

Between 1979 and 1983 membership of the Campaign for Nuclear Disarmament, the main anti-nuclear group in Britain, grew from 3,000 to 80,000.[2] It encompassed professional organizations such as Scientists Against Nuclear Extermination (SANE), Teachers for Peace, and hundreds of local groups. In June 1982 250,000 people took part in a march and rally at Hyde Park in London. In October 1983, again in London, a similar event involved an estimated

Table 8.1 *Stories covered in routine peace movement news, June 1982 and 10 May–8 June 1983*

CND blockade of RAF Upper Heyford, May 1983	10
CND protests at RAF Upper Heyford, May 1983	2
Anti-Reagan protests, June 1982	6
CND Hyde Park rally, June 1982	4
New York nuclear freeze rally, June 1982	4
UNSSDII protests, June 1982	7
Anti-MX protests in Washington, May 1983	1
IWDD* protests, May 1983	1
Anti-peace movement march, June 1983	1
Greenham women evicted, May 1983	4
Benn condemns Greenham violence, May 1983	1
END conference, Berlin 1983	1
Green MPs arrested in East Berlin	4
Vatican, Heime, Kent, May 1983	2
Comiso Peace Camp, May 1983	1
Anti-nuclear theatre, May 1982	1
The peace issue in East Germany, May 1983	1
Thatcher at the UNSSDII**	1
	Total 54

Notes:
* International Women's Day for Disarmament.
** Second United Nations Special Session on Disarmament.

400,000 people. The demonstration of Easter 1983, news coverage of which is discussed in this chapter, involved an estimated 70,000 people. In other NATO countries demonstrations were equally large. Internationally, the peace movement became the major social protest movement of the post-war era, involving trade unions and members of all political parties. The nuclear issue was discussed at the Church of England synod in 1983, in the form of 'The Church and the Bomb Report'. Against this background *peace movement news* became a significant quantitative category on television news. The movement found itself on the news agenda.

Peace movement events tended to be large and spectacular, and thus attractive to routine journalistic news values. It was as a spectacular protest lobby that the anti-nuclear movement most frequently made news. Forty-two of the fifty-four items recorded over the routine sample period reported demonstrations and other forms of peace movement protest.[3]

During this period peace movement events, such as the CND rally of 22 October 1983, frequently commanded headlines.[4]

On the other hand, some large-scale peace movement events were given surprisingly little coverage. Such an event was the American 'freeze' movement rally in New York on 12 June 1982. BBC news reported that 'it was billed as the biggest-ever rally in the history of the United States. With the final figures not yet in it's hard to know if it's achieved that, but it is huge' (1 2115 12/6/82). On 13 June the BBC reported that the protest had ended with 'a gathering of half a million people in Central Park' (1 1330 13/6/82). The next day BBC estimates of the numbers in attendance doubled: 'almost a million people marched through the city' (2 1900 14/6/82). Despite the unprecedented size of this event it was not reported by ITN on any of its bulletins.

Coverage of peace movement demonstrations tended to reflect their generally non-violent, good-humoured character. In coverage of the events of Easter 1983 journalists spoke of 'the carnival spirit of the day'.

Of course, not all peace movement protests are, or could be represented as 'carnival'. Many involve much smaller numbers of people engaging in forms of civil disobedience and minor lawbreaking, such as the blockading of nuclear bases, 'die-ins', and vigils. During the sample period television news frequently reported events at the Greenham Common peace camp,[5] such as that on 12 May 1983 when Newbury District Council successfully evicted the peace campers and confiscated their property to pay for legal costs:

> Police and bailiffs fought with women peace protesters today. The fighting broke out when the bailiffs tried to seize cars and property to pay for the High Court eviction order ... the peace women swarmed over the vehicles. (3 2200 12/5/83)

Peace movement news, then, is primarily about spectacle, but it is not simply a question of the numbers involved in protest which attracts the journalists to these events and defines them as newsworthy. Some demonstrations, like that of Easter 1983, receive more coverage than others despite the fact that less people have participated. Clearly, if 70,000 people turn out to form a human chain on a cold weekday this may have more news value than the fact that 250,000 turn out to march on a warm summer weekend. Numbers gain news value in particular contexts, combining with the form of the protest to constitute 'the event'. The Easter demonstrations were spectacular and made good pictures. Likewise, the blockades of Greenham Common by a few hundred women made news across the world. Indeed, it was through their exposure in the mass media that the relatively small-scale Greenham Common protests were made into international foci for the disarmament lobby. These, too, were spectacular events, but their newsworthiness went beyond 'the event' itself. The newsworthiness of the peace movement during the sample period also related to the political environment in which they took place, and the reactions they engendered in high places.

The reactions of officialdom to social protest (of whatever kind) are a part of what has made the peace movement 'news'. Political élites – the *primary definers* of news – have a privileged access to the media. But this can sometimes prove to be a double-edged sword. By defining 'problems' in the media, opinion-leaders contribute to creating them as media issues. They put in motion a process of agenda-setting which, while reflecting the media's structural relationship to dominant groups, also creates a space for oppositional views to be heard. Connell suggests that the range of definitions of issues which appear in the news is determined in 'the struggle between contending political and economic forces' (1980: 144). The British government began in the early 1980s to show that it regarded the peace movement – CND and the Greenham Common women in particular – as a serious contender in the political struggle surrounding defence policy. As it did so the movement *became* news to an extent that might not otherwise have been the case.

Michael Heseltine's suggestion in 1983 for an anti-CND advertising campaign funded by public money and costing £1 million, condemned at the time by Labour and Alliance members of parliament as an abuse of government's power and subsequently shelved, unwittingly gave CND headline publicity on television news. We might express the relation between the political establishment and CND's public profile – 'Heseltine's Law', as it were – in the following way: as key figures in the government publicly condemned the peace movement the more newsworthy it became. Hall *et al.* note that:

> if the tendency towards ideological closure [in news media] is maintained by the way the different apparatuses are structurally linked so as to promote the dominant definitions of events, then

> the counter-tendency must also depend on the existence of organized and articulate sources which generate counter-definitions of the situation. This depends to some degree on whether the collectivity which generates counter-ideologies and explanations is a powerful countervailing force in society; whether it represents an organized majority or substantial minority; and whether or not it has a degree of legitimacy within the system or can win such a position through struggle.
>
> (1978: 64)

In the defence and disarmament debate CND had won a position of limited legitimacy as 'an organized and articulate source' of opposition to dominant definitions of defence and disarmament issues. It had become a 'powerful, countervailing force in society'.

This was reflected not just in the appearance of peace movement news as a quantitative content category but in reportage which spoke directly of the seriousness, commitment, and political weight of the movement. In coverage of the Easter 1983 demos ITN spoke of 'the challenge it posed to the government' (3 2200 1/4/83), and 'the seriousness of the issues'. One journalist conceded that 'critics might argue with their viewpoint, but surely not with their commitment', adding, 'the sheer size of the rally will give added weight to those who are opposing the siting of new American missiles, not only in Britain but anywhere in Europe'. BBC coverage spoke of 'the serious point of the demonstrations' (1 2100 1/4/83).

During the Second Special Session of the United Nations on Disarmament, BBC coverage of a demonstration involving several hundred people at the New York diplomatic missions of the five nuclear-armed UN members stressed that this was a 'serious political protest and many of the people taking part will be back to try again just as soon as they are at liberty to do so' (1 1740 14/6/82).[6]

The presence of the peace movement on the news agenda in the early 1980s was also reflected in coverage of the 1983 General Election. In some fifty-five items of coverage of the defence debate in the election, three were concerned with the participation of CND. Indeed, such was the quantity of peace movement news on television during this period that some observers identified a media 'bias' in favour of the anti-nuclear viewpoint.

Peace movement news in the British media as a whole was held to be responsible for what Roy Dean, Director of the Arms Control and Disarmament Research Unit at the British Foreign and Commonwealth Office, identified as 'a loss of confidence in governments' security policies and feelings of frustration at the slow progress in the reduction of armaments by negotiation' (1983). Dean observed that:

> There has been widespread media coverage of rallies in western cities against nuclear weapons; these are portrayed as popular manifestations of opposition to the defence policies of western governments. In Britain, for example, the activities of the anti-nuclear campaigners have been reported as domestic news items, with no assessments of their arguments and naturally no attempt to relate their activities to the current nuclear arms control talks.

One prominent broadcaster, Sir Alastair Burnet of ITN, argued that the organization of large-scale demonstrations was a publicity tactic designed to manipulate the mass media, and gave his own view that as such they should not be given 'automatic credence and coverage'. On 3 February 1984 Sir Alastair wrote (an unpublished letter) to a critical viewer on the subject of news coverage of political demonstrations:

> Many demonstrations are organized simply to attract the attention of the media, without adding anything to the basic discussion of the issues. In the past television gave almost automatic credence and coverage, and this merely encouraged even more demonstrations. Now we try to be more discriminating in news programmes which attempt to give a balance of subjects for a wide variety of viewers.

On 15 February 1984, he added in a further letter (also unpublished) that:

> stage managed demonstrations which do not add to the debate of ideas may well be of interest to the organizers, but are going to be looked at with increasing care by the media. Some viewers and readers are getting restless about the uncritical coverage of such demonstrations.

Television news coverage *has* to some extent been 'uncritical' of the peace movement. The pattern of coverage in our sample supports Connell's assertion that 'while it can by no means be said that the media have operated as an advertising agency for CND and the other organized peace movements, neither have they operated explicitly and systematically against them' (Aubrey 1982: 31).

However, coverage of the peace movement cannot be seen in isolation from the broadcasters' tendency to reinforce the core assumptions of the Soviet threat. The two phenomena are frequently linked both by the defence establishment, as we will see in the next section, and by journalists themselves, as in an example from 1981 referred to in Chapter 7:

> The peace rallies have delighted Moscow because they are seriously undermining the resolve of the West German government to have the NATO missiles on their soil. And it's speculated the Soviets might try to spin out the Geneva talks in the hope that NATO plans for new missiles could fall apart under democratic pressure. And then Russia wouldn't have to give up any of her missiles at all.[7]
>
> (3 2200 18/11/81)

Furthermore, as Dean observes, there has been very little 'assessment of their arguments' within peace movement news. We shall not suggest that this is a consequence of 'bias' *against* the peace movement but rather of the grammar of television news, which tends to emphasize the spectacular aspects of events at the expense of explanatory themes. Essentially *descriptive*, peace movement news signals the existence of dissent but rarely develops the arguments put forward by the movement. Consequently, coverage has signified the existence of popular dissent from dominant views on the defence issue, but there has been little examination of the rationale which underlies it. From the context of his remarks quoted above it would appear that Dean regards this as a kind of media 'favouritism', but from another perspective it could be seen as an inadequacy in coverage.

Background explanatory items are not completely absent from television news coverage of the peace movement, but they are largely confined to minority audience programming.

A third reason why the appearance of the peace movement on television news cannot be equated with a pro-peace movement 'bias' relates to the privileged access enjoyed by dominant groups to counter the movement's media-presence with 'counter-propaganda' of their own. Through skilful news management, and because of the media's structured relationship to the powerful, dominant groups have the capacity to 'frame' images of the peace movement with countering images. The importance of this privileged access, and the degree to which political élites have used it to counter the peace movement's media presence with images of the Soviet Union can be seen in coverage of the demonstrations of Easter 1983.

Easter 1983: anatomy of a propaganda war

The following discussion chiefly refers to evening bulletins on BBC1 (*9 O'Clock News*) and ITV (*News at Ten*) between 30 March and 1 April 1983.

As we noted in the introduction to this chapter, Easter 1983 was the occasion of a major British peace movement protest, focused on the nuclear establishments at Burghfield, Aldermaston, and Greenham Common. The first day of the protest, 31 March, involved the blockading of the Burghfield factory and Greenham Common air base. These blockades were the prelude to a larger event planned for 1 April, a 'human chain' linking CND supporters by hand along a fourteen-mile route between the three nuclear establishments. Reported estimates of the numbers of people who took part in the human chain varied from 40,000 (the police) to 100,000 (CND). A later figure of 70,000 was generally accepted.

These demonstrations were one of the major peace movement events of recent years. Numerically larger demonstrations may have occurred before and after these protests, but this particular event took on a special significance which outweighed the numbers factor. Although it was not known then, the General Election was just over two months away. It *was* known by all that Cruise missiles would be coming to Britain that year. For these reasons Easter 1983 represented an important stage in the battle between the pro and anti-nuclear lobbies in Britain for the hearts and minds of public opinion.

Coverage of the demonstrations was discussed in the previous section. We noted that they were reported prominently in bulletins (the second item on 31 March, and headline coverage on 1 April); that correspondents reported the event in terms of the 'commitment' of the protesters, the 'seriousness' of the issues, and the 'carnival', 'holiday mood' of the events. Of greater interest in this section is the manner in which the actions of the British and American governments in response to these events, while confirming that the European peace movements were regarded at that time by NATO leaders as a major political threat, shaped coverage over the Easter weekend. In a two-pronged 'counter-propaganda' assault western leaders attempted to contrast their own flexibility and sincerity – in the shape of a new arms proposal, unveiled as a major compromise – with harsh, threatening images of the USSR, particularly the images of 'Russian spies' and the Berlin Wall.

There were three stages in the campaign. First, on the eve of the demonstrations, a major US arms control proposal was announced (the Interim Zero Option of 30 March). Second, the British government chose the first day of the Easter demonstrations, 31 March, to expel three Soviet diplomats from the London Embassy on charges of spying. And third, also on 31 March, the Defence Secretary paid an official visit to the Berlin Wall, drawing attention to the Soviet presence in eastern Europe. With the full resources of the British and American governments behind them, these three events competed with the peace protests for news time.

Over the three days of the sample period as a whole, there were seventy-six reported statements on main evening bulletins (see Table 8.2). Forty-six of these came from official western sources: statements by President Reagan were reported twelve times, as were those of Michael Heseltine, the Defence Secretary. Next in frequency of access came the Prime Minister, with nine reported statements, and there were a further thirteen statements from other official western sources.

By contrast there were three reported statements from Soviet sources, and twenty-two from representatives or supporters of CND.

The 'Interim' Zero Option, President Reagan's main contribution to the Easter counter-propaganda battle with the European peace movement, was announced on 30 March, the day before the peace movement protests were scheduled to begin. According to NATO Secretary-General Joseph Luns in *The Times* this timing was 'not unconnected' with the Easter demonstrations. As with the earlier proposal of November 1981, satellite communications broadcast the President's speech to western Europe in time for the main news programmes, and it received headline coverage.

Viewers of ITN that evening were informed that the President had 'offered *a compromise* to the Soviet Union today on nuclear weapons in Europe' (3 2200 30/3/83). The BBC reported that 'zero-zero remains the ultimate objective – no medium-range missiles at all on either side, but the President's message today was that *he'd be willing to settle for what he could get rather than end up with no agreement at all*' (1 2100 30/3/83). ITN's correspondent interpreted the proposal to mean that:

Table 8.2 *Reported statements in peace movement news, Easter, 1983*

	BBC	*ITN*	*Total*
Prime Minister	4	5	9
Defence Secretary	6	6	12
President Reagan	5	7	12
The Americans/America	2	3	5
Foreign Office	1	2	3
Foreign Secretary	–	1	1
European leaders/western governments	1	1	2
CND	10	12	22
Michael Foot (Labour)	1	–	1
Burghfield workers	2	–	2
Police	3	1	4
Moscow/Soviet commentators	2	1	3
	37	39	76

the American negotiator has been let off the leash of the Zero Option and will have *much more flexible* ideas to discuss.

The flexibility of the proposal was questionable, however.

It adhered to the basic principles, if not the detail of the original Zero Option. Where the latter had proposed (see Chapter 6) that the USSR give up all of its existing medium-range nuclear weapons in Europe in return for no future deployment of American Cruise and Pershing II missiles, the new proposal suggested a reduced deployment of 300 or so new American weapons in return for the removal of 300 or so Soviet ones. It 'did not change the essence of US policy in any significant respect' (Talbott 1984: 181).

Given the continued exclusion of British, French, and US forward-based systems from the European nuclear balance, many commentators argued that its main function, like the Zero Option before it, was not to achieve an arms control agreement with the USSR but to create a positive image of the Reagan administration's arms control policy on the eve of what were anticipated to be major anti-nuclear protests throughout western Europe.

Indeed, journalists reported the 'public relations' dimension of the proposal. 'The President's *real audience*', noted a BBC correspondent, was 'European public opinion, an attempt to convince the Europeans of the flexibility of America's position'. ITN reported that the proposal was 'very much a gesture towards

Europe'. The BBC suggested that 'The Americans are still giving nothing on some important points ... the compromise, such as it is, is a fairly unyielding one and designed to impress the Europeans rather than the Russians in the first place.' ITN predicted: 'Russia is certain to find little that's acceptable in the proposal.'

Fourteen statements in favour of the proposal were reported. These included lengthy excerpts from President Reagan's speech, journalists' own accounts of the speech, and the views of numerous official sources. 'Western governments, including Britain, welcomed the proposal,' reported the BBC. 'The Foreign Office urges the Russians to consider the offer with the utmost seriousness and to respond positively.' 'The Foreign Secretary', reported ITN, 'said the American offer had Britain's whole-hearted support.'

'Balancing' the fourteen reported statements in favour of the proposal, only two critical opinions were reported. Both of these came at the end of ITN's item. The sources for these critical comments were Bruce Kent, General Secretary of CND, and commentators on the Soviet newspaper *Izvestia*, reported together at the end:

> Monsignor Bruce Kent, the CND Chairman, said Russia was unlikely to accept the Reagan plan as a serious starting point for negotiations. He said it gave a distorted view of the European nuclear balance because it concentrated on land-based missiles. There's no official Russian reaction yet, but a commentary on the plan in the government newspaper *Izvestia* said nothing would come of it. *Izvestia* said President Reagan was engaged in farce while trying to appear flexible.

BBC news reported *no* critical comments.

In the next two days of coverage a further three critical statements were reported: two of these were by Soviet sources, and one came from the Chairperson of CND, Joan Ruddock. Over the three days of the sample as a whole a total of twenty-four statements about the Interim Zero Option were reported, of which nineteen were favourable.

While definitions of the proposal as flexible and compromising were contested at times, by journalists themselves and CND or Soviet sources, the Interim Zero Option pre-empted coverage of the Easter demonstrations with headline coverage of a President 'deeply disappointed' at the Soviet rejection of the original Zero Option, but 'willing to settle for what he can get rather than end up with no agreement at all'.

The administration's ability to shape coverage in this way at a key moment in the propaganda war with the European peace movement is another example of the media's structured relationship to dominant groups – a relationship which permits official views to command headlines and score relatively easy propaganda points.

The British government entered the propaganda war on 31 March, the first day of the peace movement protests, choosing that day to expel three Soviet diplomats from the London Embassy for 'activities incompatible with status'. At the same time Defence Secretary Michael Heseltine visited British troops on the border between East and West Germany, on what was openly declared to be an 'Easter counter-propaganda exercise'. The effect of these interventions on the structure of news that evening can be seen in the following headlines from BBC1's main bulletin:

> Three Russians expelled from Britain tonight for spying.
>
> Thousands of peace campaigners gather in what they call Nuclear Valley.
>
> Mr Heseltine says our missiles keep the Soviets behind the Wall.

ITN's bulletin was similarly structured, with news about the peace movement sandwiched between officially sponsored images of the Soviet threat.

Spies, of course, *are* sometimes discovered working from embassies in foreign countries. But official allegations of 'activities incompatible with status' are often the justification for what are essentially *political* acts in which one side attacks the other by making life difficult for its diplomats.

Diplomatic expulsions are effective propaganda tools because reporting of the facts can be restricted on the grounds of national security. Journalists may receive little or no elaboration from their unnamed official sources of the 'crimes' allegedly committed. The events of 31 March appeared to be in this category. No information was provided by the government to substantiate the charge that spying had taken place (at the very least, none was reported by journalists), as the BBC correspondent noted: 'Whitehall has been particularly tight-lipped about what these spying activities were'; and a possible link between the expulsions and the events going on that day in Nuclear Valley was noted by ITN:

> It seems to be more than a coincidence that the Russians are being thrown out on the very day Mrs Thatcher and Mr Heseltine are denouncing the Russians as part of their criticism of the Easter anti-nuclear demonstrations.
>
> (3 2200 31/3/83)

Despite this, the validity of the allegations was taken for granted on the news. Journalists assumed the truthfulness of information from 'tight-lipped' official sources, and that spying had occurred. Reports were accompanied by 'Soviet threat' graphics depicting the Union Jack being consumed by a hammer and sickle (see Figure 8.1). Statements by unnamed 'intelligence sources', such as the claim that the majority of Soviet diplomats in Britain (the figure given was 60 per cent) were 'involved in intelligence work', were presented as 'factual' background:

> In future there will be 43 Russian diplomats and 105 civilians allowed to base themselves here. Intelligence sources reckon that at least 60 per cent of those are involved in intelligence work to a greater or lesser degree.
>
> (1 2100 31/3/83)

Items on both channels contained interviews with the individuals concerned. These proceeded from the assumption of 'guilty as charged':

> Igor Titov talked about his expulsion behind a table laid with caviar and sandwiches, sheltered by his wife and by his occupation as a journalist. His column in the Russian *New Times* magazine *is now exposed as the cover for a spy . . . in addition to Mr Titov*, tonight's announcement named *two spies* who worked at the Soviet Embassy.
>
> (3 2200 31/3/83)

No firm evidence that the diplomats were spies was available, as was apparent from journalists' accounts of what they had done. In the absence of any hard factual information, these were entirely speculative:

> Mr Primakov's diplomatic title would *appear to be* a cover for an officer in the KGB
>
> (3 2200 31/3/83)

Figure 8.1 'In future there will be 43 Russian diplomats and 105 civilians allowed to base themselves here. Intelligence sources reckon that at least 60 per cent of those are involved in intelligence work to a greater or lesser degree' (1 2100 31/3/83)

> This *strongly suggests* that British counter-intelligence has an actual list of spies, *possibly provided* by the Russian who defected to Britain last June from Iran.
>
> (1 2100 31/3/83)

This coverage illustrates the ease with which establishment sources can plant stories at strategic points in bulletins, in the knowledge that their assertions and allegations will go largely unchallenged.

With these images of the Soviet threat fresh in mind, viewers of both BBC and ITN bulletins were now taken to Berkshire and the CND events, but before film reports from correspondents at the scene of the demonstrations, both bulletins reported the comments of the Prime Minister – the first in a series of official statements linking the peace movement to the Soviet threat, the Berlin Wall, or both:

> Mrs Thatcher has already reacted sharply to the demonstration. They'd be better off linking hands around the Berlin Wall, she said.
>
> (1 2100 31/3/83)

> Mrs Thatcher agreed with the Tory backbencher who said the protesters were blinkered and dangerous even if sincere.
>
> (3 2200 31/3/83)

Film of the demonstrations followed, before coverage returned once again to the Prime Minister:

> The demonstrations prompted some anger in the House of Commons. The Prime Minister agreed with the Conservative backbencher who called the women of Greenham Common blinkered and dangerous.
>
> (1 2100 31/3/83)

> The Prime Minister told the Commons that it would make far more sense for the peace women to go and link hands around the Berlin Wall.
>
> (3 2200 31/3/83)

Both bulletins broadcast the following section of Mrs Thatcher's speech:

> *Thatcher*: It would make far more sense for those women to go and link hands around the Berlin Wall. If by doing so they managed to get the Soviets to take it down, to remove the guns, the dogs, and the mines there to kill those who attempt to escape to freedom they would be doing something.

In the BBC report Mrs Thatcher continued:

> If they do not succeed in taking it down they will prove that [their] freedom and the freedom of all people in this country still needs to be defended.

The BBC also reported a statement by Labour leader Michael Foot, which 'defended the women saying that they believed the deployment of Cruise missiles would make arms limitation more difficult'. The views of Mrs Thatcher and her Defence Secretary were reported twenty-one times over the sample period. This was the only reported statement by a member of the Opposition.

The Defence Secretary's main role in the counter-propaganda campaign was to be filmed at the Berlin Wall. Both bulletins followed reports of the Prime Minister's views on the subject of the Berlin Wall with coverage of the Defence Secretary's visit there, the purpose of which was openly declared. As Mr Heseltine put it:

> It reinforces the point that we are here to defend the peace and freedom of the west. This is the point where the marching has to stop.

Outside broadcast units accompanied the Defence Secretary to Berlin, where he inspected British troops and explained to ITN's correspondent that 'over there, where the real threat is, there won't be any marches'. Television news commentaries reinforced this image of 'the threat'. BBC's report set the scene in the following way:

> The border and wall ringing West Berlin stretches for a hundred miles, so it was here that Michael Heseltine came in what he freely acknowledged was an Easter counter-propaganda exercise. The East German border guards were *out in force* in their watchtowers and beside the perimeter fence. On this side it is *patrolled* by the men of the Royal Irish Rangers. The force here is a trip-wire, easily overwhelmed by the 95,000 Russian and East German troops based in the twenty-mile ring around the city.
>
> (1 2100 31/3/83)

In Chapter 3 we noted the differential language used to describe the military forces of east and west in Berlin. Western forces 'assured and protected' the West German population against 'the Russians who ruled on the other side'. Similarly here, East German soldiers are 'out in force'. British soldiers are merely 'patrolling'. Western forces are 'easily overwhelmed' by the Soviet army which is kept in check only by the 'trip-wire' of British forces. Over film of Heseltine inspecting the Royal Irish Rangers a correspondent noted:

> Just to emphasize the nature of the enemy one of the fusiliers was sporting a Russian uniform.

Significantly, BBC2's *News Review*, a weekly digest of news broadcast on a Sunday, chose to highlight the same scene: 'One man wore a Russian uniform to show who the real enemy was' (2 1825 3/4/83).

In these reports assumptions about the reality of the Soviet threat are built into the commentary, taken for granted not only by the conservative politicians who originate this definition of the problem, but by the journalists who are reporting the debate.

Substantial parts of these items comprised interviews with Mr Heseltine. These were deferential, functioning mainly as cues for him to expound on his preferred themes. On BBC he was asked only one question, 'What purpose had this visit served?', to which he replied:

> It reinforces the point that anyone who holds my job knows. That we are here to defend the peace and freedom of the west. There's going to be a lot of protest in the west in the course of the next couple of days. There will be marching, protests, and this is the point where the marching has to stop. There won't be any protests over there, you've only got to stand here to understand why. The interesting thing is that the very success of the policies the various governments of the NATO alliance have pursued for thirty-seven years has not only kept our freedom but has kept the freedom of the people to march and protest. That's one of the privileges of a free and democratic society.

The 'interview' ended at this point, with no attempt by the journalist to represent competing views on the themes of freedom and NATO's role in keeping it, or on any of the statements made by the Defence Secretary. On the contrary, these comments were contextualized with references to 'the nature of the enemy' and Warsaw Pact troops 'out in force' to 'easily overwhelm' the British 'trip-wire'.

ITN's correspondent did not question Mr Heseltine's underlying view of the Soviet threat, but differed from BBC1's coverage in raising an objection to the deployment of Cruise missiles as a response to it. The interview as a whole was conducted in the same deferential style as BBC1's, but this question represents the only occasion during the sample period when any television journalist challenged government policy:

> *Journalist*: Now there are many people in Britain who would share your views on the Soviet system but still believe that Cruise should be opposed because they are an unnecessary addition to NATO's nuclear arsenal.

To which Mr Heseltine replied:

> I'm rather closer to the Russian SS-20 missiles than the people in Britain. You see they have already deployed that particular class of nuclear weapon in the Soviet Union facing us. They've got 350 missiles with over a thousand warheads, and two-thirds of them are actually facing western Europe. What we've said is if they'll take them away we won't deploy and that would be the best option.

On this the interview ended.

We can contrast the interviewing style adopted towards Mr Heseltine in both of these examples with that seen in an appearance by Joan Ruddock, CND Chairperson, on BBC2's *Newsnight* of 31 March. On this occasion the journalist forcefully presented the opposing side of the argument, playing 'devil's advocate' with the interviewee's position.

This example shows that when representatives of oppositional viewpoints gain access to television news, their views tend to be presented within the terms of the debate pre-established by the primary definers of the issue. They must respond, as Hall *et al.* put it, 'to privileged definitions' of the problem (1978: 64) already established. As his starting point for the interview with Joan Ruddock the journalist chose a comment made earlier in the day by Margaret Thatcher to the effect that the women of Greenham Common should 'link hands around the Berlin Wall':

> *Journalist*: Well Joan Ruddock, I'd like to ask you first about the government remarks today about the Berlin Wall. Now, when Mrs Thatcher said it would make more sense for you to be linking hands around the Berlin Wall she argued that if you couldn't persuade the Soviets to take the Wall down that would remind you of the freedom which we enjoy, which the people behind the Wall don't enjoy, a freedom which still has to be defended. How do you reply to that argument?
>
> *Joan Ruddock*: I am very conscious of the fact that people have died on the Berlin Wall, and I really feel that the Prime Minister and indeed the Minister for Defence should not be using the Berlin Wall, as I see it, in a cheap propaganda trick, because I see it as nothing more than that. [Journalist attempts to interrupt.] If she is to suggest that in fact we should have that sort of situation in Britain, if that is what she is saying, that we should not have the freedom to demonstrate – I can't see the point she is making. If she is saying there is a problem in eastern Europe, that it is a

divided continent then she finds an echo in our sentiments. We have always opposed the Soviet regime *vis-à-vis* eastern Europe and indeed we want to bring back real peace and detente in Europe, and the best way to do that is through disarmament.

Although at this point in the interview Ruddock has clearly given a lengthy answer to the question about the Berlin Wall, stating that 'we [CND] have always opposed the Soviet regime *vis-à-vis* eastern Europe', the journalist presses the subject further, again putting Mrs Thatcher's views (in an expanded version of what he assumes her to have meant) about freedom, democracy, and what 'the people behind the Wall are doing to menace us':

> *Journalist*: Her real point really, I think, is that we enjoy freedom here to debate and to demonstrate at Greenham Common and other places, the people behind the Wall do not enjoy that freedom and the people behind the Berlin Wall might want to menace our freedom and that the best way of keeping that menace at bay is by being properly defended.

A willingness to criticize and question the participants in an important political debate is properly regarded as a necessary element in good journalism. But journalists appear less likely to criticize those whose views remain within the dominant explanatory framework than those who are outside it. As the authors of *Televising Terrorism* note, in television journalism 'the aggressive style is most apparent when the witness is putting an alternative or oppositional view' (Schlesinger, Murdock, and Elliot 1983).

In news coverage of the nuclear debate examined here, officials such as Mr Heseltine were never challenged on the news as Joan Ruddock was in the above example. Indeed, to illustrate the *availability* of alternative interviewing styles for representatives of the dominant viewpoint we must move temporarily out of the news format. This example, in which Mr Heseltine is interviewed critically, accompanied the screening on 10 December 1983 of the American Broadcasting Corporation's film about a hypothetical nuclear war, *The Day After*.

The live studio debate which took place after *The Day After* was the first time Mr Heseltine had appeared as Defence Minister on the same programme as a representative of the British peace movement (again Joan Ruddock). Refusing to engage in direct debate with Ruddock he was interviewed live before the debate proper began in order, as he put it, to 'balance the film'. In the course of his interview Mr Heseltine was attacked on the grounds that he would not take part in the full debate, and for his alleged intolerance of criticism of the government's nuclear defence policy. It represents a relatively rare example of a style in which journalists 'choose the role of devil's advocate, quizzing their establishment witnesses from a perspective which incorporates alternative or even oppositional elements' (Schlesinger *et al.* 1983: 40).

In the first part of the interview the Defence Secretary had condemned *The Day After* as 'propaganda'. As the interview was nearing its end Mr Heseltine was challenged on his refusal to debate the issues with a representative of CND:

> *Journalist*: Thank you very much. I'm afraid that I can't help contrasting your interview with us tonight with the fact that you would not take part in the subsequent debate.
> *Heseltine*: Well can I just answer that point? I think that that film has a message of propaganda and I think it is critically important therefore that I should have the chance to answer it, and I do not believe I would be doing that adequately if I was set in the context where I was being balanced within itself. I wanted, and I believe rightly, to balance the film.
> *Journalist*: But I must just repeat the point: it is surely very authoritarian to suggest that it is propaganda if one questions defence policy and suggests that the present defence policy might not succeed?
> *Heseltine*: I don't believe it is authoritarian. When I was faced with the decision that you put to me – do I think people should watch the film – I said I thought they should. Now that is encouraging debate but when the film is shown I believe there should be a real debate and that is why I asked for the opportunity to comment upon it, so there would be a balance to the discussion. If I hadn't had such a chance I believe there would have been an unbalanced discussion and I think that would be wrong and not in the highest keeping of the democratic tradition, so I thank you for giving me the opportunity to respond.
> *Journalist*: If somebody made a film about an international crisis in which the deterrent was a success and did work, would that be unbalanced?
> *Heseltine*: But constantly people are, and constantly there are the opportunities to discuss these matters.

Journalist: But you don't say they're unbalanced.
(3 *The Day After Debate* 10/12/83)

The style of this interview constrains the Defence Secretary from setting the terms of the debate. His opinions of those opposing nuclear defence are referred to as 'authoritarian'. His use of the term 'propaganda' to dismiss the ABC film is criticized. His basic assumptions about the defence issue are contested. The deferential interviewing style extended by journalists towards the Defence Secretary at Easter is here replaced by a detached, critical journalism as the interviewer distances himself from the government's position and acknowledges the existence of a credible opposing view. There is nothing intrinsic to television news which could be seen as preventing the adoption of such styles 'routinely'.

Finally, on 31 March, both bulletins reported President Reagan's views on his own anti-nuclear lobby, the American freeze movement. In a speech given in California Mr Reagan, like Mrs Thatcher and Mr Heseltine, drew links between the Soviet military build-up, Soviet nuclear superiority, and the activities of the anti-nuclear movement. Like Mrs Thatcher and Mr Heseltine, his views were not qualified. BBC's report, broadcast *before* the speech had actually been made, noted that:

> President Reagan is expected to launch another attack on the Soviet military build-up in a speech in Los Angeles in half an hour's time. It's thought he'll criticize the nuclear freeze movement for undermining arms control negotiations.

An hour later, after the speech had been made, ITN confirmed the essence of the BBC's speculation:

> President Reagan attacked his own nuclear freeze movement. He said a freeze would pull the rug from under the American negotiators at disarmament talks and benefit the Russians who had more nuclear weapons. If we appear to be divided, the President said, they'll dig in their heels.

On 1 April, official sources were again reported warning about the Soviet threat. Coverage of the demonstrations that day was followed on both channels by reports of a news conference by the Defence Secretary, returned from Berlin, with what the BBC called 'a warning for the peace movement'. According to ITN:

> *Journalist*: The Defence Secretary said the anti-nuclear demonstrators were going down a naïve and reckless road. He said it would be an unforgiveable gamble for the west to do what they advocated. The Soviet Union would use force ruthlessly wherever it thought it could win.
>
> *Heseltine*: So I have got the simplest of messages for those who marched today. You do so in freedom and that freedom is your right and I am charged with its defence, however much I may deplore the inconvenience and the cost you impose on the majority of us who don't share your views. But don't believe for one moment that we will risk that freedom, our freedom as well as yours, by following you along a naïve and reckless road.

BBC news transmitted the same section of Mr Heseltine's statement.

Coverage of the peace protests of Easter 1983 was 'framed' by a sequence of officially generated stories emphasizing the Soviet threat. A weekend of defence and disarmament news which had opened with a 'flexible' and 'compromising' arms control proposal from the Reagan administration closed with images of the 'ruthless force' of the USSR and the 'naïvety and recklessness' of the peace movement. This feature of coverage was not primarily a consequence of a conscious media 'bias', but of the privileged access to the media enjoyed by the powerful in society.

Whether openly declared as 'counter-propaganda' (the Berlin Wall visit) or not (the diplomatic expulsions), the routine structure of access to official sources enabled them to intervene in images of 'peace' with 'balancing' images of the 'enemy'. Coverage on BBC and ITN showed a remarkable degree of uniformity in presenting this 'counter-propaganda'.

Of course, it cannot be assumed that images of the Soviet threat which dominated coverage at Easter 1983 successfully constructed a preferred reading of the peace movement protests as 'at best misguided, at worst dangerous and subversive' (3 2200 1/4/83), but clearly television news is a major arena within which official attempts to do so are organized.

We will end this chapter with a postscript. In 1984 the peace movement began to decline in news value. On 26 November that year the *Guardian* reported that:

> some papers have not mentioned CND for months. Now there is no interest in Fleet Street. CND's national conference at Sheffield was not even staffed by most national newspapers, even though the organization is one of the most active in Britain.

Keeble notes that 'since the 1983 election the peace movement has been effectively ignored by the media' (Curran *et. al.* 1986: 56). One possible explanation for this is that 'Heseltine's Law' began to operate in reverse. Britain's political leaders apparently became aware of the relationship between their attacks on CND and public interest in the organization, and revised their tactics. The *Guardian* article further noted:

> the Defence Secretary no longer flies to the Berlin Wall to divert attention from CND demonstrations, he simply stays quiet and hopes they will not be reported.

Television coverage of one large demonstration lends some support to the view that the Conservative government's revised strategy of ignoring CND rather than attempting to counter its activities with public relations stunts of its own (such as those discussed above) coincided with the falling-away of media interest in the peace movement. On 27 October 1984 20,000 people attended a demonstration at Barrow-in-Furness to protest against the Trident submarine system (Barrow houses the Vickers shipyard where the submarines will be constructed). ITN's main evening bulletin covered the demonstration in thirty-five words, mainly in the context of another newsworthy story at that time, the famine in Ethiopia:

> The CND leader Monsignor Bruce Kent told 20,000 demonstrators at an anti-nuclear rally in Barrow-in-Furness that the arms race was an insult when millions were starving in Ethiopia. Trident submarines are to be built at Barrow-in-Furness.
>
> (3 2215 27/10/84)

BBC1's main evening bulletin did not cover the event at all.

A systematic analysis of the reasons for the declining newsworthiness of the peace movement are beyond the scope of this book. It does, however, seem possible to conclude that the agenda-setting role of the establishment, which contributed to making the peace movement a media issue, has latterly worked to exclude 'peace' from the news.

9

The nuclear election

The nuclear debate also concerned the political parties. In the 1983 General Election the arguments about pro and anti-nuclear, Cruise and Pershing, Trident and Polaris, crystallized into a set of relatively clear electoral choices. This chapter analyses the 'nuclear election' campaign of 1983 through the 'window' of television.[1]

The nuclear debate in the 1983 General Election

When the election was called the first Cruise missiles were only six months away from their planned deployment at Greenham Common. The label of 'the nuclear election' applied by some commentators to the campaign reflected the centrality of defence issues to it.

Mrs Thatcher herself 'put defence at the top of her agenda' when she declared in the House of Commons on 10 May that there would be 'no more important issue'. Michael Foot in turn identified defence as 'the supreme issue' for the Labour party. Defence appeared as an election theme on fourteen days of the twenty-one-day sample of television news on which the following account is based, rivalled in importance only by the issue of unemployment.

When the votes had been counted on 9 June the Conservatives emerged as clear winners with 42 per cent of the votes cast, compared with 28 per cent for Labour and 26 per cent for the Alliance. The Conservative vote was almost 2 per cent down on the election of May 1979 but a 9 per cent swing from Labour to the Alliance split the opposition and increased Margaret Thatcher's majority in the Commons to 144. The Conservative party won the nuclear election resoundingly, although even towards the end of the campaign opinion polls were recording something which had long been evident in Britain: public opposition to major elements of the Conservative party's nuclear defence policy and corresponding support for a substantial part of Labour's unilateralist programme. On 26 May, at the height of the Labour party's internal crisis over defence, ITN was reporting the results of a Marplan poll that 'a majority of voters still oppose Cruise and Trident, 54 per cent in each case' (3 2200 26/5/83). However, the same poll recorded that 45 per cent of voters considered the Conservatives (who supported Cruise and Trident) to have a better policy than either Labour (who opposed both) or the Alliance (who supported Cruise but opposed Trident). This, the journalist suggested, 'would seem to indicate that while the majority don't want Britain to abandon existing nuclear weapons unilaterally, they also don't want to add to the nuclear weapons on British territory'. Regardless of public opinion polls, the majority of the electorate opted for the latter policy. Television news coverage of the campaign provides some clues as to why.

Opening shots

The date of the 1983 General Election was announced by Margaret Thatcher on 9 May, and electioneering began the next day. On defence the Conservatives took the initiative, setting the pace of the campaign and the agenda for public debate during the first week. They set about denouncing Labour as 'extremist', 'irresponsible', and 'dangerous', and although they did not begin campaigning officially until 20 May dominated television news in the first week with a series of interventions in which these themes were elaborated. Of twenty-one defence-related news items recorded in the first week, thirteen contained Conservative denunciations of Labour and the anti-nuclear lobby. One event in particular, the Scottish Conservative party conference, was used by the government as a platform from which to launch dramatic and widely publicized attacks on Labour.

The battle began on 10 May. That day in the Commons the Prime Minister demonstrated that she was prepared to confront the defence issue head on. By calling the election when she did the Prime Minister had effectively prevented a long-awaited two-day debate on defence and disarmament, prompting the accusation from Michael Foot that she had 'cut and run'.

To this the Prime Minister replied that she was 'only too delighted to discuss defence', and that she herself regarded it as the most important electoral issue. Election news that evening was dominated by these exchanges. ITN reported that 'Mrs Thatcher is going to concentrate her attacks on Labour's defence policy' (3

2200 10/5/83). *Newsnight* noted that 'in the Commons Mrs Thatcher picks up Labour's gauntlet on defence' (2 *Newsnight* 10/5/83). A flavour of Conservative tactics in the coming campaign was provided in accounts of the rest of Mrs Thatcher's speech. She had attacked Labour's defence policies as 'misguided and naïve' (4 1900 10/5/83). They would 'bring rejoicing only in the Kremlin'.[2]

These early exchanges showed how important to the Conservative campaign would be the theme of the Soviet 'threat'. In most of the news items in which Conservative views on defence were reported the Soviet Union was referred to either as a reason for supporting the Conservatives' nuclear build-up, or for rejecting Labour's non-nuclear policy. The British people were warned of the consequences if 'our sworn enemies' had nuclear weapons and Britain did not. In one memorable statement, illustrative of the general tone of the campaign, Defence Secretary Michael Heseltine doubted Michael Foot's ability to 'defend us from the ravages of a feather duster, let alone the menacing imperialism of Soviet ambition' (3 2200 24/5/83). The election campaign of 1983 confirmed the centrality of images of the Soviet Union to the nuclear debate.

On 11 May the Prime Minister appeared on the *Jimmy Young Radio Show*. In the course of her interview, which was reported on three of the four sampled bulletins that day (BBC1 being the only exception) she appealed for a Conservative victory. Otherwise, she argued, the USSR would not negotiate seriously at Geneva. On BBC2 she was reported as having taken 'a fundamental swipe at Labour's unilateralism' (2 *Newsnight* 11/5/83):

> *Thatcher*: If you really hate nuclear weapons, as I do, you do not have one-sided disarmament, throw out all the American bases and leave all the weapons in the hands of our sworn enemies.

News at Ten emphasized the Prime Minister's claim that 'the Russians were a big reason for calling the election early' (3 2200 11/5/83).

Two days into the campaign defence was thus established as a major election issue on television news. Furthermore, Mrs Thatcher was demonstrating her absolute faith in the correctness of her policies and her readiness to engage in battle with the Labour party on the issue.

The next salvo of the campaign was launched at the Scottish Conservative party conference, which began on 12 May in Perth. In a major speech Michael Heseltine attacked Labour for proposing 'the most dangerous gamble the British people have ever been invited to take'. From the conference hall ITN reported gravely that there were 'no smiles at Michael Heseltine's warning' (3 2200 12/5/83). Channel 4 news reported Mr Heseltine's reference to Labour policies as 'naïve, destabilizing and dangerous ... they might tempt the Russians towards adventurism in Europe' (4 1900 12/5/83).

On Friday 13 May the conference was addressed on the subject of defence first by Francis Pym, the Foreign Secretary,[3] and then by the Prime Minister herself, who reiterated the themes of the preceding days in a rousing and passionate speech which was covered on all bulletins, with the exception of BBC1's *9 O'Clock News*.[4] ITN reported that during the speech Mrs Thatcher had 'reserved her most withering fire for the unilateral disarmers, contrasting the protesters of Greenham Common with the brave young men of the armed forces who recaptured the Falklands' (3 2200 13/5/83).

Thus it was the Conservatives who prioritized the defence issue in the first week of the campaign. The sights and sounds of the Prime Minister and the Defence Secretary addressing their own party faithful in sympathetic surroundings, with stirring references to 'banishing the dark, divisive clouds of marxist socialism' made potent political spectacle. If Mrs Thatcher's decision to call the election on 9 May was unrelated to the Scottish Conservative conference, the close proximity of the two events was certainly a happy coincidence. This timing provided the Conservatives with a platform through which, with the aid of the *Jimmy Young Show* on 11 May, they dominated the defence debate on three of the four campaigning days available that week.

If this initial dominance was partly the result of the Conservatives' skilful use of the media, it was also due to the comparative weakness of Labour's input to the election debate on defence. Labour's opening line of attack amounted to Mr Foot's accusation on 10 May that the Tories had 'cut and run' for an early election because they were afraid to confront Labour on defence. Given the obvious enthusiasm with which Mrs Thatcher tackled the issue, Foot's accusation rang hollow. And while the Tories launched a fresh initiative on defence every day, this was Michael Foot's only contribution to the defence debate during the first week. If television news revealed anyone to be reluctant to debate the defence issue, it was Labour.

Labour's case on defence was largely put on television by Denis

Healey, the party's Foreign Affairs spokesman.[5] Replying to Mrs Thatcher's comments on the *Jimmy Young Show* on 11 May Healey gave his view that 'neither she nor President Reagan have the slightest interest in reaching agreement with the Russians on stopping the nuclear arms race' (3 2200 11/5/83). This was the only direct assault by a Labour leader on the substance of Conservative policy reported by television during the first week. As we shall see, Healey's remarks thereafter tended to lack the populist rhetorical flair of Thatcher and Heseltine, whose simple emotive language was ideally suited to a television campaign. Healey was further handicapped by a reluctance to spell out in clear terms what unilateralism was and why Labour felt it to be necessary. The reason for this soon became clear – he did not believe in the policy.

This aspect of the campaign, to which we shall return, was a self-inflicted wound for the Labour party, but it also became clear in the first week that journalists were adopting a more critical approach to Labour's defence policy than to those of the other two parties. Television news coverage of the debate tended to amplify what was rapidly coming to be seen as Labour's 'defence problem'.

Reporting the policies

The party manifestos were published on 11 May (Labour), 12 May (Alliance), and 18 May (the Conservatives). An analysis of television news coverage reveals some significant variations in the approach taken by journalists.

On 11 May the National Executive Committee of the Labour party met and agreed on the contents of their manifesto. In the evening Labour representatives appeared on two bulletins to discuss their policies. Labour's manifesto was quickly identified as problematic, and defence policy in particular rigorously dissected. Channel 4 news described the manifesto as 'just a balancing act' (4 1900 11/5/83) and asked Denis Healey if it was not 'a sign of the problem of reconciling opinions within the party that you've had to stick to these very precise golden words on the key issue of defence?' Healey replied that precision was not necessarily a bad thing in an election manifesto. With her next question the interviewer then suggested that (contrary to the implication of her opening question), the manifesto was not precise at all:

Journalist: You say it's precise but would a vote for Labour mean unilateral or multilateral disarmament?
Healey: It will mean some unilateral measures like ending the Trident programme and stopping the purely American Cruise missiles from being based in Britain but it will also mean multilateral negotiations about the Polaris force.
Journalist: But doesn't there come a point where the two are incompatible? What happens for example if, during the negotiations you talk about with our allies, they say 'no, we don't want you to close down US bases'?
Healey: Well there of course we'll have to make a choice, but I've been discussing this with leading American experts and their view, like mine, is that it's very unlikely the Americans will need their submarine base at Holy Loch once they get their Trident submarines into service because that'll be based in the United States. And Mrs Thatcher told Jimmy Young this morning ... that the American bombers based in Britain are clapped out and obsolescent.
Journalist: But do you really think that NATO can do without American bases of any kind in this country?
Healey: Not of any kind, of course, but of nuclear bases I think that's quite possible.

Later that evening Eric Heffer, Vice-Chairman of the Labour party, was interviewed on *Newsnight*. Attention again turned quickly to defence policy. In this case the journalist chose to assert that Labour's policy '*must*' imply leaving NATO:

Journalist: You say that you want to have a non-nuclear defence programme within the lifetime of a Labour government. Now the chances are that that could mean considering leaving NATO within that because NATO is not going to cease having a nuclear defence policy in that time, is it?
Heffer: No, we haven't said we would leave NATO.
Journalist: No, what I'm saying is that the implication *must be*, if you want to have a non-nuclear defence programme.
(2 *Newsnight* 11/5/83)

Such a combative approach is not of itself the object of criticism, particularly in the context of a major public debate, but one might have expected that it would be applied consistently to the defence policies of all three major parties. Analysis of the coverage shows that it was not.

Conservative plans for expanding Britain's nuclear arsenal with the Trident system and to accept new American Cruise missiles were no less radical, and by the evidence of opinion polls no more popular than Labour's defence programme. Yet, unlike Labour, when the Conservative party manifesto was published on 18 May its contents in the field of defence policy received no critical coverage. On Channel 4, for example, it was reported only that the manifesto attacked Labour: 'Labour's non-nuclear defence policy also comes under attack in the manifesto. It's condemned as "reckless and naïve". The Conservatives warn, "Soviet nuclear strength continues to grow" – so – "we will not gamble with our defence"' (4 1900 18/5/83).

News at Ten also reported warnings about the Soviet threat, with a brief summary of Conservative defence policy:

> The manifesto warns that Soviet nuclear strength continues to grow. The Conservatives would maintain Britain's independent nuclear deterrent and if the Geneva talks fail deploy the Cruise missiles by the end of the year. But they would continue to support all realistic efforts to reach arms control agreements.
>
> (3 2200 18/5/83)

There was no examination by journalists of the manifesto commitment that the Conservative party would 'continue to support all realistic efforts to reach an arms control agreement'. This major claim, with its implication that the Conservatives *had* previously supported such efforts, was unchallenged. Nor was it related to the Tories' other stated objective of increasing Britain's nuclear force with the Trident system. Unlike Labour, there were no questions put to leading Conservatives about the 'incompatibility' or 'irreconcilability' of these policy goals, nor were there any statements about what the implications of these policies 'must' be for arms control. Defence was perceived by journalists as a relatively minor and non-controversial area of Conservative policy. Indeed, defence was not referred to at all in BBC1's coverage, where the issue of trade union reform was presented as the most newsworthy aspect of future Tory plans. Cecil Parkinson, Conservative party Chairman and the only Tory leader to be interviewed on evening bulletins that day, was not questioned on defence.

As for the Alliance, there was known to be substantial disagreement between the SDP and the Liberals on defence, although the Alliance leadership maintained a public front of unity. As with the

Tories, television news coverage paid little attention to Alliance defence policy.[6]

Despite variations in the approaches of journalists to the defence programmes of the three parties, it is not suggested here that media criticism was responsible for Labour's subsequent debacle on defence. The most serious problem faced by the Labour leadership was a difficulty in expressing its own defence policy, as some leading party activists recognized.

The lull before the storm

On 26 May, when the Labour party was in full retreat on the defence issue, Channel 4 news interviewed Chris Mullin, editor of *Tribune* and author of an editorial attacking the party leadership's handling of the defence debate. The editorial had observed that 'The rift between Mr Foot on the one hand, and Messrs Hattersley, Healey, and Shore on the other has distracted attention away from the real reasons for Labour's opposition to nuclear weapons ... no wonder the public is confused about Labour's defence policy when half the Shadow Cabinet doesn't seem to understand it either.' In his Channel 4 interview Mullin asked: 'Why are the Labour leaders not putting forward the real reasons for Labour's opposition to nuclear weapons? They haven't so far been argued by most of Labour's leaders. It appears, so far, that most members of the Shadow Cabinet don't understand [Labour's defence policy], and one feels that if the nation had the actual arguments put to them people would understand it a great deal better' (4 1900 26/5/83).

In the first week of the campaign (and subsequently) Mr Healey and the Labour leadership in general did not shift the ground on which the Conservatives were conducting the defence debate. They rarely challenged an agenda, set by the Tories and shared in its essentials by the Alliance, which took as given the reality of the Soviet 'threat' and the effectiveness against that threat of forty years of nuclear deterrence. In his Channel 4 interview of 11 May Mr Healey's argument for removing American nuclear bases from Britain relied exclusively on the claim that 'it's very likely that our allies do not believe that it's essential for us to have American nuclear bases in Britain'. When the journalist suggested to him that Labour's traditional working-class vote would desert the party because 'people will think that you're committed to leaving the country undefended', Healey replied that 'I was Defence Secretary for six years'. He, Mr Healey, would never allow anyone with whom he was connected to do anything 'which threatened the defence of our country'. Such appeals were used to the exclusion of any positive *reasons* for getting rid of nuclear weapons and bases.

Despite the centrality of the Soviet threat concept to the nuclear debate Healey's only reference to the issue on television news was to note in the 11 May interview that 'we have a rough balance between Russia and the west at the moment'. Indeed, only one other Labour representative was reported engaging in a criticism of the Soviet threat. This rare example of negotiation with the Conservative 'consensus' came in the context of a speech by Tony Benn, reported on Channel 4 news on 26 May:

> *Benn*: I'm talking about the ways in which [the Tories] try to persuade people that if it wasn't for Mr Heseltine and Trident the Russians would be in Liverpool by 9 June.

The Conservatives, as already noted, clearly understood the importance to their own campaign of *asserting* the existence of a Soviet threat. Labour, while proposing to break with a well-established bi-partisan policy, locked itself into a debate conducted within the terms of the pro-nuclear lobby and in which its views were presented almost exclusively by a well-known former member of that lobby. This had important consequences for Labour's television presentation, as became increasingly apparent in the second week of the campaign.

On 16 May *Newsnight* organized a debate on defence between Michael Heseltine, David Owen, and Denis Healey. Mr Healey's comments in this debate signalled the beginning of the 'scandal' which would erupt eight days later, on 24 May. The debate began with a question directed to Mr Heseltine:

> *Journalist*: The charge commonly made against the Tories is that their defence posture is aggressive in rhetoric, needlessly dependent on Mr Reagan and the United States, and increases the nuclear armoury in an unnecessary way. How would you answer that charge?
>
> (2 *Newsnight* 16/5/83)

Mr Heseltine replied that no one who had followed the debate 'could possibly make it'. Nuclear deterrence had kept the peace for 'the longest period of contemporary history in Europe'. The continued presence of a Soviet threat necessitated a nuclear defence.

He added that the Labour party, not the Tories, had broken with the consensus and suggested that Mr Healey was himself one of 'the few' within the Labour party who disagreed with its defence programme.

As the debate continued both Mr Heseltine and Mr Owen warmed to this theme: Healey was a multilateralist, like them.

Healey was reminded that he had been a key member of pro-nuclear Labour governments. Mr Heseltine pointed out that Healey had been party to the original decision to deploy Cruise missiles in Britain. Healey's ability to counter these challenges was hampered by the fact that they were in most respects true. In replying to Heseltine's point about Cruise Mr Healey was forced to concede that while a member of the Callaghan government he *had* supported the decision to modernize NATO's medium-range nuclear force.

In so far as it became an assault on Labour's integrity, this debate can be seen as a paradigm for the election campaign as a whole. Mr Healey's preferred public image as elder statesman was used against, rather than for Labour's non-nuclear defence policy. In the course of a debate which lasted for nearly forty-five minutes Mr Healey's main attack on the Conservatives (one which he repeated three times) was to suggest that money spent on nuclear weapons was depriving 'the 2nd Paratroop Regiment, the heroes of Goose Green', who were 'having to buy with their own money the protective equipment they need because they're not satisfied with that provided by Mr Heseltine'.

The section of the debate that caused deeper controversy, however, was that in which Mr Healey attempted to explain Labour's own defence policy. This statement, in combination with others made by himself and the Labour leadership team in the following days, would be fanned by the media and the opposition parties into the event of the election.

We recall that in his Channel 4 interview of 11 May Healey had stated that Polaris would be entered into 'multilateral negotiations' with the USSR. On this occasion, when questioned on the future of Polaris under a Labour government Healey asserted that its phasing-out would be conditional on Soviet concessions. In short, the Labour party would *not* necessarily implement a non-nuclear defence policy within the lifetime of a parliament:

> *Journalist*: Could you explain ... given that you will have a non-nuclear defence policy at the end of the lifetime of one Labour government, that would mean that the unilateral commitment takes precedence over the multilateral one, I mean that is absolute, isn't it?
>
> *Healey*: Mr Callaghan's group of ministers decided before the last General Election to put the Polaris force into the disarmament negotiations and that implied a readiness to give it up *if we got adequate concessions from the Soviet Union, and that is still our position.*

With this statement the foremost Labour spokesman on defence set in motion a process of public declaration and counter-declaration by party leaders attempting to set the record straight. As this process gathered momentum the substantive issues of the debate seemed to lose their relevance for journalists and receded into the background. Media attention focused increasingly on the leadership's inability to present a coherent defence policy.

Before examining this phase of the campaign in detail it is worth noting that a positive rationale for a non-nuclear defence policy *was* presented and covered on the news. Ironically, the author of this view was a leading representative of the right in British politics – Enoch Powell MP – who found himself on this issue to be on the same side as the Labour party. Powell's critique of the philosophy of nuclear deterrence, published in the *Guardian* of 1 June and reported three times in the course of our sample, was arguably the most effective and direct to be made during the entire campaign:

> Nobody disputes that our nuclear weaponry is negligible in comparison with that of Russia – if we could destroy sixteen Russian cities she could destroy practically every vestige of life on these islands several times over. For us to use the weapon would therefore be equivalent to more than suicide – it would be genocide. An officer may in the hour of his country's defeat and disgrace commit suicide honestly and rationally with his service revolver. But in any collective context the choice of non-existence, of the obliteration of all future hope, is insanity. Whatever it is, who can call it defence?

Back on the campaign trail, following the *Newsnight* debate of 16 May, Labour had begun the slide into confusion and contradiction. Over the next few days the Conservatives and the Alliance shifted their tactics from attacking the content of Labour's defence policy to mocking its presentation. David Owen 'called Labour's defence policy nonsense. He said Labour was the party of verbal elastoplast. They couldn't even stitch up their splits and divisions' (3 2200 17/5/83). Michael Heseltine was also on the offensive:

> *Heseltine*: [Healey] cannot rewrite the Labour manifesto in speech after speech, or in television programme after television programme. If he believes in the Labour party manifesto then he should stand up and fight for it. He cannot turn himself into the fastest moving target in post-war defence history and retain a shred of credibility.
>
> (1 2100 18/5/83)

However, the party had a few more days of uneasy calm on the defence front before the 'splits and divisions' alleged by David Owen finally overtook them.

Labour routed

> Their leaders are at odds, their manifesto is in shreds.
>
> (Roy Jenkins 27/5/83)

On 24 May Labour's confusion over defence developed into what Michael Heseltine described with some justification as a 'scandal'.

The previous day, press and television journalists had arrived at Labour's regular morning press conference asking for clarification on the conflicting signals coming from the party leadership, such as Roy Hattersley's statement on BBC's *Question Time* that if 'there was no reciprocation from the other side of the Iron Curtain then a Labour government would have to think about Polaris again'.

That morning's press saw a number of articles about the apparent split. Foot, it was reported, had reaffirmed Labour's commitment to a non-nuclear policy before the end of a single parliament. Healey nevertheless maintained, as the *Guardian* reported on 23 May, that 'if the Russians do not respond Polaris should not be scrapped'.

Suddenly, in response to what looked like open conflict between the Leader and the Deputy Leader, television news promoted the dispute to headline status. On 24 May defence came to the centre of the election stage, if not quite in the way Labour had anticipated:

> Defence has been brewing up as an issue since the beginning of the campaign and today in an effort to confront it Labour itself was forced onto the defensive ... the underlying difference over defence between Mr Foot and Mr Healey which the manifesto is supposed to bridge has again been exposed in the last few days ... Mr Healey has stretched Labour's nuclear defence policy to include the possibility of retaining Polaris if arms reduction negotiations fail.
>
> (4 1900 24/5/83)

That evening Channel 4 news conducted a major interview with Michael Foot in which he was reported to have made it clear that 'at the end of a Labour parliament Britain would have no Cruise, no Trident, no Polaris'. In Birmingham he made a major clarifying speech which was reported on all four evening bulletins. In this speech he committed Labour to putting Polaris into the superpower negotiations with the aim of reducing nuclear weapons on all sides. Phasing out Polaris, he said, would be 'part of that process'. Mr Healey, meanwhile, was reported as saying that 'we will review our commitment [to give up Polaris] if the Russians make no concessions'. Throughout the evening of 24 May Healey was repeatedly quoted apparently contradicting the Labour manifesto and Michael Foot:

> *Healey*: We want to put the Polaris force which we already have into negotiations with the Russians so that we don't get rid of that unless the Russians get rid of their weapons aimed at us, and that seems to me common sense.
>
> (1 2100 24/5/83)
>
> *Healey*: If in fact the Russians break the promise they've made to cut their missiles aimed at us when we're negotiating with them as they've asked us to do, that'll be a new situation and we'll have to consider it when it comes.
>
> (3 2200 24/5/83)

The confusion engendered by these remarks was compounded by Mr Foot's inability to assert his authority. His response to valid questioning was evasive and defensive:

> *Journalist*: Mr Foot, can I ask you, would a Labour government get rid of Polaris even if the Russians did not cut their forces?
>
> *Foot*: What I want you to do is to study this document carefully –

Journalist: I have.

Foot: well, to study the whole of our manifesto and you will see that we propose to proceed stage by stage. We are going to establish a non-nuclear defence policy for this country, we are going to start off by having a, seeking to give British backing to the nuclear freeze. We think it's quite wrong that the British government should have rejected that policy and we can move stage by stage to the non-nuclear defence policy.

(3 2200 24/5/83)

On the one hand Labour's leaders were presenting a muddled and confused image of what their policy was, while on the other Mr Foot appeared unable to assert his authority over those of his colleagues who were contradicting the manifesto. The resulting assault by Labour's opponents added the leadership issue to the defence issue.[7] It was argued that Healey's refutations of unilateralism, coming as they did from such an experienced elder statesman, showed how extreme Labour's policy was. Labour's opponents also alleged that Foot's performance had destroyed his credibility as a serious candidate for Prime Minister. Charges of extremism were combined with increasingly personal attacks on Mr Foot:

Heseltine: Quite frankly, Mr Foot has lost control. In the public gaze is Denis Healey, the man that Michael Foot beat for the leadership but who wouldn't lie down. In the shadows, there wait Mr Foot's left-wing masters, Labour's new élite, the extremists to whom he owes the leadership of the Labour party, and in the middle is the yawning gap of Michael Foot's credibility. I wouldn't trust him to defend us from the ravages of a feather duster, let alone the menacing imperialism of Soviet ambition.

(3 2200 24/5/83)

Owen: The trouble is that he's been rumbled. Michael Foot's been rumbled, and the trouble is that the left are not prepared to allow Healeyspeak to continue to be the acceptable face of the defence policy that actually isn't in the Labour party manifesto, and we're all beginning to realize that Michael Foot and Denis Healey have been playing about with the nation's defences.

(3 2200 24/5/83)

On 24 May the media spotlight was turned on a party whose leaders were apparently at odds, unable to agree on the defence policy which they claimed to uphold. The Labour party was shown to be in 'disarray' over defence. The crisis intensified on the 25th when former Prime Minister Jim Callaghan spoke out in favour of the Thatcher/Reagan position at the Geneva talks, and against Labour's non-nuclear defence policy. Callaghan's speech was widely reported, coming as it did from so authoritative a former member of the defence establishment.

On the 26th, so grave was Labour's own assessment of its public image that the party's General Secretary, Jim Mortimer, decided it was necessary to reaffirm his support for Michael Foot's leadership. However, a statement intended to strengthen Foot's position further weakened it in the eyes of television journalists. Again, Labour's defence 'problem' stole the headlines. Channel 4 news described Mortimer's statement as 'a classic own goal' which had 'raised the issue of Michael Foot's leadership right in the middle of the campaign' (4 1900 26/5/83). Other bulletins agreed with this interpretation of the day's events.

The propaganda war continued with an attack by David Owen on Michael Foot's alleged unfitness to govern. Foot, declared Owen, was 'a gentle, kind person', but 'totally unable to grapple with the whole complexity of nuclear weapons and nuclear issues ... That man is not fit to be Prime Minister.'

Owen's opinion, of course, was never put to the test. On 9 June Labour polled its lowest vote since the 1930s, following a television campaign which had largely bypassed the substantive issues of the nuclear debate, and concentrated on the Labour leadership dispute. This was not the result of a deliberate or conscious exclusion of the issues by the journalists concerned. Partly, it was the byproduct of normal election journalism in which, as Jimmy Carter once put it, 'the peripheral aspects become the headlines, but the basic essence of what you stand for and what you hope to accomplish is never reported'.[8]

More importantly, the development of the election defence debate in the direction we have outlined was the consequence of Labour's inadequate input to the news process. The party's crucial defence policy appeared to be contradictory and incoherent. In presenting it, Labour's leadership consistently avoided the central issues of *why* Britain's defence should, and could be non-nuclear. The 'peripheral aspects' were allowed by Labour leaders to eclipse the defence debate as such. A debate about the relative worth of Labour, Tory, and Alliance policies was superceded by a debate about the various interpretations of *Labour*'s policy within the Labour leadership itself. In this sense the nuclear debate was not resolved in 1983. It was never really engaged.

Postcript: 1987

In the General Election of 1987 the British people were again presented with three very different defence policies. Again, with the anti-government vote split between Labour and the Alliance, the Conservatives won. Unlike 1983, however, the Labour party fought a skilful media campaign, using television effectively to project its leaders and its policies. Although Labour was unable to mobilize a majority of voters for its non-nuclear defence strategy, the arguments were put with a unity and confidence which had been singularly lacking in 1983. Echoing Gorbachov in the Soviet Union, the Labour party leadership under Neil Kinnock appeared to have learnt the rules of the modern media game.

But that in itself was not enough to overcome the widely held belief, reinforced by years of media coverage of the kind discussed in this book, that in the Soviet Union Britain has an enemy held in check only by our possession of nuclear weapons. The cumulative effects of that coverage were not to be overcome in the course of a four-week election campaign, no matter how skilfully fought.

One of the lessons of 1987 was that the assumption of the Soviet threat remains a powerful influence on British society. The reluctance of the media to contest that assumption continues to be a major source of its legitimacy.

Conclusion

I have tried in this book to show how television news does not construct a merely factual account of the defence and disarmament debate, but one in which certain perspectives are dominant.

In so far as television news reinforces the concept of the Soviet threat in much of its coverage, and tends to reproduce stereotypical images of the USSR which have their roots in conservative ideology, it is not 'neutral' or 'impartial'.

In coverage of specific exchanges between east and west, such as have occurred during the Korean airliner and Chernobyl crises, and in the arms control talks, the Soviet viewpoint tends to be constructed as a less credible, less truthful account than that of western sources. This continues to be the case, despite the positive impact of Gorbachov and *glasnost* on Soviet public relations.

But throughout this book examples have been given which qualify these conclusions: occasions when 'images of the enemy' have been contested on television news. Although they are concentrated overwhelmingly in the minority-audience programmes, they are important none the less as indicators of what an 'objective' coverage of east–west issues might look like.

The 'currently dominant' notion of the Soviet threat was the focus of a critical *Newsnight* item in October 1983, on the eve of the Cruise and Pershing II deployments. In June 1982 and May 1983 news items explicitly challenged the sincerity of the Reagan administration's arms control policies by contrasting its words with its deeds. The administration's view of the Korean airliner incident as an example of 'Russian barbarism', reinforced in the greater proportion of television news coverage, was contested in a handful of news items during the crisis itself, and in several items in the period following the crisis.

It is clear that the minority-audience format consistently presents lengthier and more detailed coverage of complex issues, and permits a wider range of views to be accessed as *serious*, *credible* views. When Soviet commentators appear on television news, it is on these programmes. The same is true, with few exceptions, for dissident establishment sources such as Admiral Noel Gaylor. These programmes, to use Schlesinger's phrase, are 'relatively open' spaces in television news. They are the spaces where television news is most likely to challenge dominant assumptions and definitions: a negotiation which, as Hartley puts it, 'is no sham' (1984: 62).

A second important conclusion of this book is that while 'bias' is a valid explanation for 'images of the enemy' on television news, it is not a sufficient one. The Soviet approach to western journalism, and to news management, is crucial to its image. The Soviets have a certain capacity, should they choose to employ it, for shaping the coverage which they receive in the west. Journalists are not mere puppets of the powerful. They work by rules and practices which, if they tend to favour the establishment in general, nevertheless create spaces for competing viewpoints, including the Soviet one, to be represented with a degree of accuracy and fairness.

If the Soviet viewpoint has tended to be underepresented, this has partly been because of constraints placed by the Soviets themselves on the routine practices of newsgathering: constraints such as those experienced by the correspondents in Moscow, and the hesitant approach to news management which characterized the pre-Gorbachov period.

In the early 1980s the United States used the media with consummate skill. With the Zero Option and Interim Zero Option proposals the administration successfully fed its viewpoint into the western European mass media, with the help of live satellite transmissions. By consistently satisfying the broadcasters' hunger for pictures and spectacle the administration gained maximum exposure for its views. In the Korean Airlines crisis the administration went public immediately, seizing the propaganda initiative and ensuring that its account of the event dominated the media in the first crucial weeks.

The Soviet Union, on the other hand, tended during this period to treat the techniques of news management with suspicion and disdain, in the long-held belief of its dominant groups that any information given to the western media would be used against it. This policy, exemplified during the Korean airliner crisis (and also apparent during the initial phase of the Chernobyl crisis), created the space for 'images of the enemy' to flourish.

But, as Chapter 7 argued, the rise of Gorbachov and the introduction of *glasnost* has shown the Soviets to be adopting news management techniques at least as slick as those of the US administration. For that reason, it is possible to end this book on a note of cautious optimism. The new cold war is far from over, and future events as yet unforeseen may cause it to flare up again. But the Soviets' new-found ability to handle the western media has undoubtedly forced a softening of the rhetoric in the superpower dialogue. Britain remains in the grip of conservatism, but Mrs Thatcher finds it increasingly difficult to make the notion of the USSR as 'our sworn enemy' stick. Whatever she may think in private, in public she must be seen to be dealing in good faith with Gorbachov.

As for television news, and the western media in general, skilful news management and *glasnost* on the Soviet side will not entirely cancel out the effects of 'bias'. The demonology of the Soviet threat will persist as it has done since 1917. What we can predict with some certainty is that the new Soviet approach to information will provide those working in our media who aspire to a more 'objective' coverage of east–west issues with better raw materials.

As we approach the end of the century committed to nuclear weapons, both our own and those of the United States, we can only hope that they will make the most of it.

Notes

1 Television news: 'a vital engine of this great democracy'

1 This trust is largely based on the fact that in Britain television news has developed within a public service framework and 'presents itself as a merely factual report of events in the world' (Schlesinger, Murdock, and Elliot 1983: 36). The Broadcasting Act, 1981 legally obliges the IBA companies to ensure that 'due impartiality is preserved as respects matters of political or industrial controversy or relating to current public policy'. The British Broadcasting Corporation is regulated by the provisions of the Royal Charter under which it was established. This means in practice, as former Director-General Howard Newby put it for the BBC, that:

> news and current affairs are broadcast in a way designed not to impose any view or foster any kind of attitude, but to put everyone in possession of the information that allows them to make up their minds for themselves.
>
> (1977: 11)

The late Hugh Carleton-Green, when Director-General, identified one of the BBC's main characteristics to be its 'impartial reflection of all kinds of controversies' (1970: 4), and the Corporation advertises its news services with the claim that:

> the BBC does not campaign. It is in the business of reporting, not crusading. It has no leader columns for the airing of its editorial views, for it has none to air. And it does not address itself to one particular class or income group, for the whole nation is its audience and the readers of every kind of newspaper watch or listen to its bulletins.
>
> (BBC General Advisory Council: 1976)

2 Ironically, during the Falklands conflict the BBC found itself under attack from the Conservatives for being excessively impartial. A substantial lobby of opinion was mobilized against the claims of the BBC that it had the right and duty to be objective in reporting the conflict. On

4 May 1982 the *Daily Mail* reported complaints by Tory MPs that BBC news had been 'unacceptably even-handed' in contrast to ITN's 'consistently less sceptical and more supportive stance'. On 7 May, the national press widely reported Mrs Thatcher's remark that 'I understand there are times when it seems that we and the Argentinians are almost being treated as equals and almost on a neutral basis.' On 11 May, following the controversial *Panorama* programme in which the Conservatives' Falklands policy was scrutinized, the Prime Minister again addressed the House on the subject of the BBC's excessive impartiality:

> I know how strongly many people feel that the case for our boys is not being put with sufficient vigour on certain – I do not say all – BBC programmes. The Chairman of the BBC has assured us, and has said in vigorous terms, that *the BBC is not neutral* on this point, and I hope that his words will be heeded by the many who have responsibilities for standing up for our task force, our boys, our people and the cause of democracy.
>
> (Hansard, 1234: 598)

3 Anderson and Sharrock, for example, have argued that content analyses of British television news overestimate the significance of the strictures of 'neutrality' adhered to by the news producers: 'the claim that the media are biased is one which it seems to us can only be assessed relative to the claims which the media themselves actually make concerning impartiality' (1980: 368).

This, of course, is a valid point: the analysis of news production should take account of the claims made for output by the news producers. But, as we have seen, in the case of British television news these claims emphasize not only the neutrality and objectivity of output but the fact that these qualities are crucial component parts of the British democratic tradition.

4 In short, content analysis is combined in this book with a production study.

Although major published examples of production studies are contained in Schlesinger's account of the workings of the BBC newsroom (1978), and in Cockerell, Hennessey, and Walker's examination of news management (1984), hitherto production studies have tended to be neglected by content analysts: partly because many journalists are unwilling to co-operate with sociologists whose motives they suspect and whose results they resent, and partly, too, because some content analysts have approached news from within an overly conspiratorial and simplistic framework of media 'bias'. This latter tends to militate against the study of news production and the problems faced by journalists, since an account of these factors often produces a more complicated picture than the crude 'bias' framework can accommodate.

The neglect of production studies has led to the criticism that many content analytical findings are unreliable, because they have been reached without consideration of the constraints working on journalists. Findings of 'bias', it is argued, are undervalued if it is not known how they relate to the 'social process' of news production. Consequently, in this book the analysis of news content is accomplished by a study of the constraints faced by the journalists who produce it. This material is not presented as a major production study (which would easily occupy a book in itself), but it does represent an attempt to take into account the views of a body of journalists who have not been canvassed in this way before.

5 In so doing, this book proceeds from the basic methodological principle that content analysis 'presupposes knowledge of the phenomena with which communication deals' (Varis 1983: 52).

This is important, not least to refute the charges of such as Anderson and Sharrock that academic criticism of the media 'usually means that the media men do not support the preferred sociological theories of the media researcher' (1980: 361).

The methodology employed here echoes that of Schlesinger, Murdock, and Elliot (1983) and the Glasgow University Media Group, in so far as its starting point is not 'the preferred sociological theories of the researcher' but 'the background of public debate' (GUMG 1976: 40).

2 The nuclear debate

1 Chomsky argues that the objective of the human rights campaign was to regain popular support – seriously depleted by the 'Vietnam syndrome' – for US intervention abroad. 'An extraordinary campaign was executed with great skill, selecting targets of opportunity, at a time when everyone knew beyond doubt that the United States had committed major crimes in Cuba, Indochina, Chile and elsewhere' (1982: 32).

2 Elements of this strategy ranged from the 'give 'em enough shovels' philosophy of such as T.K. Jones, US Under-Secretary of Defence (the view that the United States could survive a nuclear exchange with the Soviets given simple preparation), to the more sophisticated positions of such as Paul Nitze, the Reagan administration's chief INF negotiator. In 1956 Nitze wrote that 'it is quite possible that in a general nuclear war one side or the other could "win" decisively' (see Mann 1983).

Mann notes that 'after the 1980 election, Reagan installed no fewer than thirty-two CPD (Committee on the Present Danger) officials in his administration', including one Colin Gray, appointed to serve as a consultant in the General Advisory Committee to the US Departments of Defence and State. Gray's view, quoted in the Mann article, is that full-scale nuclear war 'is likely to be waged to coerce the Soviet Union to give up some recent gain. Thus, a president must have the ability not merely to end a war but to end it favourably.'

3 Cockburn argues that inaccuracies are built into the methods of estimating Soviet military power:

> Satellites can watch over enemy territory with an ease that would have been unimaginable before the Space Age, but they still cannot see through clouds. This is why, for example, the output from the tank factory at Kharkov in the Ukraine is regularly listed as 500 tanks a year in unclassified intelligence publications. Through a meterological quirk, Kharkov is covered by clouds most of the time, rendering the specialists in watching Soviet tank production effectively blind to the scale of the plant's operations. 'That is why they give the figure of 500,' one former intelligence officer told me. It's the number they use when they don't know if it's zero or 1,000.
>
> (1983: 19)

4 Another example of this number-juggling concerns the debate about troop numbers in Europe. US Defence Department figures show an impressive Warsaw Pact superiority of 1,400,000 (1983: 63). But this number does not show that Warsaw Pact figures for troop deployments include 1,000,000 personnel in non-combat roles (construction workers engaged in military projects and members of the internal security services in the Warsaw Pact countries). NATO's estimate of its own troop deployments, on the other hand, excludes French forces, an omission once legitimized on the grounds that French forces would not be available for use by NATO in a conflict. Now, however, this rationale is greatly weakened, as the *Financial Times* noted on 3 May 1983:

> General Bernard Rogers, NATO's top commander, caused a little embarrassment in Paris the other day at a public function when he warmly praised the 'extremely close co-operation and co-ordination that now exists with the French military forces'.

5 The question then arose, and was put most forcefully by the disarmers – if the new American weapons were not a response to the Soviet SS-20, what *were* they for? The BBC *Panorama* documentary *Beyond Deterrence* interviewed scientists who had been employed by the United States government as consultants in this field. One, John Steinbruner, argued that Pershing II in particular was a qualitatively new weapon, not comparable to the SS-20 or the Pershing I which it replaced. The Pershing II was a *strategic* weapon, capable of hitting targets inside the Soviet Union from European soil:

> It threatens their basic command structure with pre-emptive attack. ... It does look as if it might enable us to undertake a first strike ... from the Soviet point of view it is an extremely provocative weapon

> that not only deals with a limited capacity for the European theatre but their entire strategic operation.

NATO had argued that Pershing II was not a strategic missile because its range fell 12 per cent short of the 100 or so strategic targets in and around Moscow. Another interviewee, Paul Brackner, replied to this by pointing out that 'any competent staff of engineers in three or four months can make changes in that missile to make it increase its range by 12 per cent'. SIPRI observed that Pershing II missiles have ten times the accuracy of SS-20s.

The Cruise missile, on the other hand, while extremely accurate, was not a first-strike weapon because of its slow flight time. It was, according to the American Brookings Institute, a second-strike weapon, useable only in the context of a protracted nuclear war. A Brookings Institute report titled *Cruise Missiles* remarked that the presence of Cruise missiles would create a:

> psychological climate in which the Russians instinct to retaliate [to a US first strike] is tempered by the knowledge that the damage of the initial strikes, though significant, is limited, and that an excessive response would inevitably be met by escalation.
>
> (Betts 1981: 184)

Cruise missiles, the report continues, are more suited to 'follow-on options when raid sizes are more likely to be larger, more targets are likely to be attacked, and the distinction between theatre and strategic use of Cruise missiles becomes blurred'. The term 'follow-on option' can be considered as a euphemism for the second strike in a protracted nuclear war.

3 Reporting the Soviet Union

1 All statements in the text attributed to journalists were obtained in interviews conducted by the author in Moscow and London, unless otherwise stated.
2 Unless otherwise stated, all emphases are the author's own,
3 The Soviet media also display 'selectivity' in coverage of dissent. Throughout 1987 the Soviet media extensively covered the hunger strike in Washington of dissident US physicist Charles Heider. While the consumers of British news have probably never heard of Mr Heider, he is a media star in the USSR for his opposition to the Reagan administration and the Star Wars programme.

The Soviets routinely cover political demonstrations which in the west are ignored, such as an anti-nuclear demonstration organized in Glasgow on Sunday, 11 October 1986. This event, which involved a few hundred peace campaigners and was ignored by British television news, was reported on the main Soviet TV news bulletin, *Vremya*.

4 One important development in the crisis was not covered on television news. The *Guardian* on 30 May reported that:

> the danger of war between Syria and Israel receded yesterday after what many sources believed was Soviet intervention to stop the sabre-rattling by Damascus ... because the Soviet Union was afraid that the confrontation with Israel was spiralling out of control.

The end of a crisis, with the possibility of a Soviet contribution to peace, was not newsworthy. The beginning of one, with 'Russia' cast as arms supplier and troublemaker, was.

5 Coverage of the White Paper shows how, within certain limits, usually those defined as legitimate by the military-political establishment, existing defence policy can be challenged. Indeed, when a branch of the services feels itself to be under threat from the government it positively encourages media debate. If, however, arguments about cuts in the navy or the design faults of new aircraft are present in news, challenges to the underlying concept of the Soviet threat are beyond discussion in the great proportion of television coverage – the Soviet threat exists in the realm of 'consensus'.

6 For a detailed analysis of television news coverage of the Falklands conflict, see *War and Peace News* by the Glasgow University Media Group (1985).

4 Making Soviet news

1 An interesting footnote to this concerns the Soviet allegation that Tim Sebastian, Brian Hanrahan's predecessor as BBC correspondent in Moscow, worked for the CIA. The allegation came in a news conference given by Oleg Tumanov in Moscow.

Tumanov, until his 'redefection' to the USSR, had been editor of the Russian service of Freedom/Radio Free Europe, a station with major CIA connections. In the course of the news conference Tumanov claimed that western journalists based in Moscow were working for the CIA. There was laughter in the hall, according to a report in the Soviet weekly *New Times* (no. 19, 1986). Tumanov then asked the assembled foreign journalists:

> Do you want me to name one of your Moscow colleagues with whom I was working at the radio station? Do you want me to?

They did, and he named one:

> Tim Sebastian, the BBC correspondent. He visited our headquarters in Munich and gave us information. He received unreliable information from me personally and I, like all the operatives at Freedom/Radio Free Europe, was connected with the CIA.

Sebastian was expelled from the USSR in September 1985, along with other British journalists and diplomats.

2 ABC's *Nightline* in the United States, writes Christopher Hitchens in the *Spectator* of 10 May 1986, 'is particularly good at getting Russians on the air, a facility which has in the past enraged the White House. Vladimir Posner and Georgi Arbatov, says Pat Buchanan, are not fit participants in the American national debate.'

5 Russia condemned: the Korean airliner disaster

1 R. W. Johnson's book about the incident, *Shootdown: The Verdict on KAL 007*, further elaborated on the evidence for a spying mission. Reviewing *Shootdown* in the *London Review of Books* of 24 July 1986, Paul Foot describes it as 'a political exposé of the highest order' and notes that 'when all the arguments pile up on one side of the scales, the rational mind hesitates ... is it really possible that responsible people in a democracy could behave in such a reckless way?'

6 The superpower dialogue

1 The Coalition for Peace Through Strength, in its statement 'An Analysis of SALT II' (reproduced in the *SALT Handbook*) exemplify this position when they claim that as a result of SALT II the United States will 'be locked into strategic inferiority and overall military inferiority. The inbalance in both strategic and conventional military power has grown worse during the period of SALT' (681).

2 As the two sides entered another round of arms control talks in January 1985 (not covered in the sample) these attitudes continued to prevail in the second Reagan administration, as the comments of influential officials like Assistant Secretary of State Richard Perle made clear: 'The sense that we and the Russians could compose our differences, reduce the treaty constraints, enter into agreements, treaties, reflecting a series of constraints, and then rely on compliance to produce a safer world, I don't agree with any of that' (*Observer*, 6 January 1985).

3 A reference to the theory of limited nuclear war. Reagan's belief in the possibility of waging limited nuclear war in Europe had caused considerable alarm. He was the first American President to make it an openly declared matter of policy that such a war could be fought in the European 'theatre'.

4 Two developments were important in this respect. First, the B-2 bomber project was accelerated by the Reagan administration when it entered office, and plans were got under way to develop a new generation of 'stealth' bomber. Second, the development of the air-launched Cruise missile greatly increased the potential of US aircraft to be used as

strategic nuclear weapons platforms. The START proposal excluded Cruise missiles from its remit.

7 Gorbachov, *Glasnost*, and Chernobyl

1 *Diverse Reports*, Channel 4, 25 March 1987.
2 The Director of Moscow's Institute of USA–Canada Studies, and a leading foreign policy adviser to Gorbachov.
3 Martin Walker relates how his 'scoop' of obtaining the first interview with Stalin's daughter when she returned from exile to the USSR was received by the Soviet authorities:

> When I found Svetlana I just went round all the hotels and went up to the *dezhurnayas* [women who supervise the floors in a Soviet hotel] until I found her. At the press centre the next day they said, 'how the hell did you find her?' When I told them they shook their heads in disbelief. This isn't what journalism means to them at all, but they rather relish it and now they're onto the idea of a scoop and how we rather like having scoops. I think they're getting more educated by us into what we need. And I think they're also getting a lot prouder of what they have to tell.

4 One of the two Soviet news agencies.
5 For an account of the disaster and its aftermath see N. Hawkes *et al.*, *The Worst Accident in the World.*
6 From the Political Report of the Central Committee to the 27th congress of the CPSU. English text published by Novosti, Moscow, 1986.
7 Quoted from 'Leaking the nuclear news' by Nohdan Bahaylo in the *Spectator*, 10 May 1986.
8 Gubaryev subsequently wrote a play about Chernobyl, *Sarcophagus*, which was performed in Britain in April 1987.
9 Prime Minister Rizhkov and Central Committee Secretary Ligachov visited the scene of the disaster on 2 May.
10 See *New Scientist*, 8 May 1986, and the article by Wilkie and Milne, 'Chernobyl: sorting fact from fiction'.

8 Peace movement news

1 For discussions of peace movement news in the British press see 'Peace in our times?' by Connell in Aubrey (1982), and 'Portraying the peace movement' by Richard Keeble in Curran *et al.* (1986).
2 For a brief history of CND's development since the 1950s see Bolsover and Minnion (1983).
3 The twelve items of peace movement news in the routine sample which

were not concerned with protests of one kind or another took a range of themes, all reflecting the growth of the nuclear debate at this time. For example, in May 1983 there was coverage of a dispute within the Catholic church about attitudes to CND:

> The Vatican has disowned an attack by its envoy in London against Monsignor Bruce Kent, leader of the Campaign for Nuclear Disarmament. Earlier this week Archbishop Bruno Heim accused CND members of being 'blinkered idiots or consciously sharing Soviet ideology'. The Vatican said the Archbishop's comments were strictly personal and were without official backing.
>
> (4 1900 20/5/83)

4 Interestingly, ITN reported this event in the context of a Marplan poll which appeared that day in the *Guardian* newspaper:

Question 1. Should Britain abandon nuclear weapons no matter what other countries do or maintain our current nuclear capability, or improve it by spending more money on nuclear weapons?

	%
Abandon	16
Maintain	63
Improve	14

Question 2. Do you approve or disapprove of the government's decision to allow the Americans to base Cruise missiles on British soil?

Approve	37
Disapprove	48

Question 3. Do you approve or disapprove of the government's decision to purchase for about £5 billion the Trident nuclear missile system to replace the Polaris fleet?

Approve	26
Disapprove	50

ITN reported:

> An opinion poll today shows that *fewer than one in six* supports unilateral disarmament, though *just under half* of those polled say they reject Cruise missiles on British soil.
>
> (3 1800 22/10/83)

Opinion polls, as all political parties know, can be interpreted to mean different things. This account could have reported that the *largest* proportion of those polled rejected Cruise (48 per cent), instead of 'less than half', or that the *largest* proportion of those polled disapproved of Trident (50 per cent). While the journalist considers it necessary to report that 'fewer than one in six' supported Britain's unilateral nuclear disarmament he fails to balance this by noting that an even smaller minority (14 per cent) supported any increase in Britain's nuclear capability (such as the purchase of Trident) or, to put it another way, that 86 per cent disagreed with the government on defence.

5 For a detailed analysis of coverage of the Greenham Common protests, see *War and Peace News* by the Glasgow University Media Group (1986).

6 Connell notes the use of 'concessionary' terms such as 'well meaning, well intentioned and idealistic' in media coverage of the October 1981 CND demonstrations (see Aubrey *et al.* 1982: 29).

7 Although one example was found during the sample period of what might be called 'criticism by association'. In June 1982 ITN covered a demonstration organized by the Reagan Reception Committee to mark the President's visit to Britain. At this time the Falklands War was still being fought. Argentina was 'the enemy'. In this context the following example of linkage was significant:

> The fall-out van was supposed to encourage the anti-bomb and anti-Reagan elements. Just ahead of them were supporters of Argentina over the Falklands.
>
> (3 2200 7/6/82)

The juxtaposition of 'anti-bomb elements' with 'supporters of Argentina over the Falklands' transfers the negative image of the latter group to the former – the peace movement, which at no time during the Falklands War supported Argentina or was linked to groups which did.

9 The nuclear election

1 Unfortunately, this book was not able to include a discussion of the 1987 General Election, in which the defence issue was again a major campaign theme. Suffice to say here that, perhaps, some of the problems in Labour's news management of the 1983 campaign identified in this chapter were resolved by 1987.

2 Mrs Thatcher's remarks referred to a letter sent by the Labour party leadership to the Soviet government. The letter had enquired what the Soviet response would be if Britain disarmed unilaterally. In Parliament, Conservative MP Harvey Proctor asked the Prime Minister if 'she agreed that the Soviet response would be to accept the Labour party's näivety in this matter and continue with nuclear weapons and, in addition, increase its nuclear capability?' (*Hansard*, vol. 42: 732). Mrs Thatcher replied: 'I agree that the Opposition's defence policy is the most misguided and näive ever put before the British people. It puts in doubt our security and the defence of our traditional way of life. I hope that it will be firmly

rejected. As regards the letter to Mr Andropov, I notice that it was Mr Andropov who was reported as saying, "let no one expect unilateral disarmament from us. We are not a näive people."'

3 Pym stated that 'Labour has done a somersault. They have decided on defence what amounts to surrender. They are wrong and dangerously wrong. They put at risk our very security' (4 1900 13/5/83).

4 BBC's *9 O'Clock News* covered Mrs Thatcher's speech but not her statements on defence. That BBC news producers were aware of a possible tendency to 'bias' in coverage of the Scottish Conservative conference was revealed in a *Guardian* article of 14 May by Dennis Barker: 'The fact that the Scottish Tory party Conference is on at the moment is not the BBC's fault, and it may not be possible to balance Mrs Thatcher there.'

5 Although Denis Healey appears to have been delegated the responsibility of speaking for Labour on defence during the 1983 campaign, John Silkin was the party's defence spokesman. During the sample Silkin's views on defence were reported only five times, while those of Denis Healey received coverage on twenty-six occasions. This was somewhat unfortunate for Labour since, as Silkin revealed in a *Newsnight* interview of 24 May, he supported the manifesto commitment of phasing Polaris out within the lifetime of a parliament.

6 Richard Keeble makes a similar point in relation to press coverage of the Alliance during the election. See Curran *et al.* (1986: 50).

7 Cockerell, Hennessey, and Walker suggest that Michael Foot was the Conservative party's greatest 'negative asset' in the campaign, but clearly, the confusion was not his alone. (1984: 214).

8 *The New York Times Book Review*, 19 June 1977.

References

Anderson, D. and Sharrock, W.W. (1980) 'Biasing the news: technical issues in media studies', in G.C. Wilhoit and H. de Bock, *Mass Communication Review Yearbook*, vol.1, London: Sage.

Aubrey, C. (ed.) (1982) *Nukespeak: The Media and the Bomb*, London: Comedia.

BBC General Advisory Council (1976) *The Task of Broadcasting News*, London: BBC Publications.

Betts, R.K. (ed.) (1981) *Cruise Missiles: Technology, Strategy, Politics*, Washington: Brookings Institute.

Bolsover, P. and Minnion, J. (eds) (1983) *The CND Story*, London: Allison & Busby.

Carleton-Greene, H. (1970) *The BBC as a Public Service*, London: BBC Publications.

Cartwright, J. and Critchley, J. (1982) *Draft Interim Report of the Special Committee on Nuclear Weapons in Europe*, unpublished discussion document, North Atlantic Assembly.

Chomsky, N., Gittings, J., and Steele, J. (1982) *Superpowers in Collision: The New Cold War*, Harmondsworth: Penguin.

Clarke, M. and Mowlam, M. (eds) (1982) *Debate on Disarmament*, London: Routledge & Kegan Paul.

Cockburn, A. (1983) *The Threat*, London: Hutchinson.

Cockerell, M., Hennessey, P., and Walker, D. (1984) *Sources Close to the Prime Minister*, London: Macmillan.

Connell, I. (1980) 'Television news and the social contract', in S. Hall *et al.* (eds) *Culture, Media, Language*, London: Hutchinson.

Connell, I. (1982) 'Peace in our times?', in C. Aubrey (ed.) *Nukespeak: The Media and the Bomb*, London: Comedia.

Curran, J., Ecclestone, J., Oakley, G. and Richardson, A. (eds) (1986) *Bending Reality*, London: Pluto Press.

Dablgren, P. (1981) 'TV news and the suppression of reflexivity', in E. Katz and T. Szecsko, *Mass Media and Social Change*, London: Sage.

Dando, M. and Rogers, P. (1984) *The Death of Deterrence*, London: CND Publications.

Dean, R. (1983) 'The Alliance and NATO', *NATO Review*, September.

Glasgow University Media Group (1976) *Bad News*, London, Routledge

& Kegan Paul; (1982) *Really Bad News*, London: Writers & Readers; (1985) *War and Peace News*, London: Open University Press.

Hall, S., Critcher, C., Jefferson, T., Clarke, J., Roberts, B. (1978) *Policing the Crisis*, London: Macmillan.

Hall, S., Hobson, D., Lowe, A., and Willis, P. (eds) (1980) *Culture, Media, Language*, London: Hutchinson.

Halliday, F. (1983) *Threat from the East?*, London: Pelican.

Hanrahan, B. and Fox, R. (1982) *'I Counted Them All Out and I Counted Them All Back'*, London: BBC Publications.

Harrison, M. (1985) *Whose Bias?*, London: ITN Publications

Hartley, J. (1984) *Understanding News*, London: Methuen.

Hawkes, N., Lean, G., Leigh, D., McKie, R., Pringle, P., and Wilson, A. (1986) *The Worst Accident in the World*, London: Pan.

Herman, E. (1982) *The Real Terror Network: Terrorism in Fact and Propaganda*, Boston: South End Press.

Hetherington, A. (1985) *News, Newspapers and Television*, London: Macmillan.

Holloway, D. (1983) *The Soviet Union and the Arms Race*, London: Yale University Press.

Hutchings, R. (1983) *The Soviet Budget*, London: Macmillan.

International Institute for Strategic Studies (1984) *The Military Balance 1983–84*: *Stragetic Survey 1983–84*, London: IISS.

Jacobsen, C.G. (1983) 'East–west relations at the crossroads', *Current History*, May.

Johnson, R.W. (1986) *Shootdown – The Verdict on KAL 007*, London: Chatto & Windus.

Kaldor, M (1982a) 'Aspects of consensus', unpublished paper delivered to the British Film Institute conference, 2 April.

Kaldor, M. (1982b) 'Is there a Soviet military threat?', in M. Clarke and M. Mowlam, *Debate on Disarmament*, London: Routledge & Kegan Paul.

Katz, E. and Szecsko. T. (1981) *Mass Media and Social Change*, London: Sage.

Keeble, R. (1986) 'Portraying the peace movement', in J. Curran *et al.* (eds), *Bending Reality*, London: Pluto Press.

Labrie, R.P. (ed.) (1979) *The SALT Handbook: Key Documents and Issues, 1972–1979*, Washington: American Enterprise Institute for Public Policy Research.

McNamara, R. (1983) 'The military role of nuclear weapons', *Foreign Affairs* (62) 1.

Mann, C. (1983) 'The holocaust lobby: the men who are dying to win', *Sanity*, October.

Medvedev, R. (1980) *On Soviet Dissent*, London: Constable.

Newby, H. (1977) *The Uses of Broadcasting*, London: BBC Publications.

Schlesinger, P. (1978) *Putting 'Reality' Together*, London: Constable.

Schlesinger, P., Murdock, G., and Elliot, P. (1983) *Televising Terrorism: Political Violence in Popular Culture*, London: Comedia.

Shatz, M. (1980) *Soviet Dissent in Historical Perspective*, Cambridge: Cambridge University Press.

Steele, J. (1983) *The Limits of World Power*, Harmondsworth: Penguin.

SIPRI (Stockholm International Peace Research Institute) (1982) *World Armaments and Disarmament, SIPRI Yearbook 1982*, London: Taylor & Frances; (1983a) *World Armaments and Disarmament, SIPRI Yearbook 1983*, London, Taylor & Frances; (1983b) *The Arms Race and Arms Control 1983*, London: Taylor & Frances.

Talbott, S. (1983) 'Playing for the future: Is the US making the right moves towards Moscow in arms control?', *Time*, 18 April.

Talbott, S. (1984) *Deadly Gambits*, London: Picador.

United Kingdom Ministry of Defence (1982) *Statement on the Defence Estimates 1982*, Cmnd 8529.I, London: Her Majesty's Stationery Office; (1983) *Statement on the Defence Estimates 1983*, Cmnd. 8529.I, London: Her Majesty's Stationery Office.

United States Department of Defence (1983) *Soviet Military Power*, Washington.

United States Senate Committee on Armed Services (1981) *Report number 97–58 to accompany Department of Defence Authorization for Appropriations for Fiscal Year 1982*, Washington: US Government Printing Office.

Varis, T. (1983) 'Media coverage of disarmament-related issues', *Current Research on Peace and Violence*, no. 1.

Wilhoit, G.C. and de Bock, H. (1980) *Mass Communications Review Yearbook*, Vol. 1, London: Sage.

Index